Marco Bussagli

Understanding **Architecture**

VOLUME II

SHARPE REFERENCE
an imprint of M.E. Sharpe, Inc.

Contents

Civilizations, Architectural Achievements, Outstanding Figures

Architecture may be defined as "the great book of humanity," as Victor Hugo said: "For six thousand years, from the remotest pagoda of the Hindustan to the Cathedral of Cologne, architecture has been the great volume written by humanity, and this is so true that not only every symbol but every human thought has its page in this immense book of monuments."

It would be impossible to synthesize more clearly the significance of architecture as the communal expression of political, religious, or merely aesthetic sensibilities, but that always expresses the commitment and aspirations of entire generations.

Architecture is also this: an immense book of stone, written with the toil and resolve of small, transient beings determined to build a giant that will represent them in the centuries to come.

The pages that follow explore the most significant architectural achievements of all periods and countries and the preeminent figures in the history of architecture. It is well to remember, in this regard, that the figure of the architect as an isolated figure who creates great masterpieces is only one possibility and one understanding. The form of a building may also be understood as the product of the consciousness of an entire people. Especially with regard to the oldest temples, lack of documentation makes it all but impossible to know who conceived the original idea. The closer one comes to the present age, the more strongly the personality of the architect emerges, finally assuming total responsibility for the basic plan and stylistic features.

Neolithic Populations and Ethnographic Cultures

Left:
An Inuit igloo,
engraving from
The Polar World,
1874.

Above:
Modern buildings
made of aluminum,
inspired by the shape
of the igloo, overlook
the enormous icebergs
floating in Disko Bay.
Hotel Arctic, Ilulissat,
northwestern
Greenland.

Below:
Interior of a hut typical
of a tribe in the
Casamance region.
Senegal, West Africa.

In his treatise *De architectura*, Vitruvius linked architecture to the origins of human civilization. Little is known about the transition stage between the Paleolithic and Neolithic periods (8000–3000 B.C.E.), the time when nomadic tribes began to adopt a seminomadic or settled life. One example is the Neolithic culture of Kelteminar (fourth millennium B.C.E.) in the Lake Aral region, where seminomadic Caucasian hunters and fishermen lived. Their collective huts, of conical shape with a round base and a hole in the middle of the roof to allow smoke to escape, had a wooden structure roofed with brushwood and stubble. Huts of this kind are still being built in some cultures today.

● ETHNOGRAPHIC CONTEXTS

Some idea of the most ancient buildings thus can be gained from examining ethnographic cultures, that is, populations which, at various latitudes on the planet, have passed down their traditional customs through the centuries. Despite the urgent appeals of anthropologists and environmentalists, their habitats are now increasingly threatened by Western economic exploitation and ecological disaster: from the rainforests of the Amazon and Central Africa to the Arctic and southern Africa, where the land is arid but rich in diamond and gold mines. It is vitally important, therefore, to at least record the ways of life and habitats of these at-risk populations before it is too late.

Often referred to improperly as Eskimos, the Inuit ("men") are a nomadic ethnic-linguistic group of still mysterious origin that crossed the Bering Strait from Asia an estimated 5500 years ago to settle on the coasts of Siberia, Alaska, Canada, and Green-

land. The Inuit differ from any other people in the world for their typical dwelling place, the igloo, a structure able to withstand the most violent storms and in which they can live even at polar temperatures. The igloo, composed entirely of blocks of ice to form a rounded structure with a semicircular entrance and a hole at the top for ventilation and discharging smoke, is a temporary dwelling used during the hunting and fishing seasons. Along the southern and northwestern coasts of Greenland, where no trees grow, traditional houses in the scattered villages were built of stone covered with moss. Only after the arrival of European colonists were these replaced by buildings constructed of wooden staves, often suspended over the rock like pile-dwellings.

Around the Bering Strait, too, the Inuit have lived since remote times in huts built on piles covered with walrus skins. In use since prehistoric times, the pile-dwelling is still common today, in a wide variety of types, in many cultures throughout the world, especially the Far East. Among the dwelling types constructed of plain natural materials in warmer climatic zones are the domed huts typical of the South African *kraal*; throughout central-southern Africa, in fact, are found huts with a cylindrical body and conical roof, or an elongated body with a flat or sloping roof.

● STONEHENGE

In addition to buildings used as dwelling places, monumental structures used for tribal worship or as meeting places were also erected in very ancient times. Perhaps the most famous of these is Stonehenge, located in the south of England; the oldest part of the site dates from the second half of the third millennium B.C.E. Stonehenge is believed to have been a sort of astronomical observatory or a temple to the sun, perhaps both. The megalithic complex rises in a series of concentric circles, or *cromlechs*, built of massive stones set vertically in the earth and topped by a horizontal slab to form a trilith (p. 90).

These enormous blocks, rising to a height of 13 feet in the newer circle (second millennium B.C.E.) and 26 feet elsewhere, are formed of hewn stones, each fixed by a tooth to a notch carved in the architrave.

● THE PUEBLO

The period of transition from a hunting-and-gathering economy to an agricultural economy can be witnessed even today in pueblos (literally, "people" or "villages") on the prairies and plateaus of Arizona and New Mexico. These settlements are made up of small, cube-shaped houses that are superimposed one upon another and backed up against the rocky side of a canyon. Located nearby them are *kiva*, sacred constructions where the spirits were believed to retire for rest.

Above:
Megalithic complex of Stonehenge, third millennium B.C.E. Salisbury, Wiltshire, England.

Below:
Aerial view of the Bonito pueblo, 850–1130 C.E. Chaco Culture National Historical Park, New Mexico. The village, once inhabited by the Anasazi tribe (in *Navaho,* "old people"), contains the remains of more than 600 dwelling places and 33 *kivas.*

Below:
Pile-dwellings on the Vinh Te Canal. Vietnam.

The Egyptians

Monumental gateway at the Temple of Queen Hatshepsut and Thutmose III. Karnak. The entrance is distinguished by the so-called pylon: two massive towers tapered at the top.

Below: *Reconstruction of the Sun Temple of Niuserre, V Dynasty (2480 B.C.E.).* Abu Gurab.
1. Monumental entrance
2. Roadway to the temple

3. Courtyard
4. Altar
5. Obelisk
6. Boat of the Sun

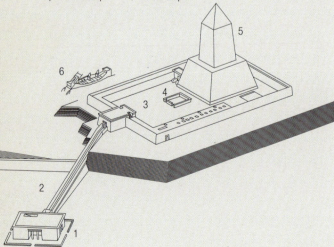

Extending almost the entire length of the Nile River, for millennia the source of its prosperity and wealth, the civilization of Ancient Egypt flourished from about the fourth millennium B.C.E. to 525 B.C.E., the year of the Persian conquest led by Cambyses II, son of Cyrus the Great. It was later, under Alexander the Great, founder of the city of Alexandria (332 B.C.E.), that ties between Egyptian and Greek cultures were consolidated. Later, having overthrown the Ptolemaic Dynasty (31 B.C.E.), Rome was to use these lands as a granary for its empire. Egypt then fell under the dominion of the Byzantium, before being definitively conquered by Islamic forces (639-642 C.E.).

● CAPITALS

The most ancient capital of Egypt was Memphis. Famous for its pyramids, Memphis was located on the boundary between Lower and Middle Egypt. During the reign of the XI Dynasty, the capital was moved to Thebes, in Upper Egypt, a city that reached its peak of splendor between the sixteenth and the thirteenth centuries B.C.E. (XVIII–XIX Dynasties). Thebes, which spread along the Nile from the sites of present-day Karnak and Luxor (east of the river) to the villages of Gurnah and Medinet Habu (west of the river), was the sacred city, consecrated to the cult of Amon. It is here that one finds the ruins of the most famous monumental temples, which evolved over the centuries into increasingly grandiose and complex structures.

● TEMPLES

Egyptian temples can be classified under three basic headings: the hy-

paethral (open to the sky), dedicated to the cult of the sun god Ra, the pharaoh's father; the peripteral, a forerunner of the Greek temple (a rectangular cell, open on the short side and surrounded by a portico of columns or pillars); and the penetralia (with a porticoed courtyard, atrium, vestibule, cell, and sanctuary all in a row, following a funnel-shaped layout).

● BUILDING TECHNIQUES

Relying mainly on poor building materials (first wood and reeds, then earth materials taken from the Nile, such as adobe, a mixture of mud and straw), Egyptian architecture began to employ limestone and sandstone around 2600 B.C.E. The adoption of these materials, which were stronger and harder (but also heavier) than their predecessors, in structures of the same forms and types,

Hypostyle hall in the Great Temple of Ramses III, XX Dynasty (r. 1182–1151 B.C.E.). Medinet Habu, Thebes.

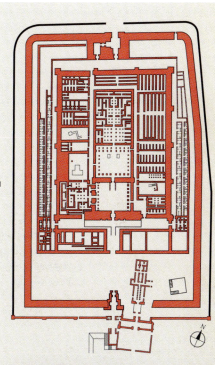

Plan of the Great Funerary Temple of Ramses III, XX Dynasty. Medinet Habu, Thebes. Near the temple dedicated to Amon, erected by Queen Hatshepsut (r. 1479–1457 B.C.E.) and enlarged by her son Thutmose III, the Pharaoh Ramses III built a great funerary complex. Similar in plan to the Ramesseum of his predecessor, Ramses II (p. 108), the temple, called "the castle of Ramses linked to eternity," was connected to the Nile by a channel.

called for complex building techniques. The first problem, that of transporting rough-hewn blocks from the quarry to the worksite, was solved by using wooden rollers on land and rafts on the river. These methods were rendered feasible by the abundance of low-cost, well-trained laborers. The blocks were put in place by rolling them up brick ramps. The spaces between columns were filled with loose earth, which was later removed, to ensure maximum stability. To make the structure more solid, the pillars were sometimes partly buried in the ground. Roofs were built according to the trilith system; great slabs of stone, or of wood in the case of dwellings, were connected to the entablatures by means of fixed joints. Along the sides of the structure, at the top of the walls, openings were provided for lighting, located to achieve the desired effects in the interior.

● OBELISKS

In addition to temples and pyramids (pp. 204–205), a monument typical of Ancient Egyptian architecture is the obelisk. Only a few remain at their original sites, as at least 30 others have been removed to the West since the time of Emperor Augustus. Monolithic and quadrangular in shape, the tower is tapered at the top and culminates in a point (thus the Greek word *obelískos*, or "skewer").

The obelisk was raised at the entrance to a temple by means of a simple but efficient technique that relied on a containing wall filled with sand. Symbolically, the obelisk is a divine ray of sun or the primordial mountain from which the earth's waters flow. Its imposing aspect—some obelisks soared as high as 130 feet—exerted a powerful fascination during the Renaissance.

Obelisk of Heliopolis, thirteenth century B.C.E. Rome, Piazza del Popolo. Dedicated to the sun god Ra, this nearly 80-foot obelisk, which originally stood before the temple of the Sun at Heliopolis (near Cairo), is covered with hieroglyphic characters engraved in granite. Brought to Rome by the Emperor Augustus in 10 C.E. and raised in the Circus Maximus, it was restored by Pope Sixtus V and placed in Piazza del Popolo in 1588.

The Pyramids

Most likely related to the Greek word *pyr* ("fire"), because of the structure's flame-like shape, the word "pyramid" is of uncertain etymology. A pyramid designates the burial site of an Egyptian pharaoh. The pyramids are thus tombs of royal rank characterized, like a geometric solid, by a square base and four triangular sides converging to a point at the top.

● FROM THE MASTABA TO THE PYRAMID

The Egyptian royal pyramid is considered a monumental evolution of the mastaba, a private tomb in widespread use during the Old Kingdom (2850–2230 B.C.E.). The shape of these tombs, a truncated pyramid with rectangular base, is reminiscent of a bench (giving rise to the Arabic word *mastaba*, or "stone bench"). The mastaba is a compact mound made of stone and terracotta, usually with two openings on the long sides that provide access to an underground shaft, which leads to the funeral chamber itself. Outside, on the eastern side of the mound, were votive altars for sacrifices, later transformed into a chamber serving the same function. Areas alluding to domestic life (courtyards, corridors, and rooms embellished with paintings and carved reliefs) were added later. The rich decorations in these rooms illustrate scenes from daily life or the journey to the "other world" undertaken by the deceased, whose features appear on the statues. The form of the royal pyramid probably developed from the idealized superimposition of these private tombs, conferring on the pharaoh's sepulcher a symbolic significance much greater than that of the mastaba. The superimposition of one mastaba on another, with the highest one necessarily the smallest, gave rise to the step pyramid, such as that of Pharaoh Djoser (p. 74), the oldest surviving pyramid today (c. 2650 B.C.E.).

● BASIC CHARACTERISTICS

The pyramid was given its definitive form by filling the gaps between each step. Unlike the mastaba, the pyramid has no underground sepulchral chambers; instead, the central chambers are contained within the pyramid itself and entered through long, narrow corridors. For the architects of the time, funerary chambers represented a prelude to experimentation with the first vaulted rooms. Since the chamber in which the pharaoh's mummy was placed stood at the center of

View of the pyramids of Cheops, Chephren (Khafre), and Mycerinus, IV Dynasty (2625–2510 B.C.E.). Giza. These majestic pyramids were built over the course of one century. In the foreground stand three small step pyramids.

the pyramid, the weight of much of the monument rested on it. Solutions such as the pseudo-arch, flat roof, and reverse-V roof served to absorb the immense weight pressing on the ceiling of the empty chamber. The pyramid was not an isolated monument, but was flanked by collateral structures in which the funeral ceremonies were held.

● ENDURING FASCINATION

The imposing form and sheer majesty of the Egyptian pyramid have exerted a deep fascination on many peoples throughout the centuries, beginning with the Ancient Romans. With the rediscovery of Egyptian culture, the Renaissance revived the concept of the pyramid as a funerary monument and symbol of eternity. The pyramid in modern architecture has lost these meanings, but it has been revived in new forms, innovative in both material and function; perhaps the best-known example is the glass pyramid designed by I.M. Pei for the Louvre (p. 364).

Antonio Canova, *Model in terracotta and wood for the monument to Titian*, c. 1795. Venice, Correr Museum.

Top:
Pyramid of Gaius Cestius, 28–12 B.C.E. Rome. The Roman pyramid tomb reflects the taste for the exotic prevailing in the Augustan Age.

Above:
Diagram of a group of mastabas

Vertical section of the pyramid of Cheops at Giza
1. Entrance
2. Descending corridor
3. Unfinished chamber
4. Queen's chamber
5. Discharge chambers
6. Pharaoh's chamber
7. The great gallery

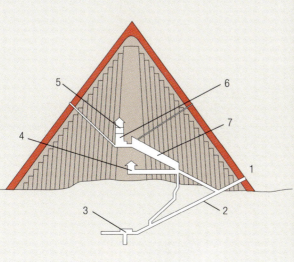

The Civilization of the Indus Valley

Aerial view of the ruins. Mohenjo-daro, Sind, Pakistan.

Reconstruction of the layout of Mohenjo-daro.

Mohenjo-daro ("hill of the dead") is the name traditionally given to a high mound of earth that rises on the right bank of the Indus River in the vicinity of today's Khairpur, Pakistan. It was at this site, in 1922, that the Indian archaeologist Rakhal Das Banerji discovered, beneath a stupa dating from the second to the fourth centuries C.E., the ruins of a much older city whose houses were made of raw and baked brick.

This was the beginning of a series of extraordinary finds that have revealed many aspects of a great civilization that flourished in the Indus River Valley, in an area roughly corresponding to today's Pakistan and northwestern India, between the late fourth and the mid-second millennium B.C.E.

● HARAPPA AND MOHENJO-DARO

The discovery of the first ruins of Mohenjo-daro immediately revealed characteristics similar to those of another archaeological site, discovered in 1860, at the center of an ancient, previously little-known civilization: Harappa, located in today's province of Punjab, Pakistan. What clearly emerged from both of these sites was a precise urban layout, an exceptional characteristic this early in the history of human civilization and architecture.

Each of the two cities was, in all probability, the capital of a kingdom made up of scattered villages nestled at the foot of a fortified hill, each of which was laid out in a checkerboard pattern with streets intersecting at right angles and a highly advanced system of sewage canals. On the basis of these discoveries, the culture of the Indus Valley must be regarded as one of the most important among all those that developed during the Copper and Bronze ages. Entirely independent of contemporaneous urban civilizations in the Mediterranean region, Mesopotamia, and China, it was in no way inferior to them in its architectural, artistic, and social achievements.

● ARCHAEOLOGICAL EXCAVATIONS

The archaeological research of Banerji and his successors at Mohenjo-daro, and those conducted at Harappa—from the discoveries of the explorers Charles Masson and Alexander Burnes to the excavations of Alexander Cunningham—have continued through the last century and up to recent times, yielding new and important finds. In the case of Mohenjo-daro, no substantial

Left:
*Remains of the citadel,
with a stupa in the
background.*
Mohenjo-daro,
Sind, Pakistan.

Right:
*Remains of the Great
Bath.* Mohenjo-daro,
Sind, Pakistan.
The Great Bath is a large
building made of baked
bricks and containing
several rooms, which
may have served a
religious function.
At the center is a pool
nearly 40 feet long and
some 32 feet wide.

Below:
*Pits covered
with terracotta
in the floor of an
artisan's house.*
Mohenjo-daro,
Sind, Pakistan.

differences have been found between the first layers and the last, indicating that the civilization was particularly advanced from the beginning. The earliest stages, in fact, reveal a precise urban plan in the grid-like pattern of roads, later blurred by the addition of smaller streets and lanes extraneous to the main checkerboard scheme. The streets were quite wide for the time, ranging from a little less than 10 feet to about 20 feet, with alleys just over three feet wide. Although the roads were not paved, some attempt to do so apparently was made with bricks and fragments of broken earthenware. One of the most striking aspects of the site is a system of channels and covered sewage lines, which collected organic and hygienic waste from a latrine in each house and carried it through a purification pit; the sewage system was strictly separated from that of freshwater and well water for drinking. At the Harappa site, a system for the collection of trash, which was deposited in rectangular bins, has recently been found.

● HOUSES

A lack of source materials or other evidence has made it is impossible to determine with certainty the functions of the various buildings. Based on their forms, however, they seem to be classifiable as temples, palaces, private residences, artisans' houses, and kilns. Private houses appear to have been either quite small (unless the buildings in question were not houses but storage depots or warehouses) or very large, with virtually nothing of intermediate size. The houses consisted of one big room, in some cases with stairs leading to an upper floor or the roof.

In the Land Between Two Rivers

The extent of the ancient capital of Babylonia at the time of Nebuchadnezzar II is compared here with that of Republican Rome and Imperial Rome.

Reconstruction of a Babylonian temple.
This pyramid-like structure, perhaps the design of the biblical Tower of Babel, reached a height of perhaps 600 feet, according to the historian Strabo. It had seven tiers, equal to the number of planets known at the time.

Great Ziggurat, second millennium B.C.E. Ur, Iraq. The building most characteristic of Mesopotamian architecture is the ziggurat (p. 49). The location of the temple at the top of the structure had symbolic significance, that of being able to contemplate the astral divinities from a closer vantage point.

Mesopotamia, the fertile "land between two rivers" (Tigris and Euphrates), corresponds more or less to the territory of modern-day Iraq, Asian Turkey, and the northern border region of Syria. Long before its conquest by Alexander the Great in 331 B.C.E., this region of Asia Minor was inhabited by a succession of different populations distinguished by highly evolved forms of urban society that were of great importance to the history of architecture (pp. 110–111).

● THE SUMERIANS

It was in the last two centuries of the fourth millennium that the Sumerians (3200–2800 B.C.E.), perhaps springing from the same stock that had given rise to the civilization of the Indus Valley, settled in Mesopotamia. Their capital city of Ur, on the right bank of the Euphrates River (near today's Tell el-Muqayyar, Iraq), was laid out in the "square grid" urban scheme, ensuring a rationalized use of space. Another important city-state on the Euphrates was Uruk (called Erech in the Hebrew Bible and *Warka* in Arabic). Here one finds some of the oldest examples of the ziggurat, an unusual structure with an underground funerary chamber and enclosed by two concentric thick walls. Another remarkable structure is the so-called Oval Temple at the site of Kafajeh (Diyala Province, Iraq), dated between 2750 and 2600 B.C.E. The building emerges as a prominent, autonomous presence in the urban grid and is also surrounded by two concentric walls. A secondary building in the complex may have been the site of the temple administration, confirming the power and economic prestige of the religious sphere, much as in other civilizations of the ancient world.

● THE AKKADIANS

With the fall of the last Lagash dynasty, the power of the Sumerians was appropriated by Sargon of Akkad (2350–2300 B.C.E.), who inaugurated a peri-

Ruins of an underground funerary construction in stone in the ancient city of Uruk, fourth–third millennia B.C.E. Warka, Iraq.

od of revival and architectural restoration that was to continue under the reign of Gudea of Lagash (2141–2122 B.C.E.) and the Third Dynasty of Ur.

● THE BABYLONIANS

Extending from the Persian Gulf to the site of modern Baghdad, the fertile Babylonian plain was marked by two great historical stages: that of the first empire (twentieth to sixteenth centuries B.C.E.), distinguished primarily by the personality and achievements of its sovereign, Hammurabi (r. 1792–1750 B.C.E.); and the domination first of the Hittites, then of the Cassites, and finally of the Assyrians during the reign of Nebuchadnezzar II (r. 605–562 B.C.E.). It was under the efficient governance of Hammurabi that architecture first flourished in the capital city, Babylon (or Babel), famous throughout the ancient world for its hanging gardens and temples. In 1531 B.C.E., the mythical city on the two banks of the Euphrates was sacked by the Hittites, inaugurating its

first period of decline. Revived under Nebuchadnezzar—its capital numbered up to one million inhabitants at the time—Babylonia was definitively conquered by the Persians in 539 B.C.E.

● THE HITTITES

The first stage in the decline of Babylonian civilization was caused by the emancipation of the Assyrian colonies and by the expansion of the Hittite Empire (fif-

teenth–thirteenth centuries B.C.E.). From the northern regions of Mesopotamia to the borders of modern-day Turkey, the Hittite Empire was to extend its political and military power as far as Egypt. The architecture of the Hittite civilization showed great vitality, although its art was clearly derived from Assyrian and Babylonian models. Architectural creations such as the imposing Lion Gate in the city of Hattusas in Anatolia (Asian Turkey) show undeniable originality.

Lion Gate, thirteenth–twelfth centuries B.C.E. Hattusas Bogazkoy, Turkey. The ruins of the entrance gate at the Hittite capital include partially restored relief carvings of two guardian lions.

The Peoples of the Iranian Plateau

Like Mesopotamia, the vast Iranian plateau has seen a succession of diverse civilizations, of greater or lesser splendor. The territory in question, known in ancient times as Arya ("land of the Aryans"), occupied much of the modern Iranian uplands as well as the areas bounded to the north by the Caucasus mountains and Lake Aral, to the east by the Tigris River, to the west by the Indus River, and to the south by the Persian Gulf and Arabian Sea. The western portion of Arya stretched from Media to Persia.

● THE CIVILIZATION OF ELAM

Around the fourth millennium B.C.E., near the border of the Iranian plateau, there emerged the civilization of Elam (or Susiana), which had its center in the city-state of Susa. By about 3500 B.C.E., Susa (today called Shush, in southwestern Iran) already covered an area of more than 60 acres. Deeply influenced by Sumerian culture, the kingdom of Elam was absorbed into the Akkadian Empire in 2300 B.C.E. It rose again some centuries later and conquered Ur in about 1930 B.C.E. Elam reached the height of its prestige with the founding of the capital of Dur-Untash (present-day Choga Zanbil), where an imposing ziggurat still stands) and with the conquest of Babylon in 1175 B.C.E.

● THE MEDES

The first major political entity in the region was the kingdom of Media, whose capital was the city of Ecbatana (today's Hamadan, 250 miles southwest of Teheran). It was inhabited by the Medes, a people of northern origin.

Mentioned in sources as early as the ninth century B.C.E., the Medes expanded first to the west, overcoming the Neo-Assyrian Empire (614–612 B.C.E.), and then, for a brief period, to the Kingdom of Persia.

Above:
Arch leading to the stairway of the Elamite ziggurat of Inshushinak and Napirisha, c. 1250 B.C.E. Dur-Untash (Choga Zanbil), Iran. With its temples of sun-dried brick, the holy city of Dur-Untash, not far from Susa, was built at the initiative of King Untash Napirisha (1250 B.C.E.) to impose unity on his domain. The urban center, surrounded by three rings of wall, contained numerous sanctuaries. The third circle of walls was to have enclosed the city proper, with private residences that were never built. Provisions had been made for supplying the city with water transferred by canal from a purification well.

● URARTU

The Kingdom of Urartu, on the border with Armenia and later annexed to the kingdom of Media, dates from the ninth century B.C.E. Urartu temples, resembling towers, were to have an important influence on Achaemenid architecture.

● THE ACHAEMENIDS

The Persians reacted to the political and military influence of the Medes during the time of Cyrus the Great, founder of the Achaemenid Dynasty. In 550 B.C.E., Cyrus overthrew King Astyages and proclaimed himself king of the Medes as well as the Persians. The Achaemenid Dynasty was a period of artistic flowering that left an extraordinary architectural legacy, from Cyrus's solemn tomb at Pasargadae (southwestern Iran) to the splendid structures of Persepolis, described in the next two pages.

● THE PARTHIANS AND THE SASSANIDS

Overthrown by Alexander the Great, the vast Achaemenid Empire was reorganized under the reign of Seleucus I Nicator (305–281 B.C.E.); it was then divided into smaller states that were not reunified until the rule of the Parthians (247 B.C.E.–227 C.E.). From the artistic point of view, Achaemenid architecture—albeit with major adaptations by Greece and Rome—established the defining style of the Western world. The Sassanid Dynasty (224–642 C.E.) revived the Achaemenid tradition with temples dedicated to fire and monumental palaces.

Above
Tomb of Cyrus the Great, 529 B.C.E. Pasargadae, Iran. Located in southwestern Iran, Pasargadae ("camp of the Persians," or "fortress of the Fars"), lies 6,200 feet above the plain of Marghab near the Pulvar River.

Upon entering the citadel complex from the southwest, the visitor immediately comes upon the Tomb of Cyrus, some 33 feet high. The great Achaemenid sovereign was the patron of a grandiose urban project, in keeping with his all-embracing vision of power.

Left:
Ruins of the ancient city-state of Susa. Shush, Iran. Destroyed in 640 B.C.E. by Assurbanipal, Susa was rebuilt by the Achaemenids, who wintered there. The ruins of the citadel stand on an artificial hill (*tell*), formed by the stratification of archaeological remains.

Above:
Ruins of the Sassanid Palace and Audience Hall ("Arch of Cosroe"), sixth century B.C.E. Ctesifonte, Taq-i Kisra, Iraq.

Right:
Ruins of the Parthian city, first century B.C.E. Hatra, Iraq.

Persepolis

Below:
View of the ruins.
Persepolis, Takht-i Jamshid, Iran.

On the broad plain covering the northern part of Persis (now Fars) province, not far from Pasargadae, the heart of Persian and Achaemenid culture, Darius the Great established the center of his empire. It was here that the splendid palaces of Persepolis welcomed the diplomatic and military delegations that came to render homage to the "King of Kings." Darius, like his successors, was to be buried in the rock tombs of Naqsh-i Rustam, located in today's Iran.

● THE STRUCTURE

A splendid colossal work that was completed in a little less than a single century (sixth–fifth centuries B.C.E.), the great building complex of Persepolis, which is now at risk of irreparable deterioration, was constructed under the direct supervision of Darius the Great.

The artificial embankment is nearly 40 feet high, 100 feet wide, and a third of a mile long. The king did not live to see the undertaking completed, and his son, Xerxes I, supervised the final details; among these were the double-ramp stairway with steps hewn from

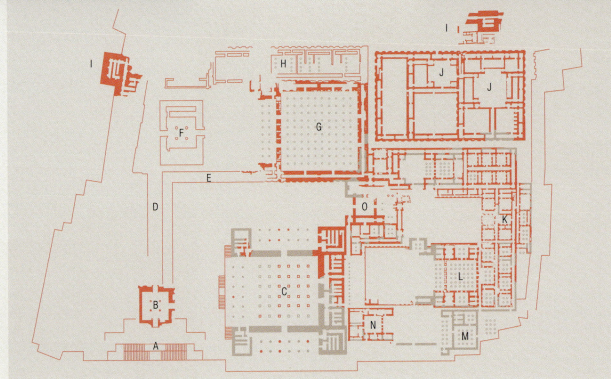

Layout of Persepolis (surviving buildings outlined in red).

A. Tiered stairway to the entrance
B. Gate of Xerxes, or Gate of the Nations
C. *Apadana* or Audience Hall
D. The Army Road
E. Wall separating the two courtyards
F. Unfinished gate
G. Throne Room, or Hall of the Hundred Columns
H. Royal stables
I. Fortifications
J. Royal treasury
K. Warehouses
L. Palace of Xerxes
M. Palace H
N. Palace of Darius I
O. Entrance to the Tripylon

blocks of stone. In front of it stands the monumental Xerxes Gate (or Gate of the Nations), square in design, with four interior columns and four stone benches. The three passages in the gate were adorned with the propitious images of lamassu, the mythological beings (human-headed winged lions) that protected the gate against entry by evil spirits (pp. 110–111).

The entranceway faced west, while the exit opened to the east onto a road that led to the Hall of the Hundred Columns. The southern opening in the gate gave access to the *apadana*, a raised hypostyle hall with double porticoes on three sides, which served as a royal audience hall (p. 111).

The complex contained a number of rooms reserved for the king and his dignitaries. Among these was the Tripylon, a small hall whose name derives from its three portals and which may have been the meeting room of the king's advisors. To the right of the Tripylon, a long wall runs beside the so-called Army Road, leading to a structure, which was never completed, in which visitors were to have been an-nounced to the king by the court marshals. The enormous complex also served as a royal residence. Two areas within it were reserved for the sovereigns themselves: the palaces of Darius and Xerxes.

The former, raised eight feet above ground level, centers around a hypostyle hall supported by twelve columns. Around it are other rooms whose outer walls, along with their doorways, architraves, and windows, have survived to this day. The Palace of Xerxes was built according to a similar plan, with a harem also in the immediate vicinity.

The treasures of the sovereigns and the material legacy of the Achaemenid Empire were safeguarded in the southeastern area.

The nerve centers of this citadel of power were the Hall of One Hundred Columns (or Throne Room), entirely decorated with scenes portraying the king in regal majesty; and the Audience Hall (the aforementioned *apadana*), where the envoys of the empire's 28 nations paid homage to the sovereign by acts of submission.

Altars in the Temple of Fire of Darius I, 521–486 B.C.E. Naqsh-i Rustam, Persepolis, Iran. Worshipers of fire, the source of life and reflection of the supreme divinity, *Ahura Mazda* ("Wise Lord"), the Persians erected tower-shaped temples with square bases, similar to those of the Urartaeans.

Above:
Lamassu guarding the Xerxes Gate, or Gate of the Nations. Persepolis, Takht-i Jamshid, Iran.

Remains of the Hall of the Hundred Columns. Persepolis, Takht-i Jamshid, Iran.

Crete and Mycenae

Ceramic plaques representing façades of individual Minoan houses, 1700–1600 B.C.E. Heraklion, Archaeological Museum, Crete. These small objects, from one to two inches tall, represent the façades of Minoan houses with several floors, appearing in a surprising variety of designs.

Both continuity and dualism are reflected in these two Aegean civilizations. As noted previously (pp. 112–113), the ancient Minoan civilization on the island of Crete, located in the eastern Mediterranean, is considered an important precursor to the Mycenaean civilization on the Peloponnesus, even though the two cultures had their own distinct characteristics. From the fifteenth to the thirteenth centuries B.C.E., the dominion of Mycenae extended as far as Crete. The Minoan culture outlasted that of its conquerors, who learned from them new techniques in gold work, jewelry, and painting, among others.

● MINOAN CIVILIZATION

The evolution of Cretan culture extended from the last phase of the Neolithic Age (2900 B.C.E.) to the late Bronze Age (1200 B.C.E.) and the civilization reached its peak between 2000 and 1500 B.C.E. with the evolution of the so-called "palace" culture, distinguished by the great architectural complexes that formed the heart of the city-state, as mentioned by Homer in the *Iliad* (XIII, 450 ff.). The adjective "Minoan" was coined by the British archaeologist Arthur Evans, who made the discovery of Knossos during excavations begun in 1900. Evans employed the term in allusion to the mythological King Minos and his labyrinthine palace, built by Daedalus, now hailed as the first great architect of antiquity. In addition to a number of large palace complexes scattered throughout the island (at Malia, Phaistos, Zakros, and Gortyn, to mention the most important), Minoan architecture also included less imposing buildings, comprising isolated houses of which rare but significant traces have been found. The most ancient is a Late Stone Age house at Zakros with an intriguing G-shaped floor plan, like a labyrinth in miniature. Some sense of the elevation as well as the various color schemes and decorations adopted for Minoan dwelling places may be gained from ceramic plaques found near the "basement of weights" in the Palace of Knossos. The distribution of the rooms and the volumetric proportions may be hypothesized from terracotta models and from evidence unearthed by a series of excavations on the island. The high level of architectural development reached in Crete is also demonstrated by the remains of terracotta pipes with modern-type joints.

● MYCENAEAN CIVILIZATION

Mycenaean civilization is named for its most important city, Mycenae, the ancient capital of Greece and the home of Agamemnon, the powerful king who leads the Achaean army against Troy in the *Iliad*. No ancient authors, however, called the Mycenaeans by that name.

Left:
Underground circular silos for conserving grain, 2000–1450 B.C.E. Malia, Crete.

Above:
View of archaeological excavations. Knossos, Crete.

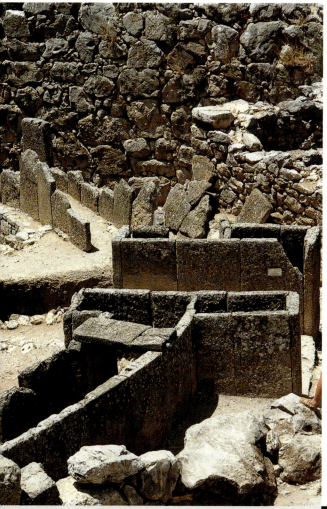

Homer called them Achaens, Danii, or Argives; what the Greeks knew of their origins came only from legends, most of them unreliable. In 1876, on the strength of research and fieldwork by the German archaeologist Heinrich Schliemann, an ardent lover of classical history, the truth of Homer's epic was revealed. In only 11 weeks of excavation, Schliemann and his team uncovered royal tombs containing splendid artifacts now known to date from a dynasty that ruled at least three hundred years before the time of the Trojan War. In the decades between Schliemann's excavations and the present, much more information about this great civilization has come to light. We now know, for example, that it spread from continental Greece to the Aegean islands and as far as the east-central Mediterranean coast.

● GOLDEN MYCENAE

"Golden Mycenae", as Homer called it, stood on a hill at the edge of the Argive Plain in the eastern Peloponnesus. At the top, surrounded by cyclopean walls, the Acropolis rose 912 feet above the plain (see map, p. 113). Another city isolated on a hilltop was "strong-walled Tyrins," where a network of tunnels within the walls was constructed with enormous polygonal blocks.

Unlike its Minoan counterpart, the Mycenaean palace was fortified. A true citadel, it was entered only through monumental gates, one of which has survived—the famous Lion Gate, decorated by a relief of two lionesses facing each other (p. 32). At the center of the hilltop stood the palace, at its heart the *megaron*: a room with a fireplace at the center, supported by four columns and preceded by an entrance vestibule and a portico. Although in reduced scale, this structure served the same purpose as the central courtyard in the Minoan palace.

Mycenaean *tholos* tombs, consisting of a circular chamber entered through a long corridor (*dromos*) are also similar to those of Crete. In both cases, burial was by interment, although circular tombs also have been found in Mycenae, erroneously proclaimed by Schliemann to be the burial sites of Agamemnon and his followers.

Above:
Royal tombs of Circle A within the citadel, thirteenth century B.C.E. *Mycenae, Peloponnesus, Greece.*

Below:
Section view and layout of Mycenaean tholos tomb (from Lord William Taylor, I Micenei, Florence 1987).

Right:
Detail of vault in the tholos tomb known as the Treasure of Atreus, thirteenth century B.C.E. *Mycenae, Peloponnesus, Greece.*

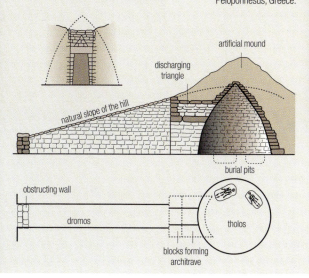

The Etruscans

The origin of the Etruscans, whose culture was one of the richest in antiquity, remains uncertain to this day. Where did this people come from? Were they native to the Italian peninsula, or did they arrive in a wave of migration? The first to raise this question was Dionysius of Halicarnassus in the first century B.C.E., who made a compendium (in *Roman Antiquities*, XXVI–XXX) of all previous theories. Today the most credible hypotheses range from that of indigenous origin to the possibility of migration from the north with the Italics, to the suggestion, deemed the most probable, that they came from Asia Minor.

● CHRONOLOGY

Bringing to the Italian coastal region their culture, the Etruscans called themselves the Rasenna; the Ancient Greeks called them Tyrsenoi (from which the name Tyrrhenian Sea). Their civilization overlapped, or perhaps succeeded, the Villanovan, named for the archaeological site (ninth–eighth centuries B.C.E.) in the province of Emilia, where necropolises have been found in which the dead were cremated and their ashes conserved in urns, a custom common to the Etruscans. In the eighth century B.C.E., the Etruscan cities were founded. By the following century, the Etruscan

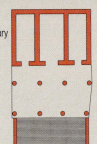

Etruscan Temple of Belvedere, fourth century B.C.E. Orvieto, Italy.

Layout reconstruction of the temple of Belvedere at Orvieto, Italy.

Limestone funerary urn in the shape of a house. Florence, National Archaeological Museum (from Chiusi). The urn looks like a miniature aristocratic palace from the Hellenistic Age, decorated with columns and Aeolic capitals, a loggia, and a rusticated bench.

Laminated bronze cinerary urn, decorated with embossed motifs, in the form of a hut, first half of the eighth century B.C.E. Rome, National Archaeological Museum of Villa Giulia (from Vulci, Necropolis of the Osteria). The circular tomb type was typical of the old society, made up of clans.

Red clay cinerary urn in the shape of a house, 650–625 B.C.E. Rome, National Archaeological Museum of Villa Giulia (from Cerveteri, Latium).

domain extended from the coast of the Campagna region to the southern Po Valley. Rome itself fell under Etruscan control, from the time of kings Tarquinius Priscus (607 B.C.E.) and Servius Tullius (578 B.C.E.) to that of Tarquinius Superbus, driven out of the city in 509 B.C.E., followed by years of conflict and strategic alliances, culminating in a truce with Rome in 351 B.C.E. Futile attempts were made to weaken the immense power of Rome during the Second Punic War (218 B.C.E.), but in the end the Etruscans were forced to finance Rome in its war against Carthage. One after another, proud Etruscan cities became colonies of the Empire, until Etruria was officially annexed in 27 B.C.E. as *Regium VII*.

● ARCHITECTURAL CHARACTERISTICS

The oldest Etruscan dwellings must have resembled their hut-shaped fu-

nerary urns, with a sloping roof and a circular plan (later to become rectangular). In addition to the arch, a feature peculiar to Etruscan architecture is the podium temple, with a ramp of front steps leading to the entrance. This led into the *pronaos*, off of which opened three contiguous cells. This defined the basic typology of the Italic temple, later adopted by the Romans and other peoples on the Italian peninsula. These buildings, with broad sloping roofs now devoid of any real pediment decoration, were occasionally ornamented with antefixes (eave carvings). Another typical feature of Etruscan architecture is the necropolis, a number of which are found across a territory roughly corresponding to today's southern Tuscany and Upper Latium. The tombs were of the pseudo-vault type (known as "vault tombs"), the mound type, or the chamber type, the latter often splendidly decorated.

Interior of the Shields and Chairs chamber tomb, middle of sixth century B.C.E. Cerveteri, Latium.

A typical "vault tomb," 620–600 B.C.E. Florence, National Archaeological Museum (reconstruction from Casale Marittimo, Volterra). The ceiling is not a real dome, but a pseudo-dome constructed of rows of soft stone laid in concentric rings and covered with a slab. A pillar at the center provides support. The tomb was discovered in 1898, transported to Florence, and reconstructed in the garden of the Archaeological Museum.

Above:
Terracotta antefix in the form of a Gorgon's head, late sixth–fifth centuries B.C.E. Rome, National Archaeological Museum of Villa Giulia (from Veio, Temple of the Portonaccio). These elements were used to decorate the ends of roof tiles, perhaps to protect the beams from humidity, or to adorn the base of pediments, which bore no other decoration. Although the antefix was introduced by the Greeks, the Etruscans used it in a unique way.

Below:
Clay frieze with race horses, sixth century B.C.E. Siena, Archaeological Museum (from Murlo). Among the important discoveries of recent decades, the remains of an aristrocratic palace, or perhaps a sanctuary, were found in 1977 at Murlo, a small town south of Siena. The decoration on the friezes and other sculpted elements is of the highest quality, indicating that the site must have been a place of great prestige.

The Seven Wonders of the Ancient World

Above:

Reconstruction of the Hanging Gardens of Babylon, with the Tower of Babel in the background. In 1899, the German archaeologist Robert Koldewey launched an extraordinary series of excavations on the site of Babylon. Within the span of 14 years, he discovered the foundations of the Tower of Babel, the palaces of Nebuchadnezzar, and

the great processional way leading through the heart of the city. It has not yet been decided, however, exactly where the Hanging Gardens were located, since the remains unearthed by Koldewey in the southern part of the citadel, which seem to match ancient descriptions, are too far from the river to make irrigation feasible. More recent research (1986) seems to indicate a

location near the Northern Palace, beyond the encircling walls, but this wonder of the ancient world remains shrouded in mystery.

Reconstruction of mechanism for irrigating the Hanging Gardens. This reconstruction is based on ancient descriptions, which mention a device that allowed water to be taken from below and conveyed to the garden terraces, where tanks were placed as reservoirs.

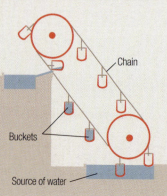

Chain

Buckets

Source of water

The ancient peoples of the Mediterranean Basin and Asia Minor produced magnificent works of architecture, amazing in the eyes of their contemporaries, that are known to us from the descriptions of geographers and travelers (especially between the first century B.C.E. and the first century C.E.). Seven in particular are marvels veiled in legend that only hint at the magnificence of a vanished time. Except for the pyramids, these "wonders of the ancient world" are known only through the writings of Herodotus, Strabo, Diodorus Siculus, Curtius Rufus, and Pliny, who describe with awestruck wonder the Hanging Gardens of Babylon, the Colossus of Rhodes, the gigantic ivory-and-gold statue of Zeus by Phidias, at Olympia; the Mausoleum of Halicarnassus; the Temple of Artemis (Artemisium) at Ephesus; and the Lighthouse at Alexandria.

● HANGING GARDENS OF BABYLON

The hanging gardens must have been located on the eastern bank of the Euphrates. Curiously enough, Herodotus, who gives a detailed description of Babylon (450 B.C.E.), fails to mention this wonder of antiquity, which is instead noted by Diodorus, Strabo, and Curtius Rufus. According to Persian tradition, the spectacular garden was conceived by Semiramis, wife of the mythical King Nino, who is said to have founded Babylon and governed Assyria for 42 years after the death of her husband. Her legendary figure was probably inspired by a woman who really existed, the Assyrian Queen Samurramat (wife of King Shamshi-Adad), who reigned from 810 to 805 B.C.E. after the death of her husband as regent for her young son,

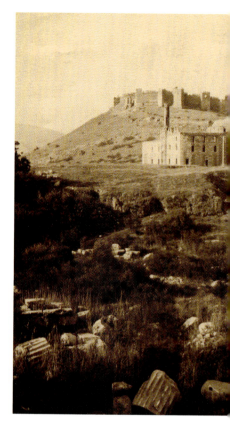

Adadnirari III. In any case, at the time of Nebuchadnezzar II, who governed the city for 43 years beginning in 605 B.C.E., visitors to Babylon marveled at its splendor. Other sources state that it was Nebuchadnezzar himself who created the hanging gardens for his wife Amyitis, daughter of the king of the Medes, who was homesick for the green meadows of Media. The gardens were unique, laid out not on ground level but on a series of terraces, with stone bases waterproofed with bitumen and covered with a layer of earth deep enough to allow enormous trees to grow (Curtius Rufus mentions trees 50 feet tall and 13 feet in diameter). The terraces were supported and surrounded by structures that delimited the garden area. Such an arrangement called for an ingenious system for draining and discharging irrigation water, taken mostly from the Euphrates, since rainfall is scarce in Mesopotamia. The city of Ur adopted a similar but much simpler solution; the flat roofs of houses were covered with a layer of soil on which small vegetable gardens were cultivated.

Ruins of the Temple of Artemis at Ephesus (Turkey), in a photograph from 1890. In the background are other ancient monuments and a castle on the hill.

● ARTEMISIUM OF EPHESUS

Dedicated to Artemis, the goddess of the hunt, a first temple dating from the sixth century at Ephesus (in modern-day Turkey) was burned to the ground in 356 B.C.E. by a madman named Herostratus, whose only aim was to be recorded in history. The monument was then rebuilt by the architect Chersiphron, who retained the original structure with 127 columns with figured bases, 36 of them sculpted by the great Scopas, as Pliny states in his *Naturalis Historia* (XXXVI, 93).

● TOMB OF MAUSOLUS AT HALICARNASSUS

Mausolus, the king of Caria in Asia Minor, governed the Greek colony from 377 to 353 B.C.E. It was his great ambition to have a tomb worthy of his rank, and he began to have it built while he was still alive. His widow, Queen Artemisia, apparently had it completed shortly after his death. The results must have exceeded all expectations. Pliny,

who describes the monument in great detail, deemed it one of the Seven Wonders of the World. Even today the word "mausoleum" is used for a tomb that is especially majestic and imposing. Vitruvius relates that the massive structure was designed by Pythius, to whom the crowning sculpture of Mausolus and Artemisia driving a chariot should probably also be attributed. Pliny's description has been confirmed in part by archaeological excavations (the first of which, led by the British archaeologist Charles T. Newton, took place in 1856), although doubts remain as to the original appearance of the tomb, which was almost certainly built of marble. In the eighteenth century, the Austrian architect and scholar Joseph Emanuel Fischer von Erlach made a reconstruction, followed by various other attempts, based on the information provided by Pliny.

The mausoleum, which measured some 160 feet tall, is believed to have stood on a base consisting of a dado, encircled by Ionic columns, on which the tomb itself rested.

Reconstruction of the Mausoleum at Halicarnassus. Built around the middle of the fourth century B.C.E., the tomb of Mausolus was severely damaged by an earthquake in the twelfth century and was exploited as a marble quarry beginning in 1402. According to the reconstruction by Krischen, the monument stood on a 72-foot-high dado resting on a tiered base. Above this rose an Ionic colonnade some 42 feet high, with nine columns on the sides and eleven on the front and back. At the top was a step pyramid 23 feet high crowned by a four-horse chariot. The proportional system was based on a multiple of the foot and the *sami* cubit, joined in a ratio of two or three multiplied by two or by the powers of two. The exterior, as related by Pliny, was decorated with relief carvings of Amazon warriors. The relief on the eastern side is alleged to have been carved by Scopas, the one on the opposite side by Leochares, and the other two by Bryaxis and Timotheus.

Mausolus, 359 B.C.E. London, British Museum (from the Mausoleum of Halicarnassus).

Greece and Rome: Architecture Compared

Remains of the bouleutérion, fourth century B.C.E. Priene, Turkey. The ancient city of Priene in Caria, laid out in a regular "square grid" plan common to other Greek cities in Asia Minor, was rebuilt around the middle of the fourth century B.C.E. on the slopes of a hill some 1,300 feet high to escape flooding of the Meander River. Resembling those of other cities in Asia Minor (p. 50) is the council hall (*bouleutérion*), with long rows of benches separated by stairways running diagonally and, at the center, the altar from which orators spoke.

Above right:
View of a Greek theater, second century B.C.E. Miletus, Turkey. The theater of Miletus, one of the largest in Asia Minor, could hold 15,000 spectators. Facing it was the western agora, with porticoes on three sides.

Compared to the millennial history of Greece, that of Rome must have seemed insignificant in the eyes of contemporaries: when the entire Greek nation was annexed to Rome in 146 B.C.E., little more than six hundred years had elapsed since Romulus had traced the borders of the city with his plow, according to tradition.

The Romans no doubt were acutely aware of this when they imposed their dominion. It was said, by the scholar Porcius Licinius, that Greece had subjugated Rome with the weapons of its culture and art more quickly than Rome had conquered Greece with its power. In other words, Roman civiliza-

tion was culturally dependent on that of Greece, which had peacefully imposed its hegemony over the Mediterranean world. Paradoxically, the political power of Rome was to become like an immense "megaphone" that amplified the echo of Greek thought throughout the known world. Through this dissemination of Greek culture, which came to be amalgamated with local idioms, the foundation was established of what has come to be known as Western Civilization. This does not mean, however, that Rome was a culture lacking in originality. This was especially not the case in architecture, where the pragmatic spirit of the Ancient Romans was masterfully expressed.

● CHARACTERISTICS OF GREEK ARCHITECTURE

The role played by the Greeks in the field of architecture was primarily that of establishing the architectural orders (pp. 114–115); consolidating the typology, already known to the Egyptians, of the peripteral temple (p. 46); and, in the course of codifying the urban agora, diversifying building types on the basis of their civic functions—from the *bouleutérion*, a council hall of the democratic government, to the theater, a place of community entertainment and catharsis. All of this was in keeping with the concept, characteristic of the Greek mentality and classical Western tradition,

Arch of Augustus, 24 B.C.E. Aosta, Italy.

Ornamental pool in Hadrian's Villa, 118–134 C.E. Tivoli, Rome. Consisting of a number of rooms linked by passageways, the villa of the Emperor Hadrian had thermal baths, nymphaeums (monuments to nymphs), and slave quarters. It also contained reproductions of the most important monuments in the empire, as seen by the emperor during the course of his travels.

that harmony coincides with rationality and logic. These were the principles that inspired Greek urban architecture, and, on a lesser scale, the layout of private houses as well.

● CHARACTERISTICS OF ROMAN ARCHITECTURE

The essential aspects of Greek architecture seem to have been entirely assimilated by the Romans, who could, moreover, bring to bear enormous resources and a range of solutions made possible only by an exceptional political and economic structure.

Roman architecture was further enhanced by the contributions of Italic culture; notable among these was the arch, borrowed from the Etruscans and used not only for buildings and decoration but also for commemorative purposes. Much as in Hellenistic culture, where monuments had been used to convey wealth and glory, Rome proclaimed its power and prestige by constructing triumphal arches in every region of its empire. The great wealth flowing into Rome also produced sumptuous villas, some of them as extensive as small cities. The rational spirit of the Romans is revealed not only in their urban planning but also in their military structures, exemplified by the *castrum* (castle or fortress), whose structure served as inspiration for a number of lavish palaces.

Model of Diocletian's Palace at Split in Croatia. The floor plan of the palace is organized like a Roman military camp, with two main roads intersecting at right angles. Here the emperor lived from the time of his abdication in 305 C.E. to his death in 316. Overlooking the sea and surrounded by walls, the palace is a forerunner of the medieval castle.

The Acropolis of Athens

The highest point in Athens, a rocky hill rising nearly 500 feet high, the Acropolis is one of the most extraordinary achievements in human history. Inhabited since the New Stone Age (second millennium B.C.E.), it was chosen by a Mycenaean prince as the site of his residence in the thirteenth century B.C.E. Among the many temples on the Acropolis dedicated to Athena, the most ancient dates to the time of the tyrant Pisistratus (561–527 B.C.E.). Called the *Hekatómpedon* because it was one hundred feet long, it replaced the temple of Cleisthenes (508 B.C.E.). The Acropolis was burned down twice (480 and 479 B.C.E.) during the wars against the Persians. Its walls were rebuilt on both occasions, first by Themistocles and then by Cymon, but it was Pericles (r. 460–429 B.C.E.), the Athenian political leader and originator

of a great artistic and intellectual flowering, who conferred on the site its unrivaled beauty. This was an exercise of political authority and personal propaganda, and a direct affirmation of the cultural supremacy of Athens over the rest of the known world. After Pericles, no one dared alter the beauty of the place.

● THE MONUMENTS

Under the governance of Pericles, from 447 to 432 B.C.E., the old temple dedicated to Athena was replaced by the Parthenon, designed by the architects Iktinos and Kallikrates. Entry into the Acropolis was barred by the new Propylaea (gateway), conceived by the architect Mnesicles (432 B.C.E.). Ten years later the temple of Erechtheus was built, followed in 421–406 B.C.E. by Kallikrates' temple of Athena Nike ("victorious").

View of the Acropolis. Athens.

Above:
Model of the Acropolis as it appeared around 400 B.C.E.

Right:
The Propylaea, 437–432 B.C.E. Acropolis, Athens.

Lower right:
The Parthenon, 447–432 B.C.E. Acropolis, Athens.

Below:
View of the Acropolis on the Propylaea side. At right, the Temple of Athena Nike, 421–408 B.C.E. Athens.

Near the Erechtheum, in the House of the Arrhephoroi, a group of young Athenian virgins worked for a year on the sacred *peplum*, a mantle donated to the goddess at the Panathenaic festival every four years. At the center of the Acropolis stood a colossal statue of Athena Prómachos ("warrior"); according to Pausanias, the tip of her lance a landmark for navigators.

THE PARTHENON

Constructed of Pentelic marble in the Doric style, the Parthenon is the largest known temple of the ancient world. Of the octostyle peripteral type (with 8 columns on the front and 17 on the sides), it has the proportions of the golden section (p. 24). It has come down to us damaged by time and by the war between the Venetians and the Turks in the seventeenth century. The two pediments were once adorned with sculptures by Phidias, which, as was customary at the time, were colored. The famous reliefs are now in the British Museum in London, while the interior frieze has remained in its original place.

THE PROPYLAEA

The Propylaea form the monumental entrance to the Acropolis. The central part of the building was adorned by six Doric columns. Behind them was a wall with five doors opening onto two vestibules. The larger, western vestibule had three naves; the center nave opened onto the *pinacoteca*, a large room in which important paintings were kept.

THE ERECHTHEUM

Famous for the Loggia of the Caryatids (p. 33), the Erectheum is a building dedicated to two divinities; on one side is the temple of Athena Poliàs ("citizen"), on the other that of Poseidon Erechtheum.

THE TEMPLE OF ATHENA NIKE

With four columns at the front and back (tetrastyle) but none on the sides (amphiprostyle), this temple likely was erected to commemorate the Greek victory over the Persians in the Battle of Platea (479 B.C.E.).

The Roman Forums

Below:
The three surviving columns of the Temple of Castor and Pollux, fifth century B.C.E.–first century C.E., Rome. Erected in 484 B.C.E. to fulfill a vow made by the son of the dictator Aulus Postumius after winning the Battle of Lake Regillo, the temple was rebuilt in 117 B.C.E. and again in 6 C.E. by Augustus.

In the provincial cities of the Roman Empire, the forum served the same purpose as the agora for the Greeks. It consisted of a public square, on which stood public and religious buildings. The situation in Rome was very different. In the broad valley between the Palatine, Capitoline, and Coelian hills, bounded by the Esquiline on the northeast, temples, monuments, and squares were crowded together in forums constructed under various emperors through the centuries. The earliest buildings, from the Bronze Age (1500 B.C.E.), have been found in the Boarium Forum (a cattle market), confirming the historical truth of ancient legend: Hercules, after having slain the fire-breathing Cacus, is said to have founded the Ara Maxima at this site. In this ancient forum, later built over completely, stood temples dedicated to the goddesses Fortuna and Mater Matuta.

● THE ANCIENT FORUM

The nerve center of Ancient Rome, the forum has a history as old as that of the city itself. When Julius Caesar, before the Battle of Pharsalus (48 B.C.E.), vowed that, in the event of victory, he would build a temple there dedicated to Venus Genitrix, the forum already had a fixed plan. Thus, two years later, Caesar was forced to purchase a high-priced plot of land on the side of the old forum. Over the centuries, the forum had reached a level of development that was to remain almost unchanged. Here stood monuments crucially important to the history of Rome: from the Curia where the Senate met (p. 50) to the Temple of Saturn and the Temple of Castor and Pollux, both of the ancient Italic podium typology (p. 217). There were also two basilicas overlooking the Via Sacra: the

Basilica Emilia (founded in 179 B.C.E., destroyed by fire, and rebuilt by Augustus) and the Basilica Julia, erected by Julius Caesar in 55 B.C.E. as a sort of restoration of the original Sempronian Basilica.

● THE IMPERIAL FORUMS

During the time of Caesar, who erected not only the Temple of Venus, protectress of the Julian clan, but also a forum of his own, a number of grandiose buildings were constructed. The forum area was extended to the southern border of the Suburra, a disreputable lower-class neighborhood. At right angles to Caesar's forum, Octavian Augustus, the

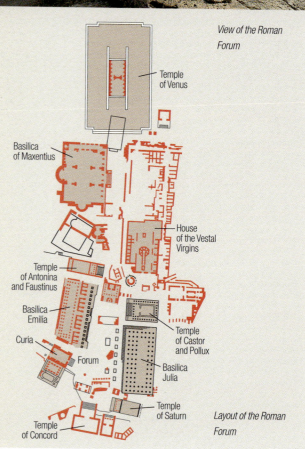

View of the Roman Forum

Temple of Venus

Basilica of Maxentius

House of the Vestal Virgins

Temple of Antonina and Faustinus

Basilica Emilia

Curia

Forum

Temple of Castor and Pollux

Basilica Julia

Temple of Saturn

Temple of Concord

Layout of the Roman Forum

Right:
View of Caesar's Forum.

Lower right:
View of the Boarium Forum.

Detail of Trajan's Column, 101–108 C.E. Rome. One of the masterpieces of the ancient world, this 90-foot column was created to commemorate Trajan's victories over the Dacians. It is covered with an unbroken band of relief sculpture containing nearly 2,500 human figures.

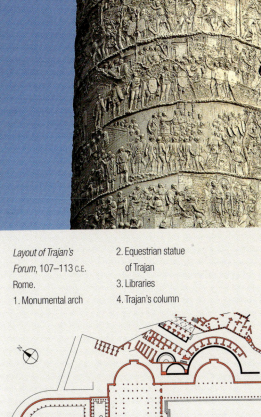

first emperor of Rome, erected his own forum with the Temple of Avenging Mars. Later, under the rule of Vespasian, came the Forum of Peace (71–75 C.E.) and the Forum of Nerva, the latter probably designed by the architect Rabirius. Of its rectangular structure, inaugurated in 97 C.E., the only remains are a pair of Corinthian columns, the "Colonnacce."

● TRAJAN'S FORUM

The last to be built (107–113 C.E.), this is the most spectacular of the imperial forums. Trajan's Forum was designed by Apollodorus of Damascus, who was also responsible for the layout of Trajan's Markets (p. 72). The forum consisted of a public square more than 100 yards long; a scenic backdrop was provided by the Basilica Ulpia (p. 50), to which it was linked by double porticoes on the northern and southern sides. In addition to the basilica, it held two libraries, between which rose Trajan's Column. Concluding the complex of buildings was the Temple of Trajan, enclosed within an exedra. To the west, overlooking the forums, stood the Basilica of Maxentius and Constantine. The last structure in the forum was erected at the initiative of the Byzantine Emperor Phocus, who had a dedicatory column erected there in 608 C.E.

Layout of Trajan's Forum, 107–113 C.E. Rome.
1. Monumental arch
2. Equestrian statue of Trajan
3. Libraries
4. Trajan's column

0   50 m

Aqueducts

Roman civilization has been defined in many ways, one of which is "the civilization of water." The problem of supplying water to cities was always an urgent need in ancient times, when there were no electric or internal combustion engines and power was supplied by animals or sheer human muscle. Eventually it came to be realized, however, that water exerts a force of its own and that its power can be harnessed by keeping its pressure constant. Another problem to be solved was that of keeping water pure enough to drink, free from polluting agents.

Complex, sophisticated networks of water distribution existed in a number of ancient civilizations, among them the Assyrian-Babylonian, the Minoan-Mycenaean, and the Greek, but it was the Romans who solved the major part of these problems with the greatest efficiency.

● HOW AN AQUEDUCT WORKS

The Ancient Romans are credited with the innovation of flowing water raised high overhead rather than at ground level or through underground channels. The water in an aqueduct flows on arched bridges that may rise to several levels, depending on the hills and valleys it traverses.

The first advantage of this system is that it carries the water easily over hills, valleys, and rough terrain. The second is that it confers the force of gravity on the water, a force that was skillfully exploited by Roman engineers for distributing the water at its final destination.

Above:
Roman aqueduct,
c. 20 B.C.E.
Pont-du-Gard,
Nîmes, France.
It was Agrippa, the son-in-law of Augustus, who decided to build this magnificent aqueduct.

The structure extends some 30 miles from Uzes to Nîmes, rising 160 feet above the Gard River, a tributary of the Rhone, in a region scattered with other vestiges of Roman architecture.

Left:
Detail of Nero's Aqueduct in a model of Ancient Rome. Rome, Museum of Roman Civilization.

The aqueduct was restored in 46 C.E. Note the arcades of varying height, in multiple combinations, designed to serve different needs and purposes.

The third is that it kept the water clean by avoiding infiltration or accidental damage to the conduit.

Hence, water channeled at its source could flow cleanly over long distances, thanks to the graded incline of the structure, and could be raised to a higher level through pressurized ducts. Already at the time of the Roman Empire, large purification reservoirs located at both ends of the aqueduct system were used to improve the quality of the water.

From there the water was let into a distribution reservoir called the *castellum*, from which it entered a network of pipes (*calices*) that conveyed it to fountains, public basins, fountains, and baths, all over the city.

● ARCHITECTURE FOR WATER

Aqueducts are genuine and elaborate works of architecture designed for the purpose of conveying water. Already in Roman times, the essential principle of twentieth-century Rationalism was being put into practice: "form follows function."

Among the most famous of these structures from the ancient world is Nero's Aqueduct in the city of Rome, derived from that of the Emperor Claudius, which brought water directly to the imperial mansion on the Palatine Hill. Today, traces of Nero's Aqueduct still survive in the heart of the city around Via Statilia.

Another important aqueduct was one that drew water from a natural hot spring at Ciampino, just outside the city, and conveyed it to the villa of the Quintili family (180–192 C.E.) near the Via Appia.

Other extraordinary works of this kind were built in outlying provinces of the empire, from Spain to France and as far as Palestine.

Especially impressive among the surviving ancient aqueducts is the multilevel Pont-du-Gard not far from Nîmes in the south of France.

Another spectacular example is the aqueduct of Segovia, on the slopes of the Sierra de Guadarrama in central Spain, with its two orders of majestic arcades.

Above:
Roman aqueduct.
Caesarea, Palestine.

Left:
Claudian Aqueduct,
38–52 C.E., Rome.

Above:
Roman aqueduct,
c. 110 C.E. Segovia,
Castile-León, Spain.
This imposing aqueduct
was built at the initiative
of the Emperor Trajan.

The Great Sanctuaries

Scattered across the east-central Mediterranean basin are the vestiges of monumental sanctuaries that, in antiquity, contributed strongly to the formation of the *koiné*, the Greco-Roman cultural community. One of the elements of cohesion between these two civilizations consisted, in fact, of a common religion. After their great expansion, the Romans continued to worship the Greek pantheon, albeit with some differences in cult and devotion, and dedicated numerous temples to the gods of Olympus.

● GREEK SANCTUARIES

A sanctuary was originally a sacred precinct, at times located far from urban centers, as at Paestum, Agrigento, and Selinus in Magna Grecia (coastal southern Italy). One of the oldest monumental sanctuary complexes in the Mediterranean basin is the Heraion ("dedicated to Hera") on the island of Samos, off the coast of Turkey. Here the ensemble of buildings (rebuilt and modified from the middle of the eighth century B.C.E. to the beginning of the sixth) began to as-

sume an organic structure of its own. With the approach of the Classical Age, the form of the citadel-sanctuary was more precisely delineated in the pan-Hellenic temples of Delphi and Olympus. Delphi, long held to be the navel of the world (*omphalós*), assumed extraordinary historical importance for its Temple of Apollo, from which the priestly oracles foretold the future. Rebuilt after a fire in 548 B.C.E., the temple received precious gifts from all Greek cities; even foreign princes sent their treasures to ensure the protection of the divinity. Beginning in the sixth century B.C.E., Delphi also became the gathering place of the Greek *anfizionía* (union of continental Greek peoples); this stimulated even further temple building, which involved the whole community. For similar reasons, the entire urban setting of Olym-

Above:
Eastern temples seen from the acropolis, sixth–fifth centuries B.C.E. Selinunte (Selinus), Italy. Founded by Greeks from Megara Iblea around the middle of the seventh century B.C.E., the Sicilian city of Selinus grew and flourished until it was conquered by the Carthaginians, who destroyed it in 409 B.C.E. Dwelling places stood on the northern heights, while the temple-filled sacred precinct lay on the acropolis and areas to the northeast. The gods to which the buildings were dedicated are unknown.

Left:
Remains of the Temple of Apollo, after 548 B.C.E. Delphi, Greece. Located on the slopes of Mount Parnassus, Delphi was already famous in the eighth century B.C.E. for the Oracle of Apollo, which predicted the future, in prophecies that exerted a strong influence on the political history of Greece.

Above:
Remains of the Heraion, sixth century B.C.E. Island of Samos, Greece. The Temple of Hera was built and renovated several times. The Hekatómpedon had an exterior colonnade and another one inside the cell, which provided a view toward the back, where the statue of Hera stood.

pia, with its Temple of Zeus (468 B.C.E.) and colossal gold-and-ivory statue of the god by Phidias (one of the Seven Wonders of the Ancient World), became a sacred city in which the sanctuary precinct was enormously extended. Delphi and Olympia are representative of the concrete communal expression of a culture that was to reign throughout the Mediterranean basin for millennia.

● ROMAN SANCTUARIES

Roman sanctuaries from the Republican Age appear to modern eyes as "macroarchitecture" of striking visual impact. Not far from Rome, at the ancient town of Preneste (today's Palestrina), the sanctuary dedicated to Fortuna Primigenia (end of the second century B.C.E., restored a century later) was originally designed as a structure with six artificial terraces and later transformed by the rebuilding projects of the Colonna family in the fifteenth and seventeenth centuries. Designed in all probability by one or more architects of the Pergamum school, the Preneste complex has no single predominating building but a unitary configuration of great dynamism and plasticity. The ramp of stairs leading to the third terrace, the design of the exedras, and the perfect integration of structure and decoration make it a unique example of religious architecture. This becomes all the more apparent in comparing it with the structure of the sanctuary of Jove Anxur at Terracina (first century B.C.E.), which had similar architectural features, such as the double-ramp stairway leading to the entrance, but simpler solutions.

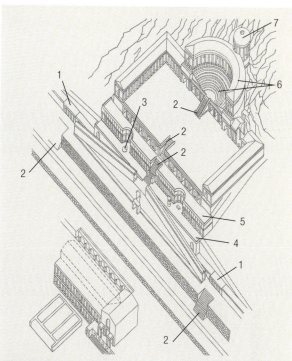

Above:
Remains of terrace constructed in opus incertum *in the sanctuary of Jove Anxur,* first century B.C.E. Monte Sant'Angelo di Terracina, Rome. The religious buildings in this sacred precinct, raised on an imposing terrace, were situated in a place of strategic importance: at the foot of the Pesco Montano, on the spectacular rock of Monte Sant'Angelo overlooking the Tyrrhenian Sea.

Right:
Arches supporting the opus incertum *terrace in the sanctuary of Jove Anxur,* first century B.C.E. Monte Sant'Angelo di Terracina, Rome.

Above:
Remains of the exedra in the Temple of Fortuna Primigenia, constructed around 80 B.C.E. Palestrina, Rome. On the third level of the sanctuary, erected on terraces rising on a hillside to a height of more than 650 feet, are two elegant exedras with a portico of Ionic columns.

At top:
Reconstruction drawing of the sanctuary of Fortuna Primigenia, second–first century B.C.E. Palestrina, Rome.
1. Fountains
2. Front ramps
3. Sanctuary of the "Fates"
4. Terrace of the exedras
5. Terrace of the fornixes
6. Theater and portico
7. Temple

Theaters and Amphitheaters

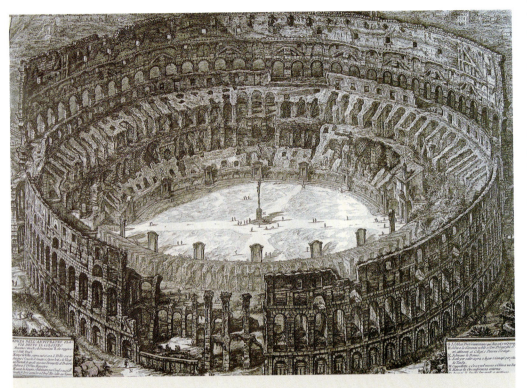

From an architectural point of view, the basic difference between the Greek and Roman theaters is that the tiered seating of the former rises on a natural slope (and sometimes carved out of the rock itself), while in the Roman theater the inclination is provided by artificial structures. Because of this difference, the Romans were able to locate their theaters almost anywhere, regardless of the natural landscape. The theater interior (*cavea*), however, was identical in Greek and Roman architecture.

As seen in the diagram on page 58, the interior structure consists of a central area; the orchestra, designated for the chorus, with side ramps leading to it; and behind the orchestra the proscenium and the stage (*skené*).

The great invention of the Romans was the amphitheater (literally, "double theater"). Theoretically, the amphitheater was formed by combining two theaters face-to-face, creating an elliptical structure supported by superimposed rows of arches. This type of structure was developed in response to the need to hold a greater number of spectators and to provide venues suited to more spectacular forms of entertainment—gladiator fights, naval battles (*naumachie*), and wild animal hunts (*venationes*).

● THE COLISEUM

The Roman amphitheater par excellence was the Flavian, known as the Coliseum because of its extraordinary size or perhaps because of Nero's statue, the Colossus, located nearby. The famous structure measures 620 feet on the outside diameter and 512 on the inside, with a perimeter of 1730 feet. It is estimated that the Coliseum could hold 45,000 seated spectators and 5,000 standees. Begun by the Emperor Vespasian in 71–72 C.E., in an area occupied by the artificial lake of Nero's Domus Aurea, it was completed by Titus and inaugurated in 80 C.E. The Coliseum provided the city with a permanent amphitheater, serving the policy of the Flavian em-

Giovanni Battista Piranesi, *The Coliseum with the Stations of the Cross*, 1746–1750. Rome, Biblioteca Casanatense.
Over the centuries, the Coliseum (72–80 C.E.) has undergone destruction, modification, and plunder. From the Middle Ages to the eighteenth century, houses and the Stations of the Cross were built inside it; it was also once used as a stone quarry. This engraving by Piranesi shows how the ancient amphitheater looked in the eighteenth century. Originally, the underground chambers, corridors, and service areas at the center housed elevator hoists and theatrical devices used to make gladiators, wild animals, or stage sets appear suddenly on the scene. The arena was covered by 11,000 feet of wood boarding, with narrow openings and access holes, concealed by a layer of sand.

Below:
The interior of the Coliseum as it appears today.

Below:
*Amphitheater
of the Roman colony
of Thysdrus,
second–third centuries
C.E.* El-Djem, Tunisia.

*Model of the Theater of
Marcellus*, 13–11 B.C.E.
Rome, Museo della
Civiltà Romana.
Built of tufa and
travertine, the theater
dedicated to Marcus
Claudius Marcellus,

grandson of Octavian
Augustus, could hold
15,000 spectators.

perors to give the people "bread and circuses" (*panem et circenses*) to distract their attention from the dictatorial power of the rulers.

On the exterior, the Coliseum presents three orders of pillared arcades; half-columns and cornices of different orders stand against the pillars: (from bottom to top: Doric, Ionic, and Corinthian, see figure, p. 89). The construction material was travertine (literally "of Tivoli," a porous rock), the blocks of which were originally held together by iron cramps (removed during the Middle Ages). The structure had 80 gates, numbered to allow each spectator to enter the assigned section. The number that appeared on the entry pass or ticket facilitated public access to the tiered seats in the cavea. As indicated by surviving inscriptions, the tiers were divided into five sections (*maeniana*), each for a different social class: the bottom was reserved for the most important personages (*senatores*), and the top was designated for common people (*clientes*). The underground facilities consisted of corridors and service areas, with elevator hoists for lifting men and animals. To shelter the spectators from the sun, the seats in the cavea could be covered by an immense velarium, or awning, divided into sections and supported by 240 poles placed in holes in the upper cornice. As many as 100 men were needed to maneuver it; sailors from the military port of Cape Miseno were known to be employed for this purpose.

The Pantheon

The Pantheon in Rome (from the Greek *pantheon*, "of all gods") is one of the supreme achievements of classical architecture. Conceived as a monument to the harmony of the universe, it was built at the order of Marcus Vipsanius Agrippa, the son-in-law of Octavian Augustus and "consul for the third time," as stated in the inscription over the portico. It was dedicated in 27 B.C.E. to the seven gods of the planets. Damaged by fire in 80 C.E., it was restored by Domitian. After another fire, it was rebuilt completely by the Emperor Hadrian (118–125 C.E.). On that occasion the inscription dedicating it to Agrippa was added and, it is thought, the portico as well. The building was part of the larger complex of the Baths of Agrippa, restored along with the adjacent Basilica of Neptune. The portico originally was framed by colonnades along both sides, which concealed the rear body of the building and produced a surprising effect on anyone who passed through the portico into the interior. The piazza in front of the temple was originally quite large. The building was restored again in 202 C.E.

● THE STRUCTURE

The supreme skill of the unknown architect who designed the Pantheon is demonstrated primarily by the ingenious combination of a cylindrical interior, surmounted by a large dome strictly in the Roman tradition, with a Greek-style portico. The latter, about 110 feet wide, features Corinthian columns nearly 40 feet high, with pink or gray granite monolithic shafts. The columns on the front stand in rows of eight, forming three naves. The

Right:
Giovanni Battista Piranesi, *Piazza del Pantheon after the renovation of 1711.* Rome, Biblioteca Casanatense. The original Pantheon—built in the time of Agrippa, dedicated to the seven celestial gods, and centered around the cult of Augustus, identified with the sun—was oriented differently from the one rebuilt by the Emperor Hadrian. The discharging arches in the cylindrical body appear on the far right in the engraving.

Right:
Giovanni Battista Piranesi, *Interior of the Pantheon,* transformed into the Church of Santa Maria ad Martyres, with the high altar erected in 1725. Rome, Biblioteca Casanatense.

Axonometric projection and layout of the Pantheon.

Right:
Interior of the Pantheon, 118–125 C.E. Rome.

bronze beams of the portico, removed in the seventeenth century by Pope Urban VIII, were melted down and used for Gianlorenzo Bernini's *baldacchino* (altar canopy) in St. Peter's and for the cannons of Castel Sant'Angelo. The cylindrical body, built of brick, is more than 140 feet in diameter and 20 feet thick. In the interior, seven large niches (four rectangular and three semicircular) alternate with eight edicules surmounted by triangular or round tympanums. The only source of light is the great oculus ("eye"), measuring 30 feet in diameter, at the center of the spectacular dome with its coffered ceiling (*lacunaria*). After the pagan temple had been transformed into the Church of Santa Maria della Rotonda (also called Santa Maria ad Martyres) in 609, the rooms behind the cylindrical hall were used as a sacristy and chapel.

● BUILDING TECHNIQUE

The Pantheon is a masterpiece of engineering. For centuries, from the time of Brunelleschi to that of Piranesi, the technique employed in constructing its open-centered dome was the subject of intense study and admiration. The first element to be noted here are the blind discharge-arches along the two registers of the cylindrical body. These served to absorb the thrust generated by the weight of the dome, which is thinner near the center and made of very light volcanic stone.

● SENSE OF HARMONY

The form of the Pantheon conveys a sense of cosmic harmony. It was imitated repeatedly over the centuries, in such buildings as the Venetian Church of the Redentore by Andrea Palladio, the Tempietto at Possagno by Canova, the Church of San Francesco di Paola in Piazza Plebiscito in Naples, and the Cisternone in Livorno, designed by Poccianti. The interior height of the great hall, from the top of the dome to the floor, is the same as its diameter (140 feet); thus, a sphere, the shape epitomizing universal harmony and balance, could be inscribed in the hall's interior. The dome, as noted by Dione Cassio (LIII, 27), alludes to the heavenly vault.

Pietro Bianchi, *Church of San Francesco di Paola*, 1817–1849. Naples, Italy.

Antonio Canova, *Tempio*, 1819–1830. Possagno, Treviso, Italy.

Pasquale Poccianti, *Cisternone*, 1829–1842. Livorno, Italy.

The Mausoleum of Santa Costanza

In Early Christian architecture, circular-plan buildings, many of them baptisteries and martyria (mausoleums dedicated to the cult of martyrs), constituted an element of continuity between the architecture of Ancient Rome and that of Late Antiquity.

● PRECEDENTS

The circular plan was not in itself a Christian innovation, as evidenced by the Roman Pantheon (see preceding pages) and the even earlier Greek *tholos* tombs. Rather, it was the Roman funerary monument, circular in design, that provided the model for these new buildings. The forerunners included such bold, innovative constructions as the Mausoleum of Augustus, of which little has survived, and the Mausoleum of Diocletian at Split in Croatia, featuring an octagonal plan, barrel-roofed peristyle, portico of Corinthian order, and interior colonnade (p. 240).

● HISTORY OF THE MAUSOLEUM

Erected in the early fourth century at the order of the Emperor Constantine—who built it as a mausoleum for his daughters Costantina (whose name was then shortened to Costanza) and Helena, wife of the Emperor Julian the Apostate, the monument rises behind the ruins of a large enclosed cemetery.

Above:
Ruins of the Tomb of Cecilia Metella (end of first century B.C.E.) in Rome, in an eighteenth-century landscape made of inlaid semiprecious stones. Florence, Museo dell'Opificio delle Pietre Dure.

Burial was prohibited within the walls of Ancient Rome, so major roads departing the city were lined with cemeteries, as demonstrated by the monumental Tomb of Cecilia Metella, of circular plan, on the Via Appia.

Remains of a tholos, 334 B.C.E. Olympia, Greece. This circular temple, erected in commemoration of the Macedonian Dynasty, contained statues of Philip and Alexander by the sculptor Leochares.

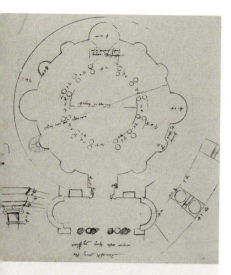

Above:

The Mausoleum of Santa Costanza in Rome in a sixteenth-century drawing. Florence, Gabinetto Disegni e Stampe degli Uffizi.

Below:

Exterior of the Mausoleum of Santa Costanza, sixth century C.E. Rome.

Of circular plan, it has an apsed narthex on the long sides. It is made of brick and presents an external ambulatory around the central body of the structure, which concludes with the curve of the dome. In these respects, the structure recalls the mausoleum of St. Helena, Constantine's mother, at Torpignattara, of which little has remained.

That structure also served as an inspiration for the church of Santo Stefano Rotondo, known as the largest circular building with a collateral, overhanging ambulatory. The interior of Santa Costanza is illuminated by twelve rounded windows in the central body of the building, which forms a kind of tambour (circular supporting wall) for the dome, some 72 feet wide at the base. Twelve pairs of granite columns with Composite-order capitals support twelve short entablatures, from which spring the arches that support the dome. The barrel vault of the ambulatory and the small apses are decorated with mosaics. The mausoleum was soon transformed into a baptistery and then, in 1254, into a church.

● FROM MAUSOLEUM TO BAPTISTERY

As shown by the art historian and archaeologist Richard Krautheimer, the reason baptisteries and mausoleums came to follow the same architectural form is explained by a passage from the *Epistle to the Romans* (VI, 3–4).

St. Paul compares baptism to death, stating that the latter is a necessary premise to resurrection in faith and in the name of Christ. The concept was then reiterated by St. Basil and St. Augustine, the fathers of the Orthodox Church and Latin Church, respectively.

Interior of the Mausoleum of Santa Costanza, sixth century C.E. Rome.

Constantinople

The history of Constantinople ("city of Constantine"), today called Istanbul (perhaps from the Greek *eis tén pólin*, or "toward the city," the cry of the besiegers on the day of the Turkish conquest in 1453), began long before its founding by Constantine the Great on May 11, 330. Strategically located on the shores of the Bosporus, a strait linking the Black Sea to the Sea of Marmara and ultimately the Mediterranean, the site has been inhabited since prehistoric times. The first urban center dates to the beginning of the seventh century B.C.E., when a Megarian colony was established there; the colony was called Byzantium, after its founder, Byzas. Independent until the second century C.E., the city was conquered by the Roman Emperor Septimius Severus (r. 193–211) who, after having reduced it almost to a village, then promoted its revival to take advantage of its strategic location.

● THE CITY OF CONSTANTINE

Preceding events partially explained Constantine's motivation for founding the new capital of his empire in the area around the Golden Horn. The sheer topography of the area—encompassing seven hills, traversed by a narrow body of water that may have recalled the Tiber—resembled that of Rome in many ways. For all intents and purposes, Constantinople was born as a second Rome, the city it was to rival in wealth and grandeur for centuries.

● MONUMENTS

The urban layout of the new capital remained basically unchanged from the time of Septimius Severus, but enlarged with a wider circle of walls. The main road, called Regia or Mese, was lined with columns. Running straight through the city, it crossed several great public squares: the Forum of Constantine, followed by the Forum Tauri, the Forum Bovis, and the Forum of Arcadius, built

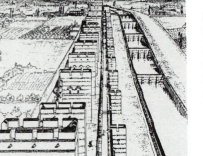

Above:
Remains of the Aqueduct of Valens, 378. Istanbul, Fahit district. As emperor of the Eastern Empire from 364 to 378, Flavius Valens reigned during one of the stormiest periods in its history. He waged war against the Alani, the Huns, and

finally the Goths, who defeated his forces in the Battle of Hadrianopolis. It was under his reign that the aqueduct of Constantinople was completed. The raised section, much of which still remains, was more than half a mile long. The structure was designed

with two orders of arcades, the first constructed of giant blocks of stone and the second of lighter materials. Restored several times, the aqueduct supplied water to the Great Palace of the emperor, later to become that of the sultans.

Left:
Reconstruction of the outer walls of Constantinople (first half of the fifth century).

Above:
Remains of the Golden Gate, sixth century. Istanbul.

from the time of Theodosius I to that of Arcadius (379–408). The true urban center was a complex erected around the Hippodrome, an extension of the one built under Severus in imitation of the Circus Maximus in Rome (p. 56), where chariot races were run and gladiator fights were held. Extending to a length of more than 1,600 feet, with a typical U-shaped plan, the Hippodrome had at its center, forming a sort of spine, an extensive collection of columns, Egyptian obelisks, and statues from throughout the empire. To the east of the Hippodrome, Constantine built his Great Palace. "A city within the city," the Palatium Magnum consisted of a network of buildings connected by porticoed courtyards. Located on the northern side were the Baths of Zeuxippus from the Severian Age, the Augusteion, the Church of St. Sophia, and the Senate.

● THE CITY AFTER CONSTANTINE

The succession of emperors who followed Constantine embellished the city with public squares, columns, palaces, baths, monumental gates, churches, and public facilities. Prominent among these was the great aqueduct, begun at the time of Constantine and completed under the reign of the Emperor Valens in 378. But the city reached its greatest extent under Theodosius II (r. 408–450), who had new walls built beyond the old Constantinian ones. By the mid-fifth century, it had emerged as a thriving capital, with 4,388 fine private residences, 322 streets, 153 private baths, five imperial palaces, and eight public baths. The city was finally conquered by the Turks in 1453, more than eleven centuries after its founding.

Above:

Constantinople before the Sack of the Turks, from the *Liber Insularum Archipelagi* by C. Buondelmonte, c. 1420. Paris, National Library. The oldest known map of Constantinople shows the extraordinary combination of natural defenses and fortifications that made the capital of the Eastern Empire

practically invulnerable for more than 1,000 years. Surrounded on three sides by the sea, the city reinforced its western side with a double line of walls. This miniature clearly shows the fortifications, gateways, great Hippodrome (to the east), emperor's palace, most important churches, and many ancient columns that characterized the city at that time.

Left:

View of At Meydani square in front of the Blue Mosque. Istanbul. The sprawling expanse of today's Sultan Ahmet Meydani (*atmeydan* means "oblong square") was the site of the great Hippodrome. Of this imposing structure, which once housed the famous bronze horses that now adorn St. Mark's in Venice, only the end section (*sphedonè*) remains.

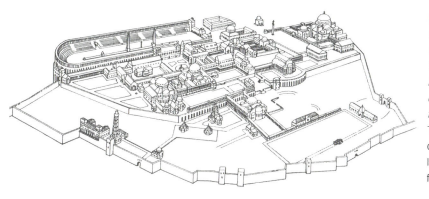

Left:

Reconstruction and plan of the Great Palace of Constantinople, with buildings and structures erected from the fourth to the tenth centuries. The vastness of the complex, described as late as 1204 as having five hundred rooms, reflected the solemnity and majestic scale of life in the court of the Eastern Empire.

Hagia Sophia

I stanbul's Church of Hagia Sophia, or Santa Sophia, was dedicated to Divine Wisdom (in Greek, *Hágia Sophía*) and considered a sort of hypostasis of God. Referred to also as the *megále ekklésia* ("great church"), it was the pride of the Eastern Empire's capital city, a temple of unrivaled beauty to which the ancient world looked with wondrous admiration.

● EARLIER STRUCTURES

Hagia Sophia was originally quite different from today's edifice. Begun under the Emperor Constantine, it was probably finished by his son, Constant II. With a basilican plan and wooden roof, it was destroyed by fire in 404 and rebuilt by Theodosius II. But Theodosius's building

was also devastated by fire, this time in 532 during the revolt against the newly ascended Emperor Justinian I. Of this building, also basilican in plan, only the remains of the portico have survived. Immediately upon assuming power, Justinian resolved to build an even more grandiose monument. Hagia Sophia would be the most beautiful church in the empire, and he summoned two of the most famous architects of the time.

● THE ARCHITECTS

The chief designer of the new building was Anthemius of Tralles. Although his date of birth is unknown, we do know that he was born in Lydia to a family of physicians and that he was famed as a sculptor and mathematician as well

Sinan, *The Suleimaniye Mosque*, 1550–1556. Istanbul.
The Turkish architect Sinan, the most famous among those who worked for the sultans, drew inspiration from the model of Hagia Sophia for his imposing mosques throughout the Ottoman Empire. Famous among these are the Selim Mosque at Edirne and the one shown here, dedicated to Suleiman the Magnificent, which still crowns one of the hills of Istanbul.

Right:
View of the Church of Hagia Sophia, sixth century. Istanbul.

Below:
Axonometric projection of the Church of Hagia Sophia.

as an architect. His only known work is the Hagia Sophia, one of history's great architectural and engineering achievements. Collaborating with him was Isidorus of Miletus the Elder, who was particularly expert in geometry. Amazingly, the great monument was erected in only five years and was consecrated by the Emperor Justinian in a solemn ceremony in 537.

● THE STRUCTURE

The building plan is difficult to classify since it is not, strictly speaking, either basilican or central. Its strikingly unique feature is the dome; measuring about 100 feet in diameter, it was designed, according to the chronicler Procopius of Caesareas, to appear "suspended in the air." The rectangular base measures nearly 230 feet long and 250 feet wide. In the interior, the piers were built of local stone, while less severely stressed elements were made of lighter brick. Divided into three naves, the church includes an apse flanked by two exedras

at the entrance, preceded by a double narthex. The ingenious division of space makes the interior seem to grow and expand without interruption.

● DIFFICULTIES

The problems encountered by Anthemius and Isidorus, of which Procopius gives a first-hand account, were fundamental. It was impossible, at the time, even to calculate the thrust and counter-thrust of structural forces and thereby ensure the stability of the building. And indeed it collapsed within 20 years of construction. Since the two architects had since died, Isidorus the Younger was called upon to restore the church. He managed to rebuild it, perfecting the original design without visible alteration. Although the extraordinary basilica was greatly admired, its features were rarely copied because of the difficulties involved. Much later, the great architect of Suleiman the Magnificent, Sinan (1489–1578), attempted to rival it in the design of his mosques.

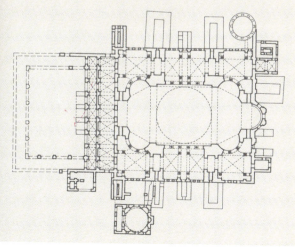

Left:
Interior of the dome of Hagia Sophia, 558. Istanbul.
The present dome is the one rebuilt by Isidorus the Younger.

Above:
Interior of the Hagia Sophia looking toward the apse. Istanbul.
The majestic building is a sort of universe in miniature; the dome represents the heavenly vault, and the hall alludes to the created world, on which shines the light of God. After the fall of the Eastern Empire, this Christian church was transformed into a mosque.

Below:
Plan of the Church of Hagia Sophia.

Theodoric's Mausoleum

Interior of the Mausoleum of Diocletian, c. 313. Split, Croatia.

The glory and dominion of Imperial Rome, the universal empire that united all the peoples of the known world under its rule, was an idea that did not die even with the historical decline and fall.

To the contrary, it was to be revived repeatedly, in different forms and with different intentions, through the centuries. One of the first to revive the imperial concept was Theodoric (454–526), king of the Ostrogoths, who considered himself the envoy in the West of the Byzantine (Eastern) emperor, who had inherited the legacy of Rome.

● THEODORIC

Raised as a hostage at the court of Constantinople, Theodoric was a member of the Amal clan, which had thoroughly assimilated Roman culture. His education gave him superior standing among his own people, who saw in him a charismatic leader.

The Goths who had settled in Pannonia now joined together under Theodoric who, after the Sack of the Balkan Peninsula in 488, was appointed *magister militum* by the Byzantine Emperor Zenone. In this capacity, he invaded Italy on behalf of the emperor and waged war against Odoacer, who had been named king in 476 after dethroning Romulus Augustulus. Apparently, Theodoric was acting as the legitimate restorer of the Roman authority.

In fact, he inaugurated the reign of the Ostrogoths ("Goths from the East"), which was to last 60 years: from 493, when Odoacer was defeated and killed, to 553, when the troops of Byzantium crushed the last Ostrogoth resistance. Although Theodoric pursued a policy of sharp division between Ostrogoths and Romans, including prohibition of mixed

Detail of wall mosaic with a view of Ravenna and the Palace of Theodoric, sixth century. Sant'Apollinare in Classe. Ravenna, Italy.

The mosaic is probably an idealized representation of the façade of the lost Palace of Theodoric.

marriages, he was obliged to revive the institutions of Late Roman culture, from its legislative apparatus to its monetary system, and finally to its religion. (His own faith was the so-called Aryan heresy, which claimed that Christ was not of the same substance as His Father, but rather the first of his creatures.) Under Theodoric's rule, the various modes of artistic expression, from mosaic to architecture, reiterated the Roman and Byzantine styles, forms, and types.

Left:
Theodoric's Mausoleum, sixth century. Ravenna, Italy. The monolithic stone that adorns the singular dome has been estimated to weigh nearly 330 tons.

Above: *Baptistery of the Aryans*, sixth century. Ravenna, Italy. Erected by Theodoric in honor of his own religious faith, the baptistery, after the condemnation of Aryanism by the Church, was adapted for use as a Catholic oratory and dedicated to Saint Mary.

● THE BUILDING

The mausoleum that Theodoric, still in his lifetime, had erected at Ravenna is difficult to classify. Art historians consider the monument unique, a distinctive and harmonious combination of Roman-Byzantine and typically Germanic elements.

The building is perfectly entitled to be included in the family of mausoleums, as confirmed by its circular plan. The lower portion is a polyhedron with a 12-sided base; the interior consists of a cruciform area with cross-vaulted ceiling, lit by narrow slits opening in blind arches around the perimeter.

The upper portion is circular in plan and narrower than the lower portion. In the interior is the sarcophagus, now empty, that once contained the mortal remains of the sovereign. The building is topped by a monolithic limestone *calotte* (concave crown) with a diameter of more than 32 feet. Similarities between the mausoleum and other buildings of the same kind appear not only in the plan but also in the suggestion of a false ambulatory deriving from the different sizes of the lower and the upper register. The differences consist primarily in the use of materials, such as Istrian stone in place of brick, as well as decorations of a geometric type, and the rostra (platforms) adorning the dome.

The Dome of the Rock in Jerusalem

If there is any building in the Islamic world that, for tradition and prestige, can be compared to the Kaaba in Mecca, it is the Qubbat al-Sakhra, or Mosque of Omar, in Jerusalem, better known to the Western world as the Dome of the Rock. At various times of war or civil strife, in fact, when it was impossible for Muslims to make the great pilgrimage to Mecca, they were allowed instead to visit the Dome of the Rock.

● HISTORY

Slightly more than sixty years after the Hegira (622 C.E.), Mohammad's flight to Medina that marked the beginning of the Islamic era, the Muslim Empire was still striving to achieve unity and to produce an architecture that would be worthy of the faith's increasing prominence on the world stage. The Ummayad Dynasty (661–750), under whose rule Islam dramatically expanded its domain, promoted internal unity and strove to create buildings that would rival those of other great empires and other religious faiths. More than any other, Caliph Abd al-Malik (685–705), at whose initiative the Dome of the Rock was built, was the promoter of reforms that were to leave an indelible mark on the Islamic world. Under his rule, the Umayyad Empire began to coin its own money; Byzantine and Sassanid coins would no longer be used. Arab became the official language of the empire and of its religious rituals. These and other measures served to strengthen the internal unity of the heterogeneous Islamic world, which was soon to expand as far east as the borders of India and as far west as Spain (p. 122).

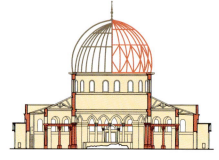

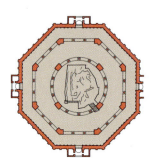

Dome of the Rock, late seventh century. Jerusalem. The building was begun in 688–689 and completed in 691–692.

Floor plan and section view of the Dome of the Rock in Jerusalem. The supporting structure of the building consists of 12 pillars alternating with 28 columns.

● THE LOCATION

For a work that would be a monument to faith in Allah and an Islamic response to the religious buildings of Christian Palestine, the choice of location was crucially important. Abd al-Malik thus chose Jerusalem, the holy city par excellence, and within it the Haram al-Sharif, or Temple Mount, where the Temple of Solomon once stood; specifically, at this site, the mosque would enshrine the rock on which Abraham (from whom the Arabs also claim descent) was said to have obeyed God's command to sacrifice his son Isaac, and from which Mohammad was said to have ascended to heaven after his miraculous night journey from Mecca on the winged horse Buràq.

● THE STRUCTURE

Built around the relic stone, the Dome of the Rock formed part of an architectural complex that included (and still includes) the al-Aqsa Mosque, which has been modified several times. The overall plan reflected to some extent the Christian model of the Rotunda of the Holy Sepulcher and its adjacent basilica, also located in Jerusalem. In architectural terms, the arrangement established a balance between different but complementary geometric forms: a parallelepiped structure (six-faced polyhedron all of whose faces are parallelograms) and a cylindrical structure, the former serving as a "container" for prayer and the latter as a casket for a holy rel-

ic. The Dome of the Rock is an octagonal building with a double ambulatory, from which the reliquary can be viewed from all angles as the faithful walk around the great mosque in a ritual known as *tawwaf*. Over the central peribolos (sacred enclosure containing votive symbols, from the Greek *períbolos*) rises a wooden dome tiled in brass. The dome rests on a masonory tambour (supporting structure) pierced by 16 windows; the lower octagonal structure has 40 grated windows, designed for Suleiman I in 1552, who had the outside of the building decorated with splendid polychrome majolica tiles. The entire structure is based on the geometric model of a star-shaped polygon, derived from Greco-Byzantine culture.

Detail of the windows and exterior decoration on the Dome of the Rock, sixteenth century. Jerusalem. The highly refined exterior decoration dates from the time of Sultan Suleiman I.

Interior of the Dome of the Rock, late seventh century. Jerusalem.

Rock-Cut Architecture

Below:
View of the ancient capital of the Nabataeans. Petra, Jordan.

Above:
Façade of el-Khazneh, first century B.C.E. Petra, Jordan. Entirely dug out of rock, this imposing funerary temple was probably erected by Aretas, king of the Nabataeans, in 85 and 84 B.C.E. The façade, measuring 130 feet high, is of the double Corinthian order. The central structure above the tympanum reflects the style of the Athenian choragic monument (p. 115).

Architecture and the earth are bound together in an ancestral relationship. The earth has often been understood as a giant edifice created by the divinity: it is thus regarded as the construction par excellence, and building "inside" it can assume the significance of perpetuating the creative act of a hypothetical demiurge. Rock-cut architecture, therefore, found in a wide range of civilizations, retains a unique fascination, used not only by many religions but also as dwelling places. The bond between architecture and the inside of the earth dates back to prehistoric times. Since the earliest stage in human history, when caves provided a kind of natural architecture, this relationship has evolved along different paths that have occasionally given rise to architectural achievements of surprising beauty.

● PETRA

As if to defy the laws of nature, between the mountains on the vast desert tableland near the southern border of modern-day Jordan—where a city should never have been built—stands Petra, a crossroads for the caravan routes linking the coasts of the eastern Mediterranean. A mercantile city that grew up as a center of trade between East and West, it was the capital of the Arabic kingdom of Nabataea beginning in the fourth century B.C.E. Served by an elaborate irrigation system, Petra remained an important urban center even after falling under Roman dominion in 106 B.C.E. Its architecture—including public baths, nymphaeums (monuments to nymphs), temples, palaces, and theaters—was strongly influenced by the Greco-Roman tradi-

tion. Much of it carved directly out of rock, Petra boasts monuments of incomparable fascination, such as the el-Khazneh Firaum ("Pharaoh's Treasure," first century B.C.E.), with an especially intricate façade. In the interior, by contrast, the tombs of Petra are bare spaces, decorated only with the great niches in which the corpses were laid.

● THE CAVES OF AJANTA

Built between the first century B.C.E. and the seventh century C.E., the complex of rock-cut temples at Ajanta, on the rocky Deccan Plateau in central-western India, was one of the most important in the world (illustration, page 152). Built at the time when Buddhism reached its peak of splendor in the area, Ajanta must have played the role of a holy citadel. Entirely forgotten as the centuries

Sotto:
Interior of Cave 57, T'ang
Dynasty, c. 618–907.
Dunhuang, Gansu,
China.

Left:
*Monumental Buddha
Amitabha in Cave 20*,
460–465. Yungang,
Datong, Shanxi, China.

Below:
*Façade of the entrance
to Cave 19*, fifth century.
Ajanta, Maharashtra,
India.

passed, it was accidentally rediscovered in 1819. Off the ancient caravan routes, but not far away, the 29 grottoes of Ajanta were likely a place of pilgrimage and devotion. Dug out of the rock as artificial caves, they served as sanctuaries and assembly halls for Buddhist monks. The decoration is of the highest quality. Its walls are embellished with great figurative murals (the most extensive living documentation of ancient Indian painting), earning it the nickname of "the Sistine Chapel of Asia."

● ROCK-CUT ARCHITECTURE IN CHINA

Rock-cut complexes are also scattered across the vast expanses of the Chinese mainland. Some, such as the one in the oasis town of Dunhuang ("Flaming Lighthouse"), along the Silk Road near the Gobi Desert in Gansu Province, are carved out of rock that is extremely hard to work. Dunhuang is famous for its wall paintings, dating from between the fifth and the eighth centuries C.E., while the 42 grottoes of Yungang ("Cloud Hill"), near the city of Datong in Shanxi Province, dug out of a wall of sandstone extending more than half a mile, contain colossal statues of Buddha. Many of the inner walls of these grottoes are decorated with striking polychrome reliefs.

● CAPPADOCIA

Nor has the Christian world been able to resist the fascination of rock-cut architecture. Testifying to this are a number of churches in the Cappadocia region of what is now central Turkey, many decorated with highly refined Byzantine frescoes.

Below:
*Ancient dwellings
carved in rock.*
Valley of Goreme,
Cappadocia, Turkey.
A historic region
in central Anatolia,
Cappadocia, like an
extraordinary "outdoor

museum," preserves not
only important examples
of rock-cut churches
and monasteries but
also underground
villages, castles, and
dwellings (some still
today in use) in a bizarre
variety of forms.

The Palatine Chapel at Aquisgrana

Below:
Interior of the Palatine Chapel, 790–805.
Aachen, Germany.

Right:
Dome of the Palatine Chapel, 790–805.
Aachen, Germany.

Axonometric projection of the Church of Saints Sergius and Bacchus (527–536) in Istanbul and plan of San Vitale (526–547) in Ravenna. San Vitale has several basic elements in common with the Church of Saints Sergius and Bacchus, such as the system of alternating the piers and columns supporting the dome, the arrangement of columns to form an exedra, the narthex, and the domed vault. But in San Vitale the octagonal plan is "exposed," while in the Constantinople church it is inscribed in a rectangle.

With the Palatine Chapel at Aquisgrana (today's Aachen, Germany), our imagined journey through the most important monuments of antiquity with the common denominator of a circular plan comes to an end. At Aquisgrana, this form took on new significance and a different function compared with the buildings that may be considered its most significant forerunners.

● THE MODEL OF BYZANTIUM

While the daring design of such a monument as the Hagia Sophia in Constantinople was practically impossible to imitate for most of the architects of the day, the model of the Church of Saints Sergius and Bacchus in the same city could easily be exported throughout the territories of the Byzantine Empire. Not by chance, the Church

of San Vitale in Ravenna (capital of that part of Italy taken back by Belisarius under the rule of the Eastern Empire in 540 C.E.) recapitulates, with certain variations, the plan of the church in Constantinople. Moreover, the Ravenna monument was the "palatine chapel" of the Emperor Justinian and his wife, Theodora, as indicated by the famous apse mosaics portraying them with members of their court.

● THE IDEAL OF CHARLEMAGNE

In two military campaigns, in 754 and 756, Pippin the Short, king of the Franks, had conquered the city and exarchate of Ravenna from the Byzantines and donated them to the pope, along with the Duchy of Rome. It is not surprising, therefore, that the Byzantine Empress Irene fiercely opposed the coronation of Charlemagne, the eldest son of Pippin, as *romanum gubernans imperium* (ruler of the Roman Empire) by Pope Leo III on December 25, 800. Despite sharp and obvious differences in their political interests, Charlemagne looked to Constantinople as a cultural center of the highest order. Determined to revive the ancient splendor of Rome, the new emperor knew only too well that he had much to learn from the culture and art of Byzantium. For this reason, when he chose to establish the capital of his empire at Aquisgrana, his Palatine Chapel was modeled after that of the Emperor Justinian in Ravenna, the most appropriate architectural representation of the emperor's ideal of renewed splendor.

● THE BUILDING

The Palatine Chapel at Aquisgrana was originally part of the palace residential complex (since destroyed) and con-nected to it by a long corridor. As known from a now-lost inscription, the chapel was designed by the architect Odo of Metz. For its construction, columns and marble blocks taken from ancient monuments were transported directly from Rome and Ravenna, with obvious symbolic intentions, under the permission of Pope Hadrian I. For the richness of its materials, its daring technical solutions, and its carefully wrought furnishings and details, this monument is the finest surviving example of Carolingian architecture. Topped by a dome more than 50 feet in diameter, the building, in whose apse stands the imperial throne, has a somewhat complex octagonal structure. The dome is supported by eight pillars connected by arches, which also form the impost for the matroneum (women's gallery). The latter, which is also vaulted, runs all round the interior like the ambulatory. The arches in the upper register are articulated by columns.

Above:
Interior of the Palatine Chapel with the "Throne of Charlemagne," 790–805. Aachen, Germany.

Ruins of a porticoed street, seventh century. Anjar, Lebanon. To build the splendid city of Anjar, Caliph al-Walid used Roman columns with decorated capitals, taken from ancient monuments.

Reconstruction of plan of the city of Anjar, Lebanon, in the eighth century. The fortified complex, with a governor's palace, mosque, and public baths (two buildings, one of them closer to the wall) was inspired by the Roman *castrum*, with porticos along the main street and avenue (*cardo* and *decumanus*), and with the territory divided into blocks (*insulae*).

1. *Cardo*
2. *Decumanus*
3. *Tetrapylon*
4. Governor's palace with facing apsidal halls
5. Mosque

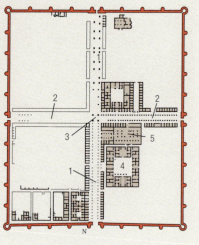

The Umayyad Castles

Under the dynasty of the Umayyad caliphs, whose capital was first Damascus (from 661 to 750) and then Cordoba (from 756 to 1031), the Islamic empire spread from the Iberian Peninsula to the Indian subcontinent. During the first phase of their rule, one of the means they employed to consolidate political power, especially in the Syrian-Palestinian region where the new faith had not been universally embraced, was that of building, along the western border of the Fertile Crescent, the so-called Castles in the Desert. These installations, which served the dual function of military outpost and desert land-reclamation facility, were built, not by chance, along an extended curved line that marked the area of most abundant rainfall. In this way, the caliphate revived the Roman-Byzantine agricultural and military organization that had once served there to protect the empire, whose boundaries been drastically contracted. Modeled on the traditional Roman "country villa," the Umayyad residences became true agricultural enterprises. First among their cities, in the rich Bekaa Valley along the route that linked Beirut to Baalbek, was Anjar (in today's Lebanon), built by Caliph al-Walid I (705–715). The urban plan and the structure of the palace and baths clearly reflect their derivation from Roman architectural tradition.

Above:
Ruins of the great square and the throne room in the palace, first half of the eighth century. Mushatta, Amman, Jordan
The only remains of the great desert castle at Mushatta are the ruins of the enormous roofed square (425 feet per side), which gives access to what remains of the *aula regia* (throne room), replicating the plan of a church with three naves and three apses.

Below:
Detail of the relief decoration in limestone on the façade of the Umayyad Palace at Mushatta, first half of the eighth century. Berlin, Staatliche Museen.
Since 1904, the Islamic collections in the Berlin Museums have possessed the right half of the façade of the desert castle at Mushatta, donated by the Turkish sultan to Emperor William I. This is one of the first examples of Islamic wall decoration, in which the prohibition against representing human figures is respected.

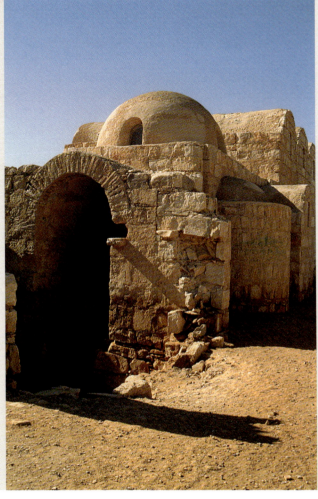

Above:
Dome over the calidarium in the baths, c. 711. Qusayr Amra, Jordan.
The dome was decorated with images of the sky and the signs of the zodiac, confirming that astrology played an important role at the court of the caliphs, who consulted a horoscope in exercising their power. The twentieth-century art historian Fritz Saxl has demonstrated that the Qusayr Amra decoration cycle is based on Greek astronomical texts.

Left:
Remains of the baths, c. 711. Qusayr Amra, Jordan.

● REFINEMENT IN THE DESERT

One of the oldest Umayyad castles, that of al-Minya on the shore of the Sea of Galilee in modern-day Israel, was most likely built during the reign of the same Caliph al-Walid. The complex consists of a mosque with three naves and a number of *bayt*, small connecting rooms used as dispensaries, following the Roman or Sassanid model. The beauty of these desert castles was also to be found in their decoration, whose richness was hard to rival, as evidenced by the remains, now in Berlin, of the Castle of al-Mushatta in Jordan, near today's capital of Amman. The square structure, encircled by a wall from which rose 25 towers, had a splendid entrance with a mosque and a ceremonial courtyard leading to a great roofed central square, beyond which stood the castle proper, which appears to have been left unfinished.

● THE BATHS

Still supplied with water by Roman aqueducts in many cases, the Umayyad desert cities also had sumptuous thermal baths. At the bath of Qusayr Am-ra's palace in Jordan, for example, the dome is decorated with a chart of the heavens and images of the zodiac. Bare on the exterior, the building containing the baths formed part of a larger complex, now lost. The interiors of the baths, decorated with wall paintings that are now almost illegible or entirely lost, were discovered near the end of the nineteenth century, and drawings made at that time still survive. The scenes, iconography, and style echo Late Roman and Byzantine models. Highly refined mosaics also decorated the baths of Khirbat al-Mafjar in Palestine, now in ruins.

Angkor

Below:

Temple of Angkor Wat,
1112–1150. Angkor,
Siem Reap, Cambodia.
Angkor Wat is the largest
religious building in the
world, even bigger than
St. Peter's in Rome.
The temple is reflected in
a symbolic lake (the
once-broad moat now
reduced almost to a
swamp), out of which
flow four rivers, recalling
those of the Garden
of Eden in the Christian
religion. In a sort of
initiatory journey, the
visitor crosses a series
of obstacles and
suddenly comes
upon an astonishing
vision in stone.

The scene of violent political upheaval in recent decades, Cambodia also boasts one of the world's largest and most fascinating archaeological sites, second in size only to the Great Wall of China. The ancient city of Angkor was the capital of the Khmer Empire from the city's founding in about 800 C.E. to about 1225. Since its rediscovery in 1860, unfortunately, Angkor has been subjected to repeated pillaging. Smothered by lush jungle vegetation, which at the same time has helped protect them from total destruction, the temples of Angkor remain very much at risk. Despite international restoration and conservation initiatives, the structures remain threatened by environmental degradation and human despoilers and are in danger of becoming only a memory, the image of neglect rather than emblem of the highest achievements of Asian civilization.

● THE KHMER

The Khmer civilization developed through a long political and military process that began in the second century C.E. in the geographical area of the Mekong Basin. It was here, according to Chinese sources, that there rose to power a kingdom called Funan, whose semilegendary origins seem to date from the marriage of a Brahman, the ascetic Kambu, and the nymph Mera (or perhaps the daughter of an indigenous chieftain). In its progressive expansion, the Funan Kingdom, whose original population was of Mongolian stock intermingled with Indian elements, subsumed the Principality of Kambuja ("sons of Kambu") in the northern Great Lake region of Cambodia, from which its name derives. Around the middle of the sixth century, however, the principality managed to escape Funan domination and moved its capital from Sambor to Angkor. At this time it began to expand, ultimately developing into the Khmer Empire. The religion of this people originally was based on the Hindu cult of the god Shiva, but in the eighth century Buddhism was introduced. At its peak, the Khmer civilization extended its cultural and architectural influence beyond the borders of modern Cambodia as far as the territories now occupied by Thailand, Laos, and Vietnam. The temple of Phanom Rung in Thailand is a significant forerunner of the one at Angkor Wat, while at Wat Phou in southern Laos, linked to Angkor by a 60-mile road, the cult of the *lingus*, especially important to the Khmer culture, was venerated. This advanced civilization, highly skilled in the fields of architecture, hydraulic engineering, and decorative arts, reached its peak under a Buddhist king, Jayavarman VII, who defeated the Champa in 1190. Immediately afterward, for a number of rea-

Left:

Detail of a naga *carved on the temple of Angkor Wat*, 1112–1150. Angkor, Siem Reap, Cambodia. The road that leads to the top of the temple is paved and lined with balustrades adorned with *naga*, two-headed cobras, the serpent of the primordial waters. The path to a higher world, where the water is pure, the trees are laden with fruit, and every animal is gentle, leads through prayer and the renunciation of worldly goods.

sons (ranging from Chinese invasions to a succession of revolts by satellite states), a period of decadence set in, culminating in 1431 with conquest by the Thais, who occupied Angkor and transferred the capital to Phnom Penh.

● IN THE STONE JUNGLE

Characteristic of Khmer art, and common to the entire Indochina region, is Buddhist iconography that derived from India and developed over time into autonomous stylistic currents. Angkor, the capital of the Khmer Empire founded in 802 by King Jayavarman II (son of a prince born in Java), contains within an area of about 15 square miles innumerable temples and grandiose monuments, roads, bridges, artificial lakes, ponds, dikes, and dams. Sophisticated hydraulic and channeling systems (100 million cubic yards of water conveyed from the Mekong River) provided for the irrigation of rice paddies and the cultivation of land. The central core of the site is the great complex of Angkor Thom (*angkor* means "capital city," *thom* means "big"). With a square plan and enclosed by walls, Angkor Thom, built during the reign of Jayavarman VII, measures nearly two miles on each side. Around it stand numerous temples, the most famous of which is Angkor Wat (*wat* means "temple"). Erected under the rule of Suryavarman II between 1112 and 1150 to commemorate his military victories, Angkor Wat covers nearly half a square mile and is surrounded by a protective moat more than 650 feet wide. The edifice is a metaphorical holy mountain, surrounded by four towers that symbolize the snow-covered peaks of Mount Meru, the axis of the world in Hindu and Buddhist cosmology. At the center, surrounded by three concentric galleries, the main tower soars to a height of 215 feet.

Below:

Plan of the Temple of Angkor Wat.

Right:

Aerial view of Angkor Wat.

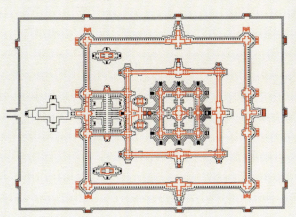

Borobudur

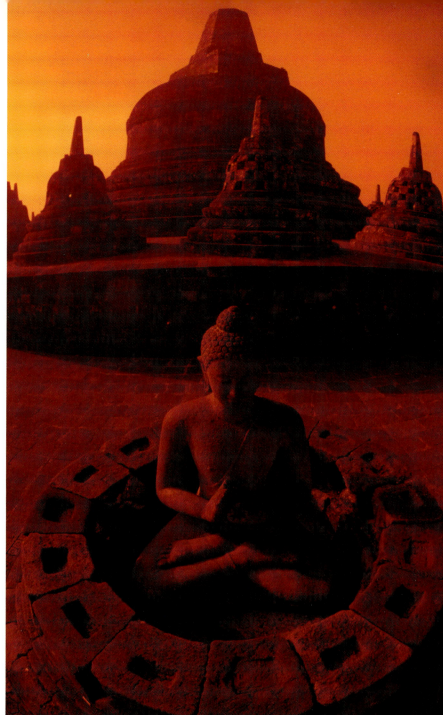

Built shortly before that of Angkor, the temple of Borobudur on the island of Java is one of the most important in all of Indonesia. Like the Khmer culture, that of Indonesia was strongly influenced by India. It was around 760 C.E., under the Sailendra Dynasty, that the skilled workers of Java built this imposing mountain of stone—some 150 feet high and 72,000 cubic yards in volume. The structure essentially consists of dozens of stupas arranged in a precise geometric pattern. Rising on the top of a hill in the Kedu Valley facing Mount Merapi, Borobudur follows a square plan and is formed by concentric terraces that become circular after the fifth tier. The top, to which access is provided by four axially arranged stairways, is dominated by a single great stupa that occupies the center of the structure. The walls between one platform and another, rising above the walking surface, serve as a balustrade for the upper corridor.

They are decorated with 1,300 relief sculptures depicting scenes from the texts that narrate episodes in the life of the original Buddha, and historical events and stories from the Bodhisattva Samantabhadra. The temple was abandoned in the eleventh century.

Left:
Aerial view of Borobudur, 760–847. Island of Java, Indonesia. Designated a UNESCO World Heritage Site in 1991, Borobudur has undergone major restoration.

Above:
Detail of one of the stupas on the circular terraces, with a statue of Buddha, 760–847. Island of Java, Indonesia. The first five square terraces from the ground up are followed by three circular ones, which carry 72 stupas.

Khajuraho

In northern India, in the central-eastern forest of Madhya Pradesh, stands one of the best-conserved temple complexes on the Indian subcontinent: Khajuraho. A city rich in date palms (its name derives from *khajur*, or "date") and the capital of the kingdom of Chandella from the tenth to the twelfth centuries, it remained isolated and unknown until the middle of the nineteenth century. Its remote location had protected it from the recurring Islamic invasions of India. Most of the 85 Hindu and Jain temples that make the complex unique were built between the years 950 and 1050 by the Chandella Rajput kings of Bundelkhand (Madhya Pradesh), who promoted architecture and literature. Today, 25 of the temples remain, of which 20 are in excellent condition, having been restored or renovated on several occasions.

● TEMPLES OF LOVE

The exteriors of the Khajuraho temples were inspired by the snow-covered peaks of the Himalayan mountain range or by the home of Shiva, the god who resides in a cave on the mythological Mount Kailash. The buildings, all in *nagara* style (p. 153), are made of sandstone. Among their signature features are splendid sculptural reliefs that decorate both the exteriors and interiors. Subjects range from representations of the divinities (Brahma, Vishnu, Shiva) to scenes of ritual, daily life, battles, and animals. Many of the figures appear in erotic poses, often highly explicit, which may be related to the spiritual significance conferred upon the sexual act in Tantrism, a mystical movement within both Buddhism and Hinduism.

Above:
Temple of Parsvanath, c. 954. Khajuraho, Madhya Pradesh, India. The typical temple has four basic parts: the entrance portico (*ardh-madhap*), hall of assembly (*mandap*), and vestibule (*antaral*) leading to the sanctuary (*garba-griha*) where the image of the divinity is kept. The larger temples have an ambulatory for the *pradakshina*, a ritual that consists of walking all around the image of the divinity while praying. The *mandap* not only embellishes the temple but also serves as a gathering place for worshipers.

Left:
Detail of an erotic scene, eleventh century. Khajuraho, Madhya Pradesh, India. The erotic scenes may be merely an augury of happiness and fertility, or they may allude to the cosmic symbolism of the union of opposites (male and female). Sexual union simulates the fusion of the two creative principles of the cosmos, allowing worshipers to enter into harmony with nature and to escape the cycle of reincarnation to achieve dissolution in Nirvana, having left the body at death.

Hildesheim

Made the seat of a bishopric in 815 by Ludwig the Pius, Hildesheim (in Lower Saxony, Germany) is the site of one of the most important architectural monuments of the Ottonian age, the Church of St. Michael, restored after having been severely damaged during World War II. This monastic complex was founded in the first decades of the eleventh century, the period of the city's greatest political importance (though it was to continue to flourish in the following centuries).

● BERNWARD AND THE ABBEY CHURCH OF ST. MICHAEL

The origins of St. Michael centered around the figure of Bernward (c. 960–1022), bishop of the city and head of its government from 993. It was he who founded the abbey and planned its defensive walls, part of which still survive. A man of great erudition, Bernward was the tutor of the boy emperor Otto III (980–1002). His interests led not only to the creation of a prominent scriptorium, but also to the embellishment and enlargement of the city's cathedral; the latter included a workshop which in 1015 produced the famous figured bronze doors, originally intended for the abbey but then placed in the cathedral itself. Despite a ravaging fire in 1162 and later damage, the Abbey Church of St. Michael retains almost the exact plan from the time of Bernward. Designed to house the first Benedictine monastery in the Diocese of Saxony, the complex centers around the abbey church, which has three naves, a double choir, and double transepts. The eastern part of the building contains three apses, while the western, which housed the emperor, is distinguished by a *Westbau*, a complex hall-like structure over a crypt that anticipated the features of the *Westwerk* (p. 129). On the exterior, four cylindrical towers on polygonal bases, with conical tops and roofs, stand adjacent to the transepts, while two towers over the crossings of the transepts create the appearance of a small city. The interior of the longitudinal body is articulated by a succession of three bays in which a straight pillar alternates with two columns, according to the Saxon system.

East transept of the Abbey Church of St. Michael, 1010–1033. Hildesheim, Lower Saxony, Germany. One of the special characteristics of the building is the perfect symmetry between the western and eastern transepts.

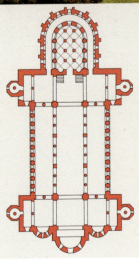

Plan of the Abbey Church of St. Michael at Hildesheim. A careful study of proportions reveals the inspiration of Greco-Roman architecture. The form of reference is the span at the crossing of the transepts, which governs the entire structure and is repeated three times in the central nave.

Interior of St. Michael. Hildesheim, Lower Saxony, Germany. The original capitals have been replaced in part, and no trace remains of the frescoes that must have existed below the register of the rounded windows. The other decorations, added at the initiative of Abbot Theodoric II (1179–1203), date from after the fire of 1162.

Cluny and Cîteaux

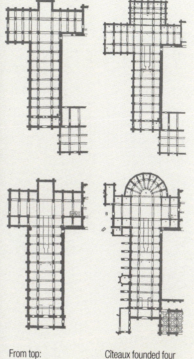

From top:
*Plans of Cîteaux II
(1130–1140);
Cîteaux III (consecrated
in 1193); Clairvaux II
(1135–1145);
Clairvaux III
(1154–1174).*
Under the English Abbot
Stephen Harding,

Cîteaux founded four
important branches of
the Cistercian order:
Ferté-sur-Grosne in
1113; Pointigny in
1114; Clairvaux; and
Morimond in 1115, all
of them similar in
design to the
"headquarters" abbey.

Above:
*Remains of the south
transept and octagonal
tower of the abbey,* first
decades of the twelfth
century. Cluny,
Burgundy, France.

*Plan of the abbey
complex of Cluny in the
mid-twelfth century*
(from Kenneth J. Conant).
The Abbey of Cluny was
built in three stages.
Above a first small

church consecrated in
926 rose Cluny II
(955–981, restructured
in 1000). It was a
basilica with three naves
and a transept, an
elongated choir, and
lateral structures. The
grand Cluny III, begun
near the end of the
eleventh century and
consecrated in 1130,
had five naves and two
transepts.

nature of Christianity—that of its origins and the Rule of St. Benedict—through reform of the liturgy and labor in the fields. Cîteaux was founded by a figure close to Bernard, Robert de Molesme.

● THE MONASTERY OF CLUNY

Founded by William of Aquitaine in 910, the Monastery of Cluny grew rich and powerful, reaching its peak under Abbot Hugo (1049–1109). Relying directly on the Holy See, it was free of obligation to any secular power. This anomalous status had been instituted by Odo (927–942), who, having succeeded the first Abbot Bernon, annexed several abbeys and imposed on them the Benedictine Rule. Of this immense complex, there remains only the base of the south transept of the church dating to the Cluny III period and its octagonal tower (Tower of the Blessed Water). As if attempting to rival Constantine's Old St. Peter's Basilica, Cluny III was the largest religious building in Europe of the entire Middle Ages, with a narthex 615 feet long.

● THE MONASTERY OF CÎTEAUX

The simplicity of Cîteaux contrasted sharply with the opulence of Cluny. The first small church at the site—about 50 feet long and 16 feet wide, with three naves concluding in a polygonal choir—dates from 1106 (Cîteaux I). Between 1130 and 1140, the building was enlarged according to a scheme that was to become typical of Cistercian architecture: a Latin cross plan, based on linear repetition of the bay module and concluding in a rectilinear choir, here very small. The choir and the left arm of the transept were enlarged in 1193.

The two great Burgundian abbeys, both destroyed between the seventeenth and nineteenth centuries, represented opposing architectural and religious worlds. It was from the older of the two, Cluny, that the reforms of the Benedictine order were begun, and its grandiosity represented the opulence and worldly prestige of the Church. Reacting against this position was the Cistercian order, founded by the French monk Bernard de Clairvaux (1091–1153), who sought to revive the "true"

Fontenay

T he Abbey of Fontenay may be considered one of the best-preserved examples of early Cistercian architecture, which more than later constructions reflects the artistic principle of the order founded by Bernard de Clairvaux. The concept was based on a particular manner of interpreting the world, human history, and God's design: the origin and essence of the cosmos is Divine reason, by which the Creator orchestrates the entire universe, according to relations of harmony and

Left:
Façade of the abbey,
first half of the twelfth
century. Fontenay,
Burgundy, France.
The masonry bases
on which the portico
rested can still be seen.

Above:
Cloister of the abbey,
first half of the twelfth
century. Fontenay,
Burgundy, France.

Below:
Interior of the abbey,
first half of the twelfth
century. Fontenay,
Burgundy, France.

beauty expressed in both mathematics and music (pp. 20–23). Accordingly, the buildings erected for this monastic order, on their own small scale, of necessity reflected this principle.

● THE STRUCTURE

Founded in 1119 by Abbot Godefroy in Burgundy, the abbey was enlarged and rebuilt during the life of St. Bernard. In 1139, the second abbot, Guillaume d'Epiry (1132–1154), welcomed Bishop Ebrard of Norwich who, with his financial generosity, contributed to its rebuilding. The new abbey complex was conse-

crated by Pope Eugenius III in 1147. The plan of the church is a Latin cross with three naves. A portico, now lost, originally stood in front of the façade. The interior is divided into eight bays with vaults and ogive arches, springing from half-columns standing against pillars. Having no clerestory, it receives light only from the small side naves and the windows in the façade and choir. On each arm of the transepts are two chapels.

The cloister is articulated by paired columns, with many of the capitals carved from a single block of stone. The refectory, restored as early as the eighth century, was rebuilt in 1750.

Durham

A town of Anglo-Saxon origin, Durham (located in a county of the same name in northern England) was founded in 995, almost a century before the Norman invasion. Rebuilt by the Normans from the ground up, Durham was an important urban center from the eleventh to the thirteenth centuries, an Episcopal See, and the site of a *scriptorium* established before 1096 and still active in the thirteenth century. The remains of the great castle, originally built of wood, were transformed into the bishop's

Left:
Detail of the galilee, c. 1153–1195. Durham, Durham County, England. The vestibule for pilgrims, erected at the western end of the cathedral at the initiative of Bishop Hugh of Pudsey, is distinguished by four rows of arcades supported by slender columns, made sturdier in 1420 as a precaution against possible collapse.

Below:
Nave of the cathedral looking eastward, begun in 1093. Durham, Durham County, England.

Above:
View of the castle, thirteenth century. Durham, Durham County, England. Despite modifications made after a fire in the mid-thirteenth century, the ensemble constitutes one of the most important English palatial complexes from the Romanesque period.

palace. The other building for which Durham is famous is its cathedral, a predecessor of the early French Gothic cathedrals. Its history is interwoven with the cult of the hermit Saint Cuthbert, the Celtic bishop of Lindisfarne (685–687), whose relics, brought to Durham in 995, made the town a popular pilgrimage destination, called "St. Cuthbert's land."

● THE CATHEDRAL

Built in stages over the area previously occupied by an Anglo-Saxon structure, the Norman cathedral, of Romanesque style, has a basilican plan with

three naves, a transept, a tower over the crossing, and towers on the façade. Its appearance was partially transformed by modifications and enlargements made during the Late Romanesque and Gothic periods; these included the addition (c. 1153–1195) of another transept and a galilee, a portico in front of the main structure that sheltered pilgrims who were not allowed to enter. The building was one of the first to be roofed entirely with stone vaulting, based on highly precise, expert stone-cutting techniques. The Romanesque apse was later replaced by a choir and transepts.

Modena

Above:
The architect Lanfranco directs work on the Cathedral of Modena, early thirteenth-century miniature from the Relatio

de innovatione ecclesie sancti Geminiani ac de translatione eius beatissimo corporis. Modena, Cathedral Archives, Ms. O.II.11, c. 1v.

Above:
Lanfranco, *Cathedral,* 1099–1106. Modena, Italy. The composite-roof plan is vertically emphasized by two buttresses that divide the façade in correspondence with the naves; horizontally, the gallery of triform windows, enclosed

in arches, confers a strong chiaroscuro effect on the surface. The central axis is dominated by the rose window (from Gothic times), while the main portal is surmounted by a prothyrum (porch) and an edicule ("little house"). The columnar lions were sculpted by Wiligelmo.

Right:
Interior of the cathedral, twelfth century. Modena, Italy.

Settled first by Ligurians and later by Etruscans, Modena, a flourishing city during Roman times, became an Episcopal See in the seventh century.

Beginning in the ninth century, when the first city walls were erected, the urban structure of medieval Modena began to develop around the axis of Via Emilia. Dating from this time is the Town Hall, later extensively modified. The city's oldest monument from the Middle Ages, and by far the most important, is its cathedral, one of the finest masterpieces of Romanesque architecture in all of Europe.

● THE CATHEDRAL

Built over an earlier church dating to the tenth century, the Modena Cathedral (begun on May 23, 1099, and consecrated by Pope Lucius III in 1184) had been substantially completed by 1106, when the relics of St. Geminianus were placed there in the presence of the Grand Countess, Matilde of Tuscany. To build this grand edifice, the Modenese had called upon the architect Lanfranco and the sculptor Wiligelmo, who carved the reliefs on the façade, a masterpiece of Po Valley Romanesque style. Lanfranco, about whom little is known, also designed the 288-foot-high Ghirlandina bell tower.

The interior of the Duomo is divided into three naves; brick pillars alternate with marble columns, while false matroneums (women's galleries) reiterate the motif of the triform mullioned windows on the façade. Sculptural decoration is concentrated mainly on the façade and interior rood screen.

Pisa

A maritime republic and an imposing political and military power, Pisa was a center of flourishing mercantile trade with the entire Mediterranean Basin and with Asia Minor. Still surviving today from its medieval urban grid are tower-houses, a number of churches, and, most notably, the great architectural landmarks of Piazza dei Miracoli: the baptistery, bell tower, Duomo, and Camposanto, all superb examples of a highly refined and original style.

Pisa has also passed on (a rare occurrence for the times) the names of the architects who designed its Duomo: Buscheto and Rainaldo, inscribed on the façade alongside those of the great masters of antiquity.

● A BUILDING "ALL IN MARBLE"

The Pisa Duomo, a colossal structure topped by an elliptical dome 158 feet high, was built after the crushing naval victory of the Pisans over the Saracens in the waters off Sicily. Begun by Buscheto in 1063 over the remains of an older building dedicated to St. Reparata, the cathedral was completed by Rainaldo and consecrated by Pope Gelasio II in 1118. A marble temple whose imposing size in no way detracts from its harmony and elegance, the Duomo immediately became the model for many of the Romanesque churches built in the city and its surroundings, as well as in Lucca, Pistoia, and the islands then controlled by Pisa, Sardinia and Corsica.

● THE BELL TOWER

Famous throughout the world as the Leaning Tower of Pisa, the campanile was begun in 1174 and completed in

Right: *View of Pisa, detail of a panel painting portraying St. Tolentino da Pisa*, fourteenth century. Pisa, San Nicola. This rare fourteenth-century view of the city of Pisa shows, within its walls, the unmistakable outlines of the Duomo and Bell Tower. Behind the two monuments rise the typical tower-houses.

Above: *View of the monumental complex of Campo dei Miracoli*. Pisa. In the great square, gleaming with white marble and pierced with intricate tracery like precious caskets in a harmonious play of solids and voids (illustration, p. 19), appear, from right to left: the Leaning Tower; the Duomo, with its great triple-naved transept and dome (illustration, p. 76); and the Baptistery, with its cupola measuring 60 feet in diameter.

Below: *Interior of the Baptistery*, 1153–1365. Pisa. At the center is the baptismal font, on the left the marble pulpit sculpted by Nicola Pisano (1260).

1372. In style it resembles the bell towers of Ravenna. Although the architect is not known with certainty, the tradition persists that it was designed by Bonanno Pisano.

● THE BAPTISTERY

Begun by the architect Diotisalvi in 1153, the building is cylindrical in shape, a departure from the octagonal design typical of baptisteries. Diotisalvi designed the first level of the structure, while Nicola Pisano and his son Giovanni built the middle loggia around 1273. The building was finished in 1365 with the completion of the cupola.

● THE CAMPOSANTO

Designed by Giovanni di Simone in 1278, the Camposanto, with its loggia of pierced windows (pp. 75 and 76), was completed by the start of the fifteenth century and later modified in part.

It was then decorated with an important cycle of frescoes by Buffalmacco, Piero di Puccio, and Benozzo Gozzoli.

Above: *Interior of the Duomo looking toward the apse*, twelfth century. Pisa. The church, with five naves, has decoration consisting of horizontal gray and white bands, which also appear in the Baptistery. Elegant columns support the walls, articulated by a matroneum (women's gallery) that extends into the wings of the transept.

Arles

Situated at the delta of the Rhône River in southern France, Arles, a city of ancient traditions, was settled by Greeks in the sixth century B.C.E. and colonized by Julius Caesar. Three centuries later, in 395 C.E., it became the seat of the Prefecture of Gaul. Named an Episcopal See in 258 C.E., it played a prominent role in the tenth century as capital of the Kingdom of Arles, which included Provence and Burgundy. In the twelfth century it became a free city, a status it retained until annexation by the Kingdom of France in the late eighteenth century, after which it gradually declined in importance. Its urban grid, and especially the remains of a Roman theater and amphitheater, testify to Arles's ancient past. The city's medieval heritage is reflected in various structures, most notably the Cathedral Saint-Trophîme, built in stages between the tenth and fifteenth centuries.

● SAINT-TROPHÎME

View of the façade of Saint-Trophîme Cathedral, thirteenth century. Arles, Provence, France.

Consecrated to St. Trophîme, the first bishop of Arles, the Romanesque cathedral, which welcomed pilgrims on their way to Santiago de Compostela

in Spain, was built on the foundation of an earlier Duomo (fifth century) dedicated to St. Stephen. (The church today thus goes by two names.)

The present-day structure has three naves, a transept, and a choir surrounded by an ambulatory. A tower rises above the crossing of the transept. The façade is adorned with a richly sculpted portal, its figures reflecting a particular sensitivity to classical art, recognizable as well in the sculptural decoration of the cloister.

View of the cloister and tower of Saint-Trophîme Cathedral, thirteenth century. Arles, Provence, France.

Cônques

The presence of a religious settlement was an entirely sufficient reason for the development of a surrounding town; when there were yet other reasons for devotion, such as veneration of the relics of a saint, the development proceeded even more rapidly. This is what occurred at Cônques, in Aveyron (south-central France), where in the eighth century an abbey had been founded and immediately benefited from the protection of the Carolingian sovereigns. The interest of the faithful intensified when, in 866, the monk Ariviscus brought from Agen in the Garonne the relics of Saint Fides (Sainte-Foy), a fourth-century martyr, consisting of a precious enameled reliquary. The town of Cônques and its abbey flourished until the fourteenth century, when competition from other religious orders in southern France and the Hundred Years' War (1336–1453) led to an inevitable decline. This culminated in the fifteenth century with the secularization of the complex, suppressed in 1790 at the time of the French Revolution. Cônques today, nestled in the forests of the Massif Centrale, preserves its medieval legacy almost intact.

● THE ABBEY

Dedicated to the young martyr (Saint Fides was only 12 years old when, during the reign of Diocletian, she was burned at the stake and beheaded), the abbey resembles such other important ecclesiastical structures as Saint-Martin in Tours and Saint-Saturnin in Toulouse. Like them, it was a pilgrimage destination and a stop on the route to Santiago de Compostela in Spain (pp. 264–265). The abbey annexed to the monastery of Cônques, begun in 1050 and finished 80 years later, had an ambulatory around the choir and a tribune extending over the body of the church and the transept, allowing the faithful to pass more easily around the relics of the saint. While the exterior is sober and clear-cut in its Romanesque forms, the interior, including the cloister and chapter house, contains significant sculptural decoration. Standing out in the façade is a richly decorated portal with a scene of the Last Judgment in which the martyred saint appears.

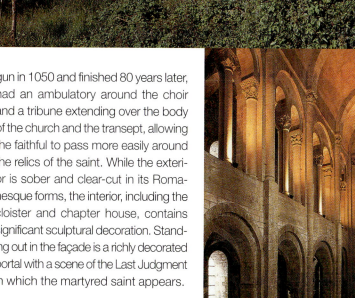

*Central nave looking
toward the apse
in the Abbey
of Sainte-Foy,*
c. 1050–1130.
Cônques, Aveyron,
France.

St. Mark's Basilica

In the year 828, Venetian merchants named Tribuno and Rustico stole the body of St. Mark from Alexandria, Egypt, and brought it to Venice. The body was consigned to the doge, who kept it in his palace while awaiting the construction of a more appropriate place in which it could be venerated. A chapel for this purpose was built at the convent of the nuns of San Zaccaria, but the structure was destroyed by fire, along with the church and much of the palace, in 976. This provided the occasion for rebuilding a church that would be worthy of both the saint and the rich and powerful city, now known as the *Serenissima* ("most illustrious").

● THE BASILICA

The first stone was laid in 1063 and, although the basilica was consecrated in 1094, it was almost continuously embellished until the fifteenth century. Despite a long-held belief that only Byzantine craftsmen worked on the basilica, St. Mark's in fact was built by local workmen with cultural ties to Constantinople. According to recent studies, the plan of the building was probably not derived from the five-domed Apostoleion in Constantinople, as some believed, but from a church of the same name built at the order of Theodosius I in Byzantium and now also destroyed. The exterior of St. Mark's is striking for its wealth of marble and mosaic (see illustration, p. 93) as well for the presence of such unique works of art as the splendid gilded bronze horses, brought to Venice from the Hippodrome in Constantinople as part of the spoils of the Fourth Crusade. The interior, preceded by a richly decorated narthex, glows with reflections from gilded mosaic, as in a precious jewel casket. Here the various styles blend harmoniously, reflecting a succession of periods within a perfectly consistent iconographic program.

Above:
Façade of St. Mark's Basilica, 1063–1095. Venice.

Left:
Aerial view of the domes on St. Mark's Basilica. The Greek cross arrangement of the domes derives from Byzantine architecture.

Above:
Interior of St. Mark's Basilica looking toward the apse. Venice. The mosaic decoration covers a span of time from the twelfth to the sixteenth centuries.

Monreale

A few miles outside Palermo, Sicily, stands a building regarded as a masterpiece of Norman architecture. Compared to St. Mark's Basilica in Venice, the Duomo of Monreale represents another Italian expression of the influence of Byzantine culture and art. The great rarity of this monument lies in its harmonious melding of Byzantine mosaics and architectural styles of Arab and Norman origin, making this church comparable to only a few other buildings in Sicily and to no other in the world.

● THE DUOMO

Erected under the reign of Guglielmo II, who ordered it built in 1174, two years after coming to the throne, the Duomo was completed in 1186, when the bronze door for the façade was commissioned of Bonanno Pisano.

Designed to serve as a dynastic mausoleum for the Norman sovereigns, the building still contains the sarcophagi of Guglielmo I and Guglielmo II. The interior, with three naves, is distinguished by the splendor of its mosaics, of Byzantine derivation, and by a magnificent wood ceiling over the presbytery decorated in *muqarnas* style, with stalactites and alveolar cells according to typically Islamic technique. In the apsidal basin, the figure of Christ Pantocrator ("Lord of all things") rises imposingly against a dazzling gold background. On the exterior, interwoven arches of obvious Islamic inspiration impart a sense of lively motion to the apses.

Another priceless jewel of this architectural complex is the cloister, which once formed part of a wealthy Benedictine abbey, now destroyed. Of typically Arab style is the fountain, where the water spurts from a stone shaft carved in the shape of a stylized palm tree, obviously alluding to the tree of life and its gifts of faith, abundance, and nourishment.

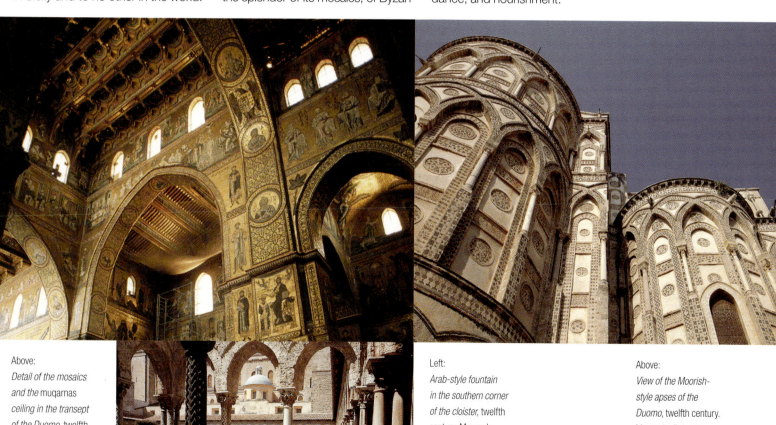

Above:
Detail of the mosaics and the muqarnas *ceiling in the transept of the Duomo,* twelfth century. Monreale, Palermo, Italy.

Left:
Arab-style fountain in the southern corner of the cloister, twelfth century. Monreale, Palermo, Italy.
The cloister of the Duomo, with arches resting on Damascene columns, is part of the original design from the time of Guglielmo II.

Above:
View of the Moorish-style apses of the Duomo, twelfth century. Monreale, Palermo, Italy.

Santiago de Compostela

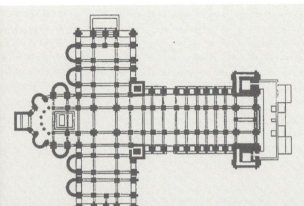

Plan of the Cathedral of Santiago de Compostela.

Below:
Façade of the Cathedral of Santiago de Compostela.

Above:
P. Derveux, *Carte des Chemins de S. Jacques de Compostelle*, 1648. This seventeenth-century map shows the network of roads and stopping places for the pilgrims who journeyed from France to Santiago de Compostela.

Throughout the Middle Ages, as well as in later times, the church of Santiago de Compostela in Galicia (north-western Spain) was the destination of pilgrims from every class of society. Legend had it that St. James the Greater (*Santiago* in Spanish) appeared in a dream to all those who prayed to him and invited them to meet him in Galicia; there, it was said, a peasant plowing his fields had found the relics of the saint after having seen a light glowing like a comet in the sky. The field was called *Campus stellae* (from which the name "Compostela" derives), and a small church was built there. According to another legend, it was a hermit named Pelagius who discovered the tomb of St. James in the year 813 and the Bishop Theodomir who moved it to the place where Santiago now stands. Sacked first by the Normans (968) and again by the Arabs under al-Mansur (997), the village of Santiago—which would grow to the size of a city over the succeeding centuries—was reconstructed by Bishop Diego Peláez, who began expanding the church in 1078. The cathedral still houses the relics of St. James, the brother of St. John the Evangelist and the first Christian martyr, killed in 44 C.E.

N

Left:
Interior of the cathedral,
eleventh–twelfth
centuries. Santiago
de Compostela,
Galicia, Spain.
With the matroneum
(women's gallery),
pilgrims could walk
all around the interior
of the church
on two levels.

Below:
*Entrance to the
cathedral from the
Pórtico de la Gloria
by Maestro Mateo,*
end of twelfth century.
Santiago
de Compostela,
Galicia, Spain.

● THE TOWN

Today's town is the result of sweeping Baroque renovation. But the urban plan has remained that of medieval times, with the cathedral at the center of the town (both geographically and symbolically). The fame of the site during the Middle Ages is evidenced by the fact that St. Francis founded a monastery there in 1213: San Francesco de Valdeidós. Santiago also has an ancient medieval seminary, called San Martín Pinario, founded in 912 and rebuilt completely in the sixteenth and seventeenth centuries.

● THE CATHEDRAL

During the years of its construction, Santiago was an outpost of Christianity in an Islamic land. In 1095, Pope Urban II raised it to the status of an Episcopal See. After the reconquest of Galicia, the Church wished to reaffirm the presence of Christianity with a strong cult, such as that of St. James. All of Europe looked toward Compostela, and the pilgrimage came to be seen as a kind of journey toward the light. In 1120, Pope Callixtus II granted a special indulgence promising that anyone who died at Santiago or on the way to it

would be received in Paradise. The great popularity of the sanctuary grew still further, making it a sort of "Jerusalem of the West." Despite major modifications in the Renaissance and Baroque periods, the plan of the Cathedral remains essentially that of the Middle Ages. The interior of this first great proto-Romanesque Christian basilica is basically unchanged. Even better preserved is the crypt, whose massive, sharply defined architectural forms both contrast with and heighten the effect of the fine sculptural decoration on the capitals and the embrasure of the main door. During the long period of construction, which began in 1075, continued through the Middle Ages, and ended in the late fourteenth century, the plans of the surrounding buildings, including the octagonal Chapel of Santa Fede and the cloister, were also defined. It was the Bishop Diego Gelmírez (1093–1140) who imparted new enthusiasm to the initiative, setting the guidelines for future architectural decisions. Santiago thus became the prototype of the church-sanctuary for pilgrims, rich in magnificent sculptural achievements; prominent among these is the Pórtico de Las Platerias and the Pórtico de la Gloria by Maestro Mateo.

Chartres

Located about 50 miles southwest of Paris in the Ile-de-France, the town of Chartres is famous the world over for its cathedral, a supreme example of Romanesque and Gothic architecture. An Episcopal See since the fourth century, Chartres became a thriving commercial center in the eleventh and twelfth centuries, benefiting from the network of roads that connected the north to the south (including Lyon, Rouen, and Orléans) and the east to the west (Blois, Le Mans, and Paris) in central-northern France. At the same time, the lower part of the city began to expand along the Eure River, a tributary of the Seine, and became a flourishing artisan's market connected to the upper city by steep lanes. Still today, Chartres preserves significant vestiges of its medieval past:

the remains of walls, ancient houses, churches, suburban abbeys (Saint-Martin-du-Val and Saint-Père), and, above all, the great cathedral. Around it, in the first half of the twelfth century, was founded a famous ecclesiastical school, of neo-Platonic inspiration, where some of the greatest philosophers of the Middle Ages studied and taught (among them St. Bernard, Theodoric of Chartres, and Bernard Silvestre). Annexed to the school was a scriptorium of such importance that it constituted its own school of miniature painting, which reached its peak around 1140 before being surpassed by that of Paris.

● THE CATHEDRAL

The first documentation regarding the site dates from 743, although it re-

ports only the destruction of the original structure.

That edifice is believed to have stood on the site of today's cathedral, over an ancient well thought to have been the place where early Christians suffered martyrdom. Around this cave, called Saint-Lubin (after a sixth-century bishop), must have stood the apse of the ancient cathedral, and it was here that the Romanesque crypt was built. The crypt and western façade alone survived the fire of 1194, which provided the occasion for rebuilding the structure. The undertaking was carried out over a span of 20 years and made Chartres the unrivaled model for other Gothic cathedrals. Erected over the ancient crypt (1020–1024), the new Chartres Cathedral, dedicated to Notre-Dame, has three broad naves

Above:
Interior of the cathedral.
Chartres, Eure-et-Loire, France. The many stained-glass windows on every wall of this magnificent structure, almost all of which date from the thirteenth century, reflect a consistent iconographic program.

Right:
Exterior of the choir with flying buttresses, 1220. Chartres, Eure-et-Loire, France.

and a choir with ambulatory divided into three chapels.

At the center, the body of the church is crossed by a broad transept; there is no tower over the crossing, which concludes on the northern and southern sides in two lateral façades. The interior soars upward above heavy pillars supporting a wall lightened by a triforium and a clerestory. The excellent building technique is apparent on the outside of the choir, where an array of flying buttresses imparts stability to the construction.

Other striking aspects of the building are its extraordinary size, the matchless splendor of its stained-glass windows, and its elaborate sculptural decoration, which is especially rich in the embrasures of the portals and on the side façades.

Above:
View of the Cathedral of Notre-Dame, built after 1194, consecrated in 1260. Chartres, Eure-et-Loire, France.

Above:
Façade of Notre-Dame, after 1134–after 1194. Chartres, Eure-et-Loire, France. The original Romanesque design of the façade has undergone various changes, including the addition of a rose window. The sculptural decoration on the Portal of the Kings, however, has remained unchanged. While it manifestly still belongs to the Romanesque period, the complex, distinguished by the harmonious integration of sculptural decoration with architectural design, is considered a turning point toward the Gothic style.

Right:
Stained glass windows in the cathedral as viewed from the bell tower, twelfth century. Chartres, Eure-et-Loire, France.

Benedetto Antelami

Benedetto Antelami, *Deposition*, detail with the artist's signature, 1178. Parma, Cathedral.

Right:
Benedetto Antelami, *Baptistery*, 1198 (finished after 1321). Parma.

Below:
Benedetto Antelami, *Northern portal of the baptistery*, 1198 (finished after 1321). Parma. At the center of the lunette depicting the *Adoration of the Magi* appears the *Madonna and Child Enthroned*. On the other two portals, Antelami portrayed *Christ at the Last Judgment* (west portal) and the *Legend of Josaphat and Barlaam* (south portal).

Right:
Interior of the Baptistery. Parma. The interior plan of the building is decahedral, differing from the octagonal shape of the exterior.

The architect's profession has always been half practical and half theoretical. During the Middle Ages, however, apprenticeship in a workshop, which provided direct contact with the materials to be fashioned into new forms, was indispensable to entering the world of art. Thus, the training of an architect went far beyond the realm of architecture itself, which explains why Benedetto Antelami (active from 1178 to 1230) was not only an architect but also a sculptor and perhaps a goldsmith as well.

● LIFE

Very little is known of this artist. The only certain information comes from inscriptions left on some of his works, such as the relief carving of the *Deposition*, signed and dated 1178, in the Cathedral of Parma. From it emerges the possibility, corroborated by another badly deteriorated but comparable slab, that this work formed part of a pulpit or rood screen designed entirely by Benedetto in his dual capacity as sculptor and architect. The name Antelami, which appears in the inscription, may indicate that the artist belonged to a group of builders called *Magistri Antelami*, about which information exists only from 1439. "Antelami" is an early medieval place name that designated the Valley of Intelvi, lying between Lakes Como and Lugano, from which Benedetto may have come. Another hypothesis is that the master came from Genoa, where these builders had also worked. None of this, however, sheds much light on the artist's life and training. On the basis of stylistic features, critics have presumed that he was familiar with Chartres Cathe-

Below:
Detail of façade of the Duomo, 1178–1196. Fidenza, Parma. The work is generally considered to have been carried out by the master's assistants, but with his participation. The reference to Chartres concerns the Romanesque version.

dral and Notre-Dame in Paris, and that he spent time in Provence, perhaps carving some of the capitals on the columns in Saint-Trophîme at Arles.

● THE BAPTISTERY IN PARMA

Signed and dated 1196 on the architrave of the northern portal, the baptistery in Parma is Antelami's masterpiece and one of the greatest monuments of Gothic architecture in Italy. Ready in time for celebration of the first baptism in 1216, it was not fully completed until after 1321, when the master builders finished the roof and pinnacles, preceded by the balustrade and an elegant register of blind arches. The exterior of the building, of traditional octagonal plan, is faced with slabs of Verona marble. A sense of rhythmic motion is imparted by the arrangement of exterior galleries, with

a striking chiaroscuro effect, and by three portals bearing reliefs carved by Antelami himself, who also executed much of the interior sculptural decoration.

● THE DUOMO OF FIDENZA

It was sometime between 1178 and 1196 that the "modernization" of the Fidenza Duomo took place. It was probably more the work of Antelami's assistants than of the master himself. Standing along the Via Emilia, the cathedral was a brickwork building constructed according to principles derived from the tradition of Wiligelmo and Lanfranco. Antelami and his assistants introduced the use of stone and designed a new façade, with three finely sculpted portals, enclosed between two towers in accordance with the most recent innovation of the French Gothic style.

Left:
Benedetto Antelami, *September*, c. 1215. Parma. Along with others still preserved in the baptistery, this work formed part of a cycle of Months and Seasons. The 16 relief sculptures, one for each of the 16 sectors of the inner structure, were placed at the height of the impost of the dome. Antelami's harmonious integration of architecture and sculpture made him one of the great masters of his age, comparable to the anonymous creators of the most innovative achievements in France.

Villard de Honnecourt

Already by the Middle Ages, architecture, while considered a mechanical art (that is, an applied technique), had developed a complex theoretical structure that was for the most part transmitted orally among workers skilled in the various procedures. At times, however, the techniques and aesthetic principles were recorded in written works that amounted to working reference manuals. Among these, the most important still extant today is the notebook of Villard de Honnecourt.

● A LIFE OF TRAVEL

Very little is known of his life, but what is known comes from his own words in the "Notebook." In it the artist relates, among many other things, that he has been to Hungary and seen the floor of a church, which he sketches in the manual. Active in the thirteenth century, he most likely came from the Picardy region in Normandy, perhaps from the town of Honnecourt-sur-Escaut, where a great abbey, destroyed in World War I, once stood. It was here that Villard, who (as he explains) came from a long line of construction engineers, must have trained as an architect and set out on his journeys driven by an interest in art. "I have been in many countries," he writes, "as you can see from this book." It is clear that Villard is telling the truth, since the notebook not only relates his many travels but also includes sketches of the monuments he visited. After seeing the rose window at Chartres, he went on to Reims, where

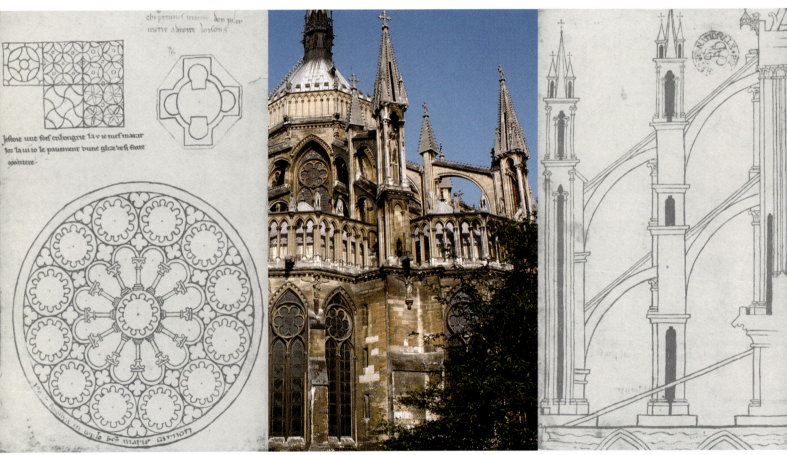

Above:
Villard de Honnecourt,
The floor of a Hungarian church, base of a pillar at Reims Cathedral, and rose window at Chartres Cathedral, from the *Livre de portraiture,*
1220–1235. Paris, National Library, ms. fr. 19093, c. 15v.

Above:
Exterior view of the apsidal chapels in the Reims Cathedral, 1220–1241. Reims, Marne, France.

Above:
Villard de Honnecourt,
Section of the wall and rampant arches on the apsidal chapels of Reims Cathedral, from the *Livre de portraiture,*
1220–1235. Paris, National Library, ms. fr. 19093, c. 32v.

he stayed for a time, and then proceeded to Laon, where he praised the beauty of the cathedral tower, and other locations. His interest was by no means purely theoretical; to the contrary, theory was assigned a secondary place in the architect's profession. In other words, Villard must have built extensively, in his native land as well.

● THE NOTEBOOK

The real title of the work, familiarly known as the "Notebook" (now at the National Library in Paris), is *Livre de portraiture* ("Book of Descriptions"). The work contains text and sketches, based strictly on first-hand experience, of the works described (see illustration, p. 23). The tone is that of a manual for students eager to learn the secrets of the art of building. The choice of material is predominantly technical, covering an impressive range of subjects: from geometry to building diagrams, from the description of machines used in construction to a definition of decorations and the geometric methods for creating them. Everything is explained with the utmost clarity and without superfluous discussion. Moreover, the book's character as an architectural manual, to be used at actual worksites, is seen in its strictly black-and-white illustrations, a choice no doubt partly intended to limit the cost of production. All of this clearly indicates that Villard's *Livre* was not intended as a work to be left on a shelf and gather dust. The author himself chose all of the examples used to illustrate specific architectural innovations and building features. At the time of his trips to Chartres, Reims, and Laon, the great cathedrals were still in the construction stage or, as in the case of Chartres, undergoing reconstruction after a fire. Villard acted as neither a tourist nor an art historian, but inspected worksites strictly in connection with his profession as architect and engineer. Beyond that, to provide his pupils with complete information, his attention ranged from the construction of machinery to representation of the human figure.

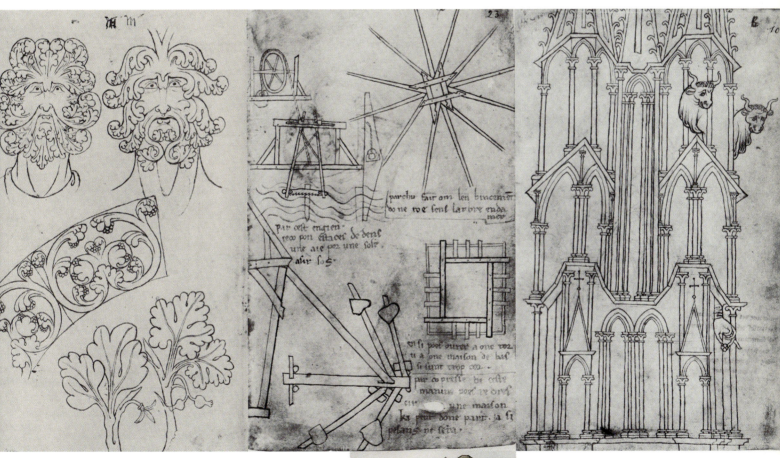

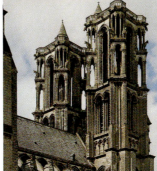

Villard de Honnecourt,
*Drawings of decorative
motifs*, from the
Livre de portraiture,
1220–1235. Paris,
National Library,
ms. fr. 19093, c. 5v.

Above:
Villard de Honnecourt,
*Machines and
instruments*, from the
Livre de portraiture,
1220–1235. Paris,
National Library,
ms. fr. 19093, c. 23r.

Left:
*Detail of the western
tower of the
Laon Cathedral*,
c. 1150–1210.
Laon, Picardy, France.

Above:
Villard de Honnecourt,
*Western tower of the
Laon Cathedral*, from
the *Livre de portraiture*,
1220–1235. Paris,
National Library,
ms. fr. 19093, c. 10r.

The Duomo of Siena and the Duomo of Orvieto

Left:
Interior of the Duomo, 1215–after 1376. Siena, Italy.
In the foreground appears the magnificent fifteenth-century inlaid flooring; in the background are the columns and facing in striped black-and-white marble.

Lower left:
View of the Duomo, 1215–after 1376. Siena, Italy.
The black-and-white stripes do not derive from the dominant influence in Tuscany of the Pisan Romanesque style, but reflect instead the heraldic motif of the Sienese *balzana* (black-and-white banner; see illustration, p. 103).

It would be hard to find two works of architecture that are so different in spirit and history, yet so similar in form and style. The Duomo of Siena was built in a city in political turmoil, the stronghold of Tuscan Ghibellines hostile to Florence until excommunication by the pope. The Orvieto Duomo, by contrast, was built in a Guelph city, albeit one torn by opposing factions, that was the site of a papal palace. The two buildings are both masterpieces of Italian Romanesque-Gothic, but the former was built almost in defiance (retaining its ancient dedication to the Madonna, the "queen of the city"), while the latter was erected as the crowning achievement of a policy that had linked Orvieto to the Roman Curia since its communal status had been recognized by Pope Hadrian IV in 1157. If these are the differences, the similarities are more obvious. To solve the problems of their cathedral, the citizens of Orvieto called upon the Sienese sculptor and architect Lorenzo Maitani, who was thoroughly familiar with the layout of the Duomo in his own city; moreover, when the Sienese completed the façade of their cathedral in 1376, they drew inspiration from that of Orvieto.

View of the Duomo,
1290–after 1330.
Orvieto, Italy.
The median pilasters on
the façade match those
of the portal, unlike
those of the Siena
Duomo, where the
discrepancy is due to
the building's
complicated history.

Below:
Detail of the south
portal of the Duomo.
Orvieto, Italy.
The choice of black-
and-white registers was
inspired by the Duomo
of Siena.

● THE DUOMO OF SIENA

The Siena Duomo emerges out of the mists of history only in the ninth century, when a church dedicated to Mary, perhaps built over a temple to Minerva, is known to have occupied part of the area where the Episcopal annex stands today. Only near the end of the twelfth century was the new Duomo given a façade facing the ancient hospital, to underscore the relationship between prayer and suffering. Some part of the church must have been in use by 1215, since records indicate that a Mass was celebrated in it that year. The interior was in use by 1264, and the planning of the new façade began around 1284. The Sienese then turned to Giovanni Pisano, who directed work on the lower register until 1296. Work on the façade thereafter came to a halt for 80 years, because the Sienese had planned to build the largest church in Christianity, of which the existing one would have constituted only the left wing of the transept. They even wanted to rival St. Peter's in Rome, but the grandiose plan went unfulfilled; in the end it was decided to complete the old plan based on the designs of Giovanni d'Agostino, the master builder from 1340 to 1350. The façade, completed by Giovanni di Cecco, reflects these events in a notable stylistic difference between the Romanesque lower register and the flamboyant Gothic upper register, and with the position of the pinnacles flanking the rose window off-center in relation to the pilasters of the central portal.

● THE DUOMO OF ORVIETO

The history of the Orvieto Duomo is less complicated. It was begun by Fra Bevignate da Perugia in 1290 and continued in the Gothic style by Uguccione da Orvieto in 1300. When it became obvious that the walls were unsteady, Lorenzo Maitani (c. 1275–1330) was called in. He was appointed *universalis caput-magister* in 1310. Not only did he solve the problem of the apse by utilizing rampant arches, but he also designed and began work on the façade. It is highly probable that Maitani was the sculptor responsible for the fine reliefs that adorn the four pilasters of the portals. The interior does not differ greatly from that of the Siena Duomo, which inspired it, except for the ceiling, a trussed-beam structure.

Todi

On a hill overlooking the Tiber Valley in central Italy rises the town of Todi, whose medieval urban and architectural plan is among the best-preserved anywhere, remaining practically unchanged through the nineteenth century. Organized as a free commune in the twelfth century, Todi, as a Guelph city, opposed Frederick II in 1240. It began to decline in political importance during the fourteenth century, progressively losing its freedom under the lordship of various families. Encircled by imposing medieval walls, parts of which are perfectly preserved, the city has its religious and political center at the top of the hill on which it stands.

There, around an oblong square extending lengthwise in an L-shape, stand the palaces of political power and the Duomo, which, with the bishop's palace, occupies the highest and northernmost point of the complex.

● PUBLIC PALACES

The oldest of those surrounding the square, the Palazzo del Popolo was built between 1214 and 1248. Above a loggia on the ground floor rise two stories crowned by an elegant ring of Guelph merlons (battlements). Connected to the building by a broad stairway without a balustrade is the Palazzo del Capitano, dating from 1290. Lastly, the Palazzo dei Priori, erected be-

Right:
Remains of the medieval walls, 1244. Todi, Italy.

Below:
Façade of the Duomo, eleventh–fourteenth centuries. Todi, Italy.

Right:
Palazzo del Popolo (or Palazzo del Podestà) and Palazzo del Capitano. Todi, Italy.

tween 1334 and 1337 and renovated in 1514, still retains its original structure with a quadrangular tower.

● THE DUOMO

Majestic and harmonious, the façade of the cathedral rises above a broad stairway. The interior is divided into three naves. Begun in the twelfth century, the Duomo was finished between the thirteenth and the fifteenth centuries.

Bruges

The most important city in West Flanders (now western Belgium), Bruges (*Brugge* in Flemish) lies just inland from the North Sea port of Ostend. The city became economically important during the eleventh century as a center of commerce that grew up around an ancient Roman *castrum* (fortified encampment), on which Count Baldwin V conferred a new political and economic role. The geographical position of the city was unexpectedly improved at that time by a sudden inundation of the Zwyn River, which transformed it into a natural port (today covered with earth). A burgeoning population from the thirteenth to the fifteenth century testified to the wealth of the city, which attracted many religious orders and led to the construction of the public and private buildings that give the city its distinctive look. An important factor in the social composition of the city was the community of Beguines, whose church, erected in the thirteenth century, was rebuilt four centuries later.

The Beguines were women who, without taking vows, lived together in a particular area of the city and led pious, industrious lives.

Among the noteworthy monuments of Bruges are the Church of Notre Dame (*Onze Lieve Vrouw*), begun in the second quarter of the thirteenth century near the Hospital of St. John (*Sint Janshospitaal*), a highly modern facility for its time.

Another notable building is the Town Hall (*Stadhuis*), erected between 1376 and 1420, whose decoration places it in the category of Flamboyant Gothic. The entire urban grid is well preserved, and many beautiful houses from medieval times can still be seen.

Left:
View of a canal lined with medieval houses and, in the background, the municipal tower of the Beffroi. Bruges, West Flanders, Belgium. The 270-foot municipal bell tower (*beffroi*), begun in 1296 and finished in 1482, dominates many views of Bruges. The city is called the "Venice of Belgium" for its lovely canals, lined with medieval houses, churches, and palaces.

Above:
View of the complex of the Beguines (Begijnhof), founded in 1245. Bruges, West Flanders, Belgium.

Right:
The Stadhuis building in Burg Square, 1376–1420. Bruges, West Flanders, Belgium. The façade of Belgium's oldest town hall is distinguished by three turrets and embellished by elegant two-light mullioned windows and rich sculptural decoration.

Canterbury

One of the best-preserved medieval cities in England and the seat of the primate of the Church of England, Canterbury has a roughly circular urban layout, enclosed by walls of which large sections are still standing. Located in southeastern England, Canterbury served as capital of the Saxon kingdom of Kent in the sixth century and was converted to Christianity in 597 by Abbot Augustine (sent by Pope Gregory the Great), who made it an Episcopal See and founded its most important landmark. Canterbury Cathedral is one of the most compelling architectural complexes anywhere in Great Britain, whose ultimate form resulted from a centuries-long process of stylistic stratification. The original church founded by Augustine was followed, between 1070 and 1077, by a Norman cathedral built under Archbishop Lanfranco of Pavia (1003–1089), a prelate imposed by William the Conqueror. The church was inspired by the impressive design, including rectangular towers, of the monastic church of Saint-Etienne in Caen, Normandy, where Lanfranco had served as bishop. Because a bishop was also an abbott in the Norman order, Lanfranco was followed by more than 100 monks; to provide more space, the complex was enlarged in 1096 and, after a fire, rebuilt entirely in 1175. In this second renovation, directed first by the architect Guillaume of Sens and then by William the Englishman, the choir, the first example of English Norman Gothic style, was built. The nave and west transept were rebuilt in Late Gothic style around 1377. The northern tower on the façade was erected in the following century, and the cloister, chapterhouse, and southeastern and central towers in the early sixteenth century.

Above:
View of the cathedral,
twelfth–sixteenth
centuries. Canterbury,
Kent, England.

Right:
Nave of the cathedral,
c. 1377. Canterbury,
Kent, England.
The nave, with its
soaring vertical lines,
was designed by the
greatest English
architect of the time,
Henry Yevele
(1320–1400). The
ribbed vaulting was
completed in 1405.

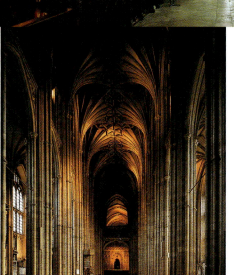

Above:
Choir of the cathedral,
twelfth–fourteenth
centuries. Canterbury,
Kent, England.
On December 29, 1170,
the cathedral was the
scene of the
assassination of Thomas
Becket, the archbishop
of Canterbury,
who was canonized
three years later.

Lübeck

A city of great importance during medieval times, and not for Germany alone, Lübeck was the founding place of the Hanseatic League (1358), the trade association (*Hansa*) that was to confer enormous economic power on the more than 200 German cities and merchant settlements near the Baltic and North Seas of which it was made up. Theirs was a true monopoly, consisting of the right to unload their own goods free of charge while re-

Left:
View of Lübeck with the Marienkirche.
The church, like the Rathaus, stands on Market Square, the city's financial and political center at the heart of the aristocratic district. At the beginning of the fourteenth century, Lübeck had a population of 25,000.

Right:
Interior of the Marienkirche, 1282–1300. Lübeck, Schleswig-Holstein, Germany.

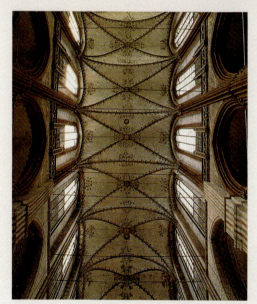

Above:
The Holstentor, from 1464. Lübeck, Schleswig-Holstein, Germany.
The Holstentor is the imposing gateway to the city.

View of the Rathaus, fourteenth century. Lübeck, Schleswig-Holstein, Germany.

quiring foreign merchants to dock in their ports and pay customs duties. In that capacity, Lübeck played a crucial role as a center for routing the cargo of the merchant ships sailing from east to west toward Prussia and Livonia (today's Latvia). A small, recently founded settlement at the beginning of the twelfth century, Lübeck was moved farther north in 1143, destroyed by fire in 1157, and soon rebuilt at the order of its overlord, Henry the Lion; the

historic center of the city today dates to that time. The economic and political growth of Lübeck is demonstrated on the one hand by the fact that it was entitled to coin its own money, and on the other hand by the construction, beginning in 1229, of an imposing ring of walls (traces of which still survive today). Enclosed between two rivers, the Trave and the Wakenitz, Lübeck had its political and religious center in the main square. On it stand the Ra-

thaus, or town hall (the city remained independent until 1937), and the Marienkirche, which was completely rebuilt after a fire; because of internal disputes and indecision, the reconstruction did not begin until six years later, in 1282, reaching completion in 1300. The Duomo, meanwhile, rose in the southern part of the city. It was consecrated in 1247, although the renovation of the choir continued from 1277 to 1329.

Arnolfo di Cambio and Giotto

The decision to discuss two such apparently different figures as Arnolfo di Cambio and Giotto together is based on the recent hypothesis that the two artists worked together at the construction site of the Upper Church of Assisi. Specifically, Arnolfo is believed to have executed his first paintings there, consisting of two works usually attributed to the so-called Isaac Master, while Giotto is thought to have learned the basic elements of architecture, which he was then to employ at the height of his career.

● ARNOLFO DI CAMBIO

A painter, but above all a sculptor and architect, Arnolfo was born at Colle Val d'Elsa, not far from Siena, between 1240 and 1245; he died in Florence, his adopted city, around 1302. Although his early work consisted mainly of sculpture, the commissions of the time often required artists to design architectural structures as well. A clear example of this may be seen in the "lesser" Fountain of Perugia, removed from its original location in 1308, on which some of Arnolfo's high-relief sculptures still remain and for which he had to solve a number of architectural problems. The same may be said of such works as his funerary monument for Cardinal De Braye at Orvieto and, in particular, the ciborium (pillared canopy over an altar) of St. Paul's Outside the Walls in Rome. It has recently been suggested that his activity at the construction site of St. Francis of Assisi in the early 1390s may have marked the occasion of Arnolfo's initial contact with the religious order that, during the same period, was to commission the first of his great architectural projects, the church of Santa Croce in

Above:
Arnolfo di Cambio,
Palazzo Vecchio,
1299–1315. Florence.

Right:
Arnolfo di Cambio,
The thirsty lame man,
from the "lesser"
Fountain, 1277–1281.
Perugia, Italy. Galleria
Nazionale dell'Umbria.
Art historians have
noted that Arnolfo
was obviously familiar
with contemporary
Parisian sculpture.

Left:
Arnolfo di Cambio,
Ciborium, 1284.
St. Paul's Outside the
Walls. Rome, Italy.

Florence. Attributed to Arnolfo on the basis of Vasari's testimony, as well as close stylistic comparison, the Palazzo Vecchio in Florence was superimposed over existing buildings that were incorporated into the new structure, begun in 1299. The central core of the palace was probably finished by 1302, but the undertaking continued even after Arnolfo's death, with construction of the 310-foot tower in 1310 until its completion five years later. The majestic, monumental building clearly evidences the sculptor's experience with molding blocks of stone by chiseling and chipping. Although many works are attributed to Arnolfo on the basis of Vasari's testimony, his commission for the Florence Duomo is also supported by a document dated April 1, 1300, in which Arnolfo is excused from paying taxes because of his position as *caput magister* ("master builder") of the Santa Maria del Fiore worksite. The new Duomo was built over the old one, Santa Reparata, which was incorporated into it. This operation was partially carried out by Arnolfo, who used portions of the outer wall of the old church for the new one. Unfortunately, no trace of the architect's stylistic choices remains, since Bernardo Buontalenti managed to have the structure demolished in 1587, planning to modernize it in keeping with the new aesthetic principles of the Renaissance. The general plan, however, remains the one designed by Arnolfo di Cambio.

● GIOTTO

With the death of Arnolfo in 1302, Giotto, his former companion from the scaffolds of Assisi, was chosen to continue the construction of the Duomo. The only certain element of Giotto's work as an architect is the 275-foot bell tower, although he completed only the lower order with its hexagonal panels. The Florentine artist served not only as master builder of the Duomo but was also appointed superintendent of the fortifications of Florence by the city government.

Left:
View of the apse and chevet, 1294. Santa Croce, Florence, Italy. These elements and the crypt are Arnolfo's only certain contributions to the building. The T-shaped transept derives from Cistercian tradition.

Above:
Giotto and others, *Bell Tower of Santa Maria del Fiore*, 1334–1359. Florence, Italy.

Right:
Plan of Santa Maria del Fiore (1296–1468). The drawing shows how the ancient church of Santa Reparata was incorporated in the new Duomo.

The Parler Family

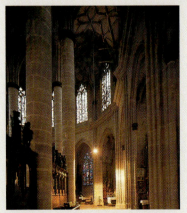

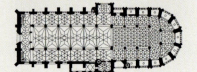

Above: *View of the Frauenkirche*, 1350–1358. Nuremberg, Germany.

Right: *Hall-type choir viewed from the ambulatory*, late fourteenth century. Freiburg in Breisgau, Baden-Württemberg, Germany.

Plan of the Heiligkreuzkirche, 1330–1351. Schwäbisch Gmünd, Germany.

When one thinks of an architect today, one may imagine an isolated figure, at the most working with assistants in his studio. In the past, however, the architectural profession was handed down from father to son, often for several generations.

It is no coincidence that the family name "Parler" derives from the German word *parlier*, the designation for the first assistant of a master builder. Parler, in fact, was also the name of one of the great families of medieval architects. With roots in the Rhineland (western Germany), the Parlers remained active in many parts of Europe from the fourteenth to the early fifteenth centuries, attaining a level of influence that invested German Late Gothic with a unique stylistic variation that came to be called *Parler-Zeit* ("Parler Age").

The most important members of the family were Heinrich and his sons Peter and Johann.

● HEINRICH PARLER

Considered the founder of the family, at least in artistic terms, Heinrich Parler was born around the first decade of the fourteenth century, perhaps in Cologne. His greatest achievement was the church at Schwäbisch Gmünd (in southwestern Germany) dedicated to the Holy Cross (*Heiligkreuzkirche*), where he directed the construction site. He was certainly working there in 1333, the year in which the birth of his son is recorded. His architectural training led him to modify the plan of the church, originally of the basilican type, transforming it into a "hall" church on the model of Notre-Dame in Paris. Heinrich also worked in Nuremberg on the

Frauenkirche, the church dedicated to the Virgin Mary and, most likely, on the Cathedral of Augsburg, where some stone blocks in the building bear the lapidary insignia of the Parlers: the *parlerhaken*, a square with a double broken line. Heinrich Parler was buried at Schwäbisch Gmünd.

● PETER PARLER

The most influential of the Parlers, Peter was born in 1333 and lived to the age of 66. He trained at his father's school, first on the site of Schwäbisch Gmünd and then on that of the Frauenkirche in Nuremberg, where he worked in his father's place until 1356. This imperial

commission (the church was built at the order of Charles IV, who had it erected next to the Castle of Lauf) procured Peter the most important position of his life, that of site director for the Prague Cathedral, succeeding the French architect Mathieu d'Arras.

A glance at the plan of the Prague Cathedral dedicated to St. Vitus is enough to see how thoroughly Peter had assimilated his father's teachings. Peter worked on the sculptural decoration as well, as was customary for the Parler family, contributing to the distinctive "Parlerian" style.

Charles IV conferred other commissions on Peter, such as the Charles Bridge in Prague, whose tower, decorated by sculpture on the façade, leads into the old city, as well as the roof on the west wing of Prague Castle.

● JOHANN PARLER

Unlike his father, Heinrich, and his brother, Peter, he preferred to be called Johann of Gmünd rather than Parler. Johann worked as master builder of the Freiburg Cathedral in Breisgau. He designed the choir, with an ambulatory surrounding a polygonal interior body, resulting in a highly original solution. The Parler family tradition continued with the sons of Peter and Johann, who followed in the footsteps of their father, grandfather, and uncles.

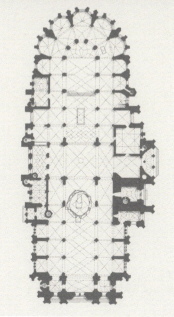

The Alhambra

Left:
Detail of ceramic mosaic in the Hall of the Ambassadors, 1333–1354. Alhambra, Granada, Andalusia, Spain.

Below:
Entrance to the Hall of the Boat from the Courtyard of the Myrtle Trees, 1333–1354. Alhambra, Granada, Andalusia, Spain.

Above:
View of the Alhambra, thirteenth–sixteenth centuries. Granada, Andalusia, Spain.

Left:
Courtyard of the Myrtle Trees, 1333–1354. Alhambra, Granada, Andalusia, Spain.

In southern Spain, surrounded by the mountains of Andalusia near the Mediterranean Sea, lies a small but highly cultivated plain. Here, protected by the peaks of the Sierra Nevada at an altitude of 2,300 feet, stands the city of Granada. The plain and the city are dominated, on the left bank of the Darro River, by La Sabica hill, which expert Arab agronomists enriched with water, woods, and gardens.

Here in 1238, Muhammad I (1238–1273), the founder of the Nasrid Dynasty, established his residence on a site well protected by nature and not far from escape routes to the sea. In the next century, under the initiatives of a succession of resident princes, one of the world's most singular architectural complexes took shape at the site: the Alhambra ("the red") palace. Part residence and part fortress, it was the last outpost of Islamic civilization in the West, resisting, with the rest of the city of Granada, the forces of Spanish sovereigns Ferdinand and Isabella until 1492.

Muhammad I had encircled the Alhambra with thick walls, fortified with imposing quadrangular towers, which, with the additions of Emperor Charles V in the sixteenth century, reached no less than 24 in number. Only eight of them remain today, but they are enough to evoke the besieged citadel in medieval times. The complex contained at least six palaces, built according to the typical Oriental plan, with courtrooms, residence, and baths situated around a patio or courtyard. In addition to the Alhambra proper, a defensive citadel called the Alcazaba and a princely palace called the Alcazar were erected on La Sabica under Muhammad I. The oldest part of the Alhambra is that built by Yusuf I (r. 1333–1354), extending around the spectacular Courtyard of Myrtle Trees; because it is also filled with orange trees, it is sometimes referred to as the Patio de las Arrayanes ("Courtyard of the Oranges"). At the center of the courtyard is a large pool called the Alberca, a deformation of the Arabic *al-birkah* (cistern, or pool of water). The eastern front of the wide patio

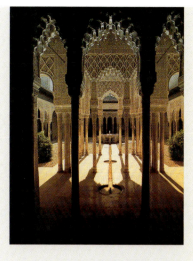

Left:
*Arches with stucco
decoration and Kufic
inscriptions,*
1354–1391.
Alhambra, Granada,
Andalusia, Spain.

Below:
*Detail of decoration
with imprinted stucco
and mosaic
in the Hall of the Two
Sisters,* 1354–1391.
Alhambra, Granada,
Andalusia, Spain.

Above:
Courtyard of the Lions,
1354–1391.
Alhambra, Granada,
Andalusia, Spain.

gives access to the Hall of the Boat, also called the Hall of Blessings (from the Arab *al-barakah*).

Behind it, dominated by the Torre de Comares, stands the splendid Hall of the Ambassadors, or Throne Room. Its ceiling is covered with stylized stars that allude to the Seven Heavens of Islamic tradition, thus identifying the prince as the center of the universe and, at the same time, serving as an omen of good fortune. This area, containing the palace courts, separates the private and residential eastern section from the area of the baths. To the west lies the Palazzo de Comares, entered through the Cuarto Dorado, named for its stucco ceiling entirely covered in gold leaf.

The rooms extending to the east of it are occupied by the baths, in the best Islamic tradition (p. 249), though their typology is clearly of Roman derivation.

At right angles to this complex, Muhammad V (r. 1354–1391) built his own residential palace, of the *ribat* type. The complex is centered around the Courtyard of Lions, named for the fountain at the center (connected through channels to four small fountains on each side of the courtyard), adorned with lions' heads. On one side of the Courtyard of Lions is the Hall of the Two Sisters, and on the other side is the Hall of Abencerrajes (named after a Moorish family said to have been murdered there).

Peking and the Forbidden City

The precise date of the founding of Peking (now called Beijing) is difficult to ascertain because, as the chronicles relate, the city (known as Ji at the time), was already rich during the Warring States Period (third and fourth centuries B.C.E.), before the unification of the country under Qin Shi Huangdi. That historical uncertainty, common to many ancient cities, is complicated by the fact that Peking developed over a span of many centuries, and even more by the fact that the last dynasty, in restoring many of the existing monuments, replaced them with copies. In other words, an urban center largely rebuilt during the eighteenth and nineteenth centuries has the appearance of a fifteenth-century city. In fact, the Qing Dynasty (1644–1911) faithfully replicated the models of the Ming Dynasty (1368–1644), which had moved the seat of the government to Peking in 1421. The city is therefore included in this section covering the fifteenth century, the period in which historic Peking began to take shape.

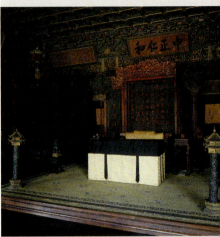

Throne Room in the Hall of Supreme Harmony, renovated around 1695. Peking, China.

The plan of the fifteenth-century city, which has remained largely unchanged to the present time, can thus be examined with chronological consistency. The plan might be called that of "Chinese boxes." At the center is the Forbidden City, enclosed within walls. Around them stood another high wall, now destroyed, that marked the limits of the so-called Imperial City. Access to it was gained through four large gates, the southern one called the Gate of Celestial Peace. The entire Inner City was protected by a third, rectangular belt of walls. The distance between the four sides ranged from four to five miles, defining an area nearly double that of Imperial Rome (a radius of less than three miles within the Aurelian walls). From the outside in, the successive sets of walls defined areas of increas-

ing power and more restricted access. In the Forbidden City, the heart of China, resided the emperor and the imperial family. The Imperial City just outside it was reserved for court officials, while the so-called Inner City beyond that was divided into a Tartar district to the north (inhabited by subjects of Mongol stock, or Manchus, who had held power during the previous Yuan Dynasty) and a Chinese district to the south.

● THE FORBIDDEN CITY

The Chinese name for the imperial compound is *Gugong*, or "forbidden city." The entire architectural complex, begun in 1404 under Emperor Yongle and completed in 1420, still reflects the original plan. The enclosed area is rectangular in shape with a north-south

orientation. At the high point of the complex is the Hall of Supreme Harmony, which served as the imperial throne pavilion (*Zi jin cheng*). The highest point in Beijing is Coal Hill, which overlooks the Forbidden City from the north in a strategically—and geomantically—defensive location. Indeed the layout of streets and arrangement of buildings were determined by the ancient art of geomancy.

The heart of the Forbidden City consists of the Three Great Halls: the aforementioned Hall of Supreme Harmony; the Hall of Complete Harmony, where the emperor rested before receiving the court; and the Hall of Preserving Harmony, where he presided over banquets and greeted state visitors. Behind them stand the private palaces and, around them, an artificial canal.

Left:

View of the Forbidden City. Peking, China.

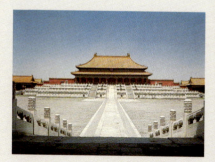

Above:
Hall of Supreme Harmony in the Forbidden City, renovated in 1695. Peking, China. Facing a vast square paved in marble, the pavilion features a double-cornice roof and covers an area of nearly 25,000 square feet.

Right:
Succession of portals in the six private palaces of the Forbidden City. Peking, China.

Filippo Brunelleschi

Below:
Filippo Brunelleschi,
Interior of the
Basilica of San Lorenzo,
1418. Florence.
The church with three
naves, inspired by the
Florentine Basilica of
Santa Croce, is
designed so that the
proportional ratio in
height between the bays
of the central nave, the
lateral naves, and the
chapels reflects the
geometric diminishing
of the optical and
perspective cone.

One of the founding fathers of Renaissance architectural style, Brunelleschi took an interest in problems apparently collateral to those of his profession. He was the first to establish the rules of perspective in painting and delved deep into mathematics and physics. Through his friendship with the physicist and geographer Paolo dal Pozzo Toscanelli (1397–1482), he became a strong supporter of the theory that the earth was round, and his writings helped to inspire the voyage of Christopher Columbus.

● LIFE

The second of three brothers, Filippo was born in Florence in 1377. After pursuing a conventional course of study, in which he learned the traditions of me-

dieval Arab philosophers and mathematicians, at the age of 21 he became a member of the Arte della Seta, whose members included goldsmiths and metal workers (under the name Arte di Por Santa Maria). In the following year, he entered the workshop of the Pistoian master goldsmith Lunardo di Matteo Ducci. On the basis of this experience, he participated in the design competition for the doors of the Florence Baptistery in 1401, an event often identified as the beginning of the Italian Renaissance. Three years later, he was a master goldsmith in the Arte di Por Santa Maria and at the same time began his career as architect. His first journey to Rome likely took place at about this time. Around 1417, he conducted his famous experiments in perspective with two painted panels (now lost), with views of the Florence Baptistery and Palazzo dei Priori from

Via de' Calzaiuoli. By 1420, Brunelleschi was already an artist of renown, engaged in carrying out the many architectural commissions conferred on him by the Florentine signoria. He died on the night of April 15–16, 1446.

● WORKS

Although Brunelleschi is most famous for the dome on the Florence Cathedral, Santa Maria del Fiore, he had many other outstanding accomplishments. He distinguished himself as a military engineer in various cities of Tuscany, including Pisa, where he was summoned to repair the Ponte a Mare. Dating from 1418 is his design for the Basilica of San Lorenzo in Florence, the first attempt to construct a new architectural syntax with the grammatical elements, as it were, of classical design. Also in 1418, Brunelleschi began work on the Old Sacristy adjacent to San Lorenzo, where he applied his ideals of proportional harmony—the domed room is double the length of the rectangular apse, which in turn is divided into three areas, the central one domed—and simple geo-

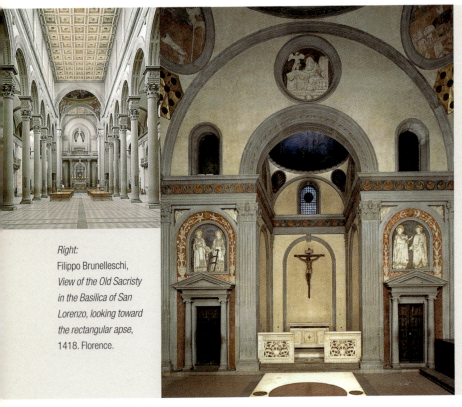

Right:
Filippo Brunelleschi,
View of the Old Sacristy
in the Basilica of San
Lorenzo, looking toward
the rectangular apse,
1418. Florence.

Right:
Filippo Brunelleschi,
Portico of the Ospedale
degli Innocenti, 1424.
Florence.

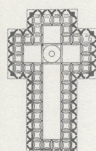

Above:
Filippo Brunelleschi,
Plan of the Church
of Santo Spirito (1436)
in Florence.

metric motifs. At the age of 47 he was appointed director of works for the Ospedale degli Innocenti, which was already being constructed according to his design but was proceeding slowly. In 1433, he began construction on the Pazzi Chapel next to the Church of Santa Croce (p. 142). And in 1436, he was commissioned to build the Church of Santo Spirito, in which he further developed the concepts of proportion he had applied in San Lorenzo, strictly reiterating the square model of the bays. He also designed the unfinished Rotonda degli Angeli (1434), a summary of the experience acquired in his study of Roman monuments, and the original core of the Pitti Palace (1440).

● THE DOME

The problem of the Florence Cathedral was constructing a dome without resorting to fixed external centering to support the masonry. Brunelleschi managed to solve the problem by following the Roman technique of laying the bricks in a fishbone pattern, which made them self-bearing.

Below:
Filippo Brunelleschi,
Paired capitals on the
edicule adorning the
outside of the apse of
Santa Maria del Fiore,
1436. Florence.

Left:
Model of the dome and tambour of Santa Maria del Fiore in Florence (architect F. Gizdulich, Florence 1995). Florence, Istituto e Museo di Storia della Scienza. Brunelleschi's dome is the largest ever built without centering. It is formed of a double calotte divided into eight sections, each composed of two vaulting ribs. The distance between opposite edges of the octagonal base is approximately 180 feet.

Above:
Filippo Brunelleschi, *Dome of Santa Maria del Fiore,* 1420–1436 (lantern, 1436–1469). Florence. The dome rises to a maximum height of 350 feet and required more than four million bricks to build. Its weight is estimated at more than 40,000 tons. The height of the lantern is 72 feet, including the copper ball at the top.

Palazzo Ducale in Urbino

Above:
*View of Urbino
and the Palazzo Ducale.*

With the Renaissance, even the relationship between subjects and their lords changed. Dukes and princes preferred to exercise their power generously, at least in appearance, without the need to shelter themselves in grim castles behind thick defensive walls. The lordly residence of the Renaissance was a palace of harmonious forms, unencumbered by offensive or defensive structures and seemingly open to everyone. The Ducal Palace in Urbino represents a moment of transition from one typology to another, although it can also be seen as unique, being not only the residence of the prince but also the seat of the municipal government. In this sense, it may be compared to the palaces of the East or the Vatican. In fifteenth-century Florence, however, while the Palazzo Medici-Riccardi was the residence of the true lords of the city, the official seat of government remained the Palazzo della Signoria, also known as Palazzo Vecchio, at least until the Medici family moved there in 1540, when it began to be called the "ducal" palace.

● A CITY WITH THE STAMP OF THE RENAISSANCE

An important urban center since Roman times, located between the valleys of the Metauro and the Foglia rivers, Urbino was conquered by Byzantine troops under General Belisarius in the sixth century and later given to the Church by the Carolingians. In reaction, the city became Ghibelline, but this choice proved to be fatal when the Swabians demoted it from the status of a free Commune to that of a vicariate and then a fief of the counts of Montefeltro (1213). Starting from that date, it was governed by the Montefeltro dynasty until 1508. In 1628 it was granted to the Papal States. The city is a splendid example of Renaissance architecture; enclosed within heavy fortification in 1507, it has remained largely unchanged since that time.

● A CITY IN THE FORM OF A PALACE

It was Federico da Montefeltro (1422–1482), a great *condottiere* (mercenary leader) and man of vast erudition, who

Below:
Turreted façade, before
1472. Palazzo Ducale.
Urbino, Marche, Italy.

Below:
Francesco Laurana,
*Winding staircase
in the Palazzo Ducale*,
before 1472.
Urbino, Marche, Italy.

This spectacular
staircase, located in one
of the two turrets on the
façade facing the ducal
stables, allowed the duke
to enter his grand palace

without dismounting his
horse. The Ducal Palace
was also one of the rare
buildings of the time in the
West that was equipped
with an indoor bathroom.

conferred a majestic new form on the modest family palace in Urbino. With this objective, between 1466 and 1468 he commissioned the Dalmatian architect Luciano Laurana (c. 1420–1479) to enlarge the original core of the building, still visible on the side facing the Duomo, which overlooks today's Piazza Rinascimento. Laurana directed the work until 1472, when he was succeeded by the Sienese architect Francesco di Giorgio Martini (1439–1502), who remained in the service of the duke until 1489 and followed the guidelines laid down by his predecessor in his work on the side of the building overlooking the Mercatale esplanade. The palace complex was linked to the valley below through the ducal stables, near the Mercatale, which could be reach by a winding stair-

case. Harmonious and balanced, the palace is organized around a great courtyard inspired by those of Florentine palaces and serving, in turn, as a model for such other architects as Bramante. From there the structure extends on one side toward the Duomo and on the other along the old perimeter, creating another courtyard known as "del Pasquino." The feature that makes the palace unique, however, is its turreted façade, whose loggias in part replicate those of the Arch of Alfonso d'Aragona in Naples (p. 141). Elegant and austere, the towers clearly symbolize the dual aspects of harmony and power that characterized Federico's reign. The most fitting definition of the edifice was coined by Baldassar Castiglione, who called it "a city in the form of a palace."

Left: *Aerial view
of Palazzo Ducale.*
Urbino, Marche, Italy.
On the far right, toward
the Mercatale esplanade,
is the building housing
the ducal stables.

Below:
*Plan of the Palazzo
Ducale in Urbino.*

Piazza
Duca Federico

Cortile del
Pasquino

Mercatale

Leon Battista Alberti

Alberti, the other father of Italian Renaissance architecture (with Brunelleschi), played the dual role of art theorist and architect. As a treatise writer, he clearly enunciated the principles of the Renaissance, making him a vital reference point for artists in the 1400s and the next centuries. As an architect, Alberti had the ability to put theoretical principles into concrete form, designing buildings that were their supreme expression.

● LIFE

The illegitimate son of Lorenzo, a wealthy Florentine merchant who had been exiled from the city for having opposed the Albizzi family, Leon Battista was born in Genoa in 1404. Educated in the best schools, he was awarded a diploma in law from the University of Bologna at the age of 24. Thanks to his wide learning (he also studied mathematics, philosophy, and literature), he was soon employed as secretary to high-ranking prelates, with whom he traveled throughout Europe on diplomatic and cultural missions. He was in Rome from 1431 to 1434 as a secretary for the Papal Chancellery. His stay in the Eternal City aroused an interest in architectural matters and inspired him to write a kind of guidebook to Rome (*Descriptio urbis Romae*). His contact with Florentine circles, beginning in 1434, led him to write a treatise titled *De pictura*, which he dedicated to Brunelleschi. After dealings with the court at Ferrara, he returned to Rome, where, in 1452, he dedicated his treatise *De re aedificatoria* to Pope Nicholas V. In 1459 he followed Pope Pius II to Mantua, returning again to Rome in 1463. In 1464 he wrote *De*

Leon Battista Alberti, *Facade of Santa Maria Novella*, 1439–1470. Florence, Italy.
The completion of the façade on this church was a lengthy undertaking. The decision to renovate it was taken at the Council of Florence in 1439, and the commission was conferred on Alberti sometime between this date and 1442. The date on the frieze under the tympanum is that on which the work was finished.

sculptura and left his post as papal secretary to more closely supervise the design of his buildings. He died in 1472.

● WORKS

Alberti's interest in architecture began rather late, as the natural offshoot of a broad cultural training that emphasized beauty in the classical tradition. This is demonstrated by his renovation of the façade of the Church of Santa Maria Novella in Florence, commissioned by Giovanni di Paolo Rucellai, which transformed the church's old medieval façade into classical terms; he confronted the same problem in restoring the Tempio Malatestiano in Rimini (pp. 140–141). Alberti's work as an architect was facilitated by his vast erudition and knowledge of such classical texts as Vitruvius's *De architectura*, which led him to propose solutions governed by a previously inconceivable philological rigor. While Brunelleschi was inspired by the monuments of Florentine Romanesque, which represented a somewhat diluted classicism, Alberti could draw directly from the source of Roman architecture. This is exemplified by the façade of Sant'Andrea di Mantova, modeled on the triple Roman arch. Alberti's architectural language is thus distinguished by his ability to employ classical codes to express new meanings. This may be seen in the Palazzo Rucellai in Florence, where the *opus reticulatum* on the backs of the benches at the base of the façade (p. 91) and

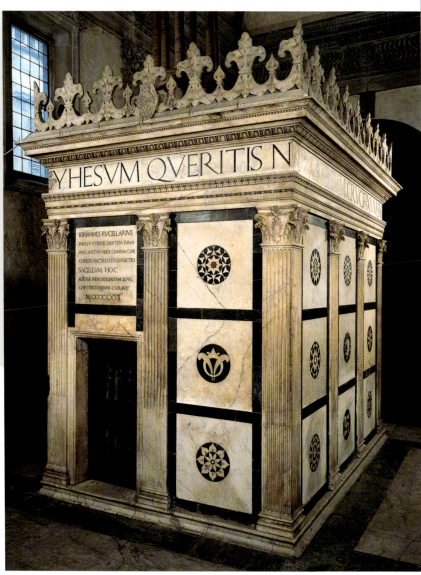

Left:
Leon Battista Alberti,
*Tempietto of the
Holy Sepulcher in
the Rucellai Chapel*,
1467. Florence, Italy.
The proportional ratio
between length and
width of the tempietto is
the musical one of 2/3.
Significant in this
regard is the choice of
Roman characters for
the inscription.
Classicism, Christianity,
and harmony came
together as a unified
whole in the new
architectural vision of
the Renaissance.

Above:
Leon Battista Alberti,
Façade of Sant'Andrea,
design from about
1470. Mantua, Italy.

Below:
*Reconstructive drawing
by Rudolf Wittkower
of the original design
for San Sebastiano
(1460) in Mantua, Italy.*
As demonstrated
by Wittkower, Alberti's
design again cites an
architectural precedent,
in this case the Arch
of Tiberius in Orange.

the superimposition of the orders of parastades reminiscent of the Coliseum clearly allude to the client's humanist culture. These elements recur in many of Alberti's designs, including those that remained unfinished and were later altered, such as San Sebastiano in Mantua. Alberti was ever concerned with proportional ratios, as in the Tempietto of the Holy Sepulcher, where they are respected down to the inscription.

Donato Bramante

It was Bramante's work in the fifteenth century that established the premises for the evolution of the Early Renaissance architectural style to that of the High Renaissance.

Not by chance, Bramante drew inspiration from the architectural achievements of Luciano Laurana and Francesco di Giorgio Martini in Urbino, from those of Brunelleschi in Florence, and especially those of Leon Battista Alberti. In his own work, Bramante introduced a greater plasticity and did not refrain from employing artifice to achieve his goals.

● LIFE

Donato di Pascuccio d'Antonio, known as "Bramante" like his father before him, was born in 1444 in the town now called Fermignano (Monte Asdrualdo, at the time), not far from Urbino. The nearby ducal city was a pole of attraction for the young man, encouraged by his father to pursue his natural talent for painting. Vasari reports that Donato was sent to school by one of the architects who worked for the duke of Montefeltro, Fra Bartolomeo di Giovanni della Corradina, known as Fra Carnevale. Little is known

of Bramante's training, although other sources report that he worked with such masters as Piero della Francesca (for perspective) and Mantegna (for the use of optical illusion). It is certain that Bramante was an engraver and painter of great skill, and equally sure that he was one of the few architects in Italy to master the structural and mathematical problems of constructing domes. His career began in northern Italy, where he lived until 1499. He then went to Rome, remaining there until his death in 1514. He was a friend and patron of Raphael, but a fierce rival of Michelangelo.

● WORKS

Bramante's first architectural achievements date from his years in Urbino, where he may have designed the Church of San Bernardino, later con-

Above and right:
Donato Bramante,
Detail of the false apse in Santa Maria presso San Satiro, c. 1482. Milan, Italy.

Right:
Andrea Mantegna,
Ceiling of the Bridal Chamber, 1465–1474. Palazzo Ducale, Mantua, Italy. Bramante most likely drew inspiration from this work in conceiving the *trompe-l'oeil* decoration of the false apse in Santa Maria presso San Satiro.

Donato Bramante, *Temple in Ruins,* 1481, burin engraving by Bartolomeo Prevedari. London, British Museum. Taken from a lost drawing by Bramante, this engraving documents his studies on perspective in Milan. The perspective scheme is so rigorously correct that it has been possible to derive the precise layout of the building.

structed by Francesco di Giorgio Martini. He then left Urbino for Milan, where documents reveal his presence in 1481 and where, in the following year, he began work on Santa Maria presso San Satiro. The building was erected to protect a miraculous image of Mary that had been painted in an edicule outside the Sacellum of San Satiro. Bramante worked intensively in northern Italy, where he designed the Duomo of Pavia (inspired in part by Brunelleschi's design for Santo Spirito in Florence, but more grandiose and spectacular), and the Church of Santa Maria delle Grazie in Milan, for which he designed the tribune area, added as an independent element to the fifteenth-century basilican plan (p.144). With the downfall of Ludovico il Moro (driven out of Milan in 1499 by Louis XII of France), Bramante went to Rome, where he built the cloister of Santa Maria della Pace (see illustration, p. 23) and further developed the principles established by Laurana. The first expression of his mature style may be seen in the Tempietto of San Pietro in Montorio, in Rome. This work, in which a colonnaded semicircle surrounds the body of the structure, was designed as a "hero's tomb." The hero in this case was a Christian one, Saint Peter, and the architect chose the Doric order to commemorate his virtue, while decorating the metopes on a circular architrave with symbols of the Mass and the Eucharist. Upon the election to the papal throne of Julius II (r. 1503–1513), Bramante became chief architect of the pope's architectural renovation program, called upon to enlarge the Vatican complex and build the new St. Peter's Basilica (pp. 298–299).

Donato Bramante,
*Tempietto of San Pietro
in Montorio*, c. 1502.
Rome.

Right:
Donato Bramante,
*Cloister of Santa Maria
della Pace*,
1500–1504. Rome.
Bramante utilizes
Tuscan and Ionic
orders in the lower
register, while relying

on the refined forms
of the Corinthian in the
upper registers. He
was one of the first
to take into account
Vitruvius's directions
regarding the
importance of the
architectural orders.

Raphael

Celebrated above all as a painter, for which he is universally praised and admired, the "divine" Raphael, born Raffaello Sanzio, was also an architect of great distinction and influence. His talent for architecture is revealed primarily in his astonishing sense of spatiality, which found expression in the adoption and invention of unique solutions for composition, so innovative as to revolutionize an era. Even his method of preparing sketches was architectural; if the structure of one of his paintings was to be symmetrical, Raphael drew only half the sketch, much as architects did with building plans. In Rome, moreover, his contacts with Bramante, an old friend who also came from the Marche region, must have heightened his interest in architecture. It is likely that Raphael turned to Bramante for assistance in designing his great fresco, *The School of Athens*. In no way does this mean, however, that Raphael was an architectural amateur. As Celio Calcagnini wrote in a letter to his mathematician friend Jacob Ziegler in 1519, Raphael was an "architect, truly, of such great talent as to invent and realize works so extraordinary that even the best engineers despair of being able to rival him in this field." Yet time and history have conspired against the fame of Raphael as an architect, since few of his buildings have survived.

● LIFE

Son of the painter Giovanni Santi, from whose name the patronymic "Sanzio"

Right:
Raphael, *The School of Athens*, detail, 1509–1510. Rome, Vatican Palaces. According to Vasari, it was Bramante himself who designed the "perspective view of Mount Parnassus in the pope's chamber."

Above:
Raphael, *Palazzo Pandolfini*, 1517–1525. Florence.

Right:
Raphael and assistants, *Interior of the loggia of Villa Madama*, designed 1518. Rome. Raphael's studio was unique in that patrons could purchase a "package" containing everything from the architectural design to the pictorial decoration.

Right:
Pietro Ferrerio, *Palazzo Branconio dell'Aquila in Borgo Nuovo in Rome*, 1655. This is the most faithful image of the palace built by Raphael between 1518 and 1520.

derives, Raphael was born in Urbino in 1483 and trained as an apprentice to Perugino. By 1500 he had already earned the nickname "Maestro." He is known to have been in Siena around 1503 and in Florence the following year. He remained there until 1508, when he was summoned to Rome to paint frescoes in the Vatican Apartments. With the election of Pope Leo X (r. 1513–1521), his opportunities in the architectural realm became more frequent, beginning with his appointment as conservator of Roman antiquities (1515) and then as architect of the Fabbrica di San Pietro, a position that had been held by Bramante until his death. In fact it been Bramante who recommended Raphael for the position, in which he was then assisted by Giuliano da Sangallo and Fra Giocondo. Raphael produced a number of designs and wrote, in collaboration with Baldassar Castiglione, a text considered fundamental to the conservation of Roman antiquities. In a letter to Leo X in 1516–1517, he proposed that a sort of architectural census be taken, recording the plans and elevations of all ancient buildings. Raphael was unable to carry out the project, however, since he died in 1520, a year before the pope.

● WORKS

Among the many of Raphael's architectural works that have been destroyed or radically altered is the Church of Sant'Eligio degli Orefici in Rome, which was completely rebuilt by Flaminio Ponzio after collapsing in 1601. Construction of Bernini's colonnade at St. Peter's in the mid-seventeenth century removed all traces of Raphael's palace of Giovan Battista Branconio dell'Aquila, the artistic adviser to Pope Leo X, and only graphic documentation of this work survives. Raphael also designed the Palazzo Pandolfini in Florence, although some modifications were made in the original plan. In Rome, Raphael's most important patron was still Pope Leo X, who commissioned him to design, build, and decorate the Vatican Loggias and Villa Madama.

Below:
Raphael, *Loggias*, 1516–1519. Rome, Vatican Palaces.

Right:
Marten van Heemskerck, *St. Peter's and the Vatican Palace, with the façade of the Loggias seen from Piazza San Pietro,* 1534–1535. Berlin, Kupferstichkabinett.

Michelangelo Buonarroti

Below:
Michelangelo, *Piazza del Campidoglio with the Palazzo dei Conservatori,* 1538–1564. Rome.

Michelangelo did not live to see the entire project completed, but only to supervise part of the construction of the Palazzo dei Conservatori.

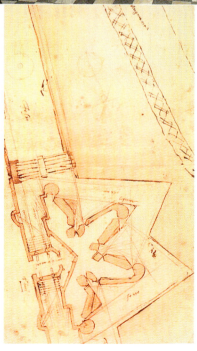

Above:
Michelangelo, *New Sacristy of San Lorenzo,* 1520. Florence. The sacristy was arranged by Vasari, who tried not to alter the original design of Michelangelo, even though the latter had not sculpted all of the necessary statues.

Right:
Michelangelo, *Plan for the fortifications of Florence,* 1527. Florence, Casa Buonarroti.

Painter, sculptor, and architect, Michelangelo is the only artist in history to have excelled in all three realms. Vasari hailed him as "divine" and unrivaled, representing the peak of genius in the history of art; the inevitable consequence, according to Vasari, was that after him it would be possible only to "descend" from the towering heights of his achievement. Yet in his painting and sculpture, as well as his architecture, Michelangelo, at least from a certain point on (the 1620s), unintentionally established the foundation of Mannerism, which was not so much a period of decadence as a movement that carried the premises of the High Renaissance to an extreme.

To fully grasp the innovational impact of Michelangelo's architecture, it is sufficient to consider the value he attached to the wall, no longer a simple barrier between outside and inside but an organic structure created to define a spatial perimeter. Two examples suffice to illustrate this point. In the interior of the New Sacristy in San Lorenzo, Michelangelo employed the same color scheme that Brunelleschi had used in the Old Sacristy, but without the latter's Quattrocento graphic effects. If a door is to be opened in a wall, the wall must be plastically molded to receive the door, and the volumetric ratios adjusted.

Michelangelo thus incorporated true door systems rather just than cutouts in the wall. This innovation also appears in the vestibule of the Biblioteca Lauren-

Right:
Michelangelo, *Wooden
model for the façade
of the Basilica of
San Lorenzo (c. 1519).*
Florence, Casa Buonarroti.

Right:
Michelangelo, *Wooden
model for the façade
of the Basilica of
San Lorenzo (c. 1519).*
Florence, Casa Buonarroti.

Below:
Michelangelo,
Tomb of Julius II,
1547. Rome,
San Pietro in Vincoli.
Despite a scaling back

of the tomb project,
Michelangelo took
personal responsibility
for its placement and
realization.

ziana (p. 62), where the wall is "mobilized" to accept the door that opens onto the reading room.

● LIFE AND WORKS

The son of Ludovico Buonarroti, chief magistrate of the Tuscan villages of Chiusi and Caprese, Michelangelo was born in 1475. Although his father intended to make him a man of letters, the boy immediately showed an extraordinary talent for art. He apprenticed at the studio of Ghirlandaio in 1488, but the next year he began to frequent the Medicean Sculpture Garden at San Marco, where he attracted the attention of Lorenzo de' Medici, who provided him with a humanist education. In the late

1490s, Michelangelo received his first important commissions, from both private patrons and the Republic of Florence. He painted the famous Sistine Chapel frescoes between 1508 and 1512, and Pope Leo X, convinced of his architectural genius, commissioned him in 1518 to design the façade of the Church of San Lorenzo in Florence; the façade was never to be built, but his drawing and a wood model do survive. Four years later, Michelangelo returned to work on the New Sacristy of San Lorenzo, and in 1524 on the Biblioteca Laurenziana. Then in 1529, he was given a chance to exercise his talents as a military architect in the defense of Florence, which was under siege by the Holy Roman Emperor Charles V. Michelangelo's

great torment was the tomb of Julius II, on which he worked off-and-on from 1505 to 1545 in Rome and Florence. The elaborate marble monument, which includes his seated *Moses,* was finally placed in Rome's San Pietro in Vincoli rather than in the Vatican, as originally planned. The finished work, scaled back from the original grand design, underscores Michelangelo's highly refined architectural sensibility and the special relationship he established, as a model for the future, between sculpture and architecture. In Rome he was assigned such other commissions as the design of Piazza del Campidoglio and, most importantly, was named chief architect of the St. Peter's Basilica (see next page). He died on February 18, 1564.

Below:
Michelangelo,
*Ceiling of the Sistine
Chapel,* detail,
1508–1512. Rome.
The immense fresco
is framed by a painted
architectural structure
of the utmost solidity.

St. Peter's Basilica

There have been at least six different St. Peter's basilicas in the Vatican, counting those that have been realized as well as those that have only been imagined. All of them have centered around the tomb of the apostle who, according to the historian Eusebius of Caesarea, was martyred in 67 C.E. in the area then occupied by the Circuses of Gaius and Nero, where condemned Christians were executed. Archaeological excavations have confirmed this account, revealing under the basilica corresponding to the present-day confessional a small plaza containing the remains of an edicule whose wall is covered with graffiti referring to Peter and his martyrdom. The first basilica, that of Constantine (p. 47), built between 319 and 350, had five naves preceded by a great portico called "Paradise." Despite certain modifications and improvements, such as the addition of benedictional loggias by Popes Boniface VIII and Pius II, the structure remained substantially unchanged until 1452, when Pope Nicholas V commissioned Bernardo Rossellino to renovate it, at least in part. Still, little work was done before the election of Pope Julius II (1503), who at first planned to build a great papal chapel (for which he commissioned Michelangelo to design his mausoleum) but later decided to rebuild the entire edifice.

● ONE IDEA, MANY PLANS

The objective in the sixteenth century was clear: to build the largest and most beautiful church in the Christian world. But how was this to be done? By retaining the existing basilican plan? Or by transforming it entirely? To solve this problem and others, Julius II summoned Donato Bramante, who opted for a Greek-cross plan. Bramante's design was based on precise symbolism intended to emphasize the concept of the new St. Peter's as

Right:
Antonio da Sangallo the Younger, *Wooden model of the design of St. Peter's, view of the apse,* c. 1520. Vatican, Fabbrica di San Pietro.

Above:
Donato Bramante, *Plan for St. Peter's Basilica on parchment,* 1505, Florence, Gabinetto Disegni e Stampe degli Uffizi, inv. no. 1A.

the image of Heavenly Jerusalem on earth. It has been shown, in fact, that the plan of the new building was inspired by the Cross of Jerusalem, or *digamma*, consisting of a large central cross and four smaller ones in the corners. Bramante thus planned to provide 12 entrances, the same number believed to exist in Heavenly Jerusalem.

His design was not immediately implemented, however, and when Raphael succeeded him as chief architect he preferred a basilican plan, perhaps inspired by his own layout of the Duomo of Pavia. Other architects made other proposals; among these were Baldassarre Peruzzi and Antonio da Sangallo the Younger, who was chosen by Pope Leo X to collaborate with Raphael. Sangallo built an immense wooden model with a central Greek-cross plan and the addition of a forestructure. Michelangelo's design reflected that of Bramante, albeit adapted to his own style and made more regular by the "mediation" of Sangallo. In any case, Michelangelo's choice was clear: St. Peter's was to have a circular plan with a dome at the center, thus representing Heavenly Jerusalem in masonry. But this was not to be, either. Pope Paul V Borghese commissioned Carlo Maderno to modify the structure that Michelangelo had designed and already partially built, transforming it into a church with a Latin-cross plan, officially for the purpose of providing more space for the faithful. This was to be Maderno's affliction for the rest of his life—to be forced to modify the masterpiece of Michelangelo. Finally, the colonnade was added by Bernini in 1656–1667.

Left:
Aerial view of St. Peter's and Bernini's colonnade looking toward Via della Conciliazione.

Above:
Michelangelo and others, *Dome of St. Peter's*, 1547–1589. Rome. The span of more than 40 years required for the construction of the dome saw a succession of architects, from Pirro Ligorio to Vignola. In the eighteenth century, Vanvitelli was engaged in the maintenance of the building, for which he had a wooden model built to facilitate the work.

Left:
View of St. Peter's and Bernini's colonnade according to the original design, with a third arm over the entrance, in a seventeenth-century drawing.

Olmecs, Toltecs, Aztecs, Mayas, and Incas

The first contact between Europe and the empires of Central and South America took place in the sixteenth century, when the Spanish conquistadors invaded these recently discovered lands. Perhaps because of the forced, violent nature of the contacts, the Europeans failed to regard them as civilizations in their own right until much later. Interest in these peoples, marred by misunderstanding and cruelty, was based chiefly on political and economic interests, and rarely went beyond curiosity for the ex-

otic. Unlike Asian cultures both before and after, the civilizations of America exerted little or no influence on the art and architecture of the European world.

● OLMECS AND TEOTIHUACÁN

The Olmecs are regarded as the founders of Mesoamerican civilization. The name derives from *Olman*, the "Land of Rubber Trees," of which they were the inhabitants. Not by coincidence, the ritual game of *tachtli*, in-

vented by this people and popular throughout Mexico from the eleventh to the fifteenth centuries, was played with a rubber ball (pp. 56–57). The Olmec civilization, which had been developing since at least the twelfth century B.C.E., flourished in the sixth to fifth centuries B.C.E. By about 400 B.C.E., however, the religious center of La Venta had been desecrated and the Olmec civilization had dissolved.

Teotihuacán ("birthplace of the gods") was the first city among the pre-Columbian Mesoamerican civilizations, emerging about 100 B.C.E. and controlling central Mexico for at least another seven centuries. The city center comprised the main temple complex (Citadel) and marketplace (Great Compound) and was dominated by the immense Pyramid of the Sun (p. 49).

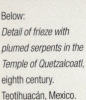

Below:
Detail of frieze with plumed serpents in the Temple of Quetzalcoatl, eighth century. Teotihuacán, Mexico.

Above:
Playing field for the game of pelota, thirteenth century. Chichén Itzá, Yucatan, Mexico. This playing field, dedicated to the plumed serpent, is found in the great ceremonial area of Chichén Itzá. The place where the ball was launched represents the universe, and the game symbolizes the struggle between the forces of light and darkness.

Left:
Plan of Tenochtitlán taken from a sixteenth-century engraving. Built on small islands, the city centered around the temple of Huitzilopochtli ("The Snake Doctor," protector of the Aztecs), which stood in the place now occupied by the Cathedral of Mexico City.

Above:
Stone ring with the coils of the plumed serpent in the playing field of Chichén Itzá. Yucatan, Mexico. The plumed serpent Quetzalcoatl, derived from Toltec culture, was known as Kukulkan in the Yucatan.

Below:
Maya-Toltec art,
Temple of the Warriors,
twelfth century.
Chichén Itzá,
Yucatan, Mexico.
The typology of the
stepped pyramid
(preceded by a portico
with square supports
and having a square cell
at the top) derives from
the Toltec structure at
Tula (p. 154).

Above:
*View of the Machu
Picchu complex,*
thirteenth–fifteenth
centuries. Cuzco, Peru.
The settlement, built at
an altitude of more than
6,500 feet, was
connected to Cuzco by a
road through the
foothills. The terraces
were built to increase
the amount of land
available for cultivation.

Right:
*View of Cuzco in the
sixteenth century.*
The most famous
of the Inca cities
(twelfth–fifteenth
centurie) was divided
into two parts: Hanana
(Upper Cuzco) and Hurin
(Lower Cuzco). At the
center was the Temple
of the Sun. All of the
streets converged on
the two main squares.

TOLTECS

The Toltec civilization ruled central Mexico from about 900, after the demise of Teotihuacán, to the mid-twelfth century C.E. The capital was Tula (p. 154), from which the name of the people derived. The Toltec king Quetzalcóatl was said to have fled Tula and later returned as the mythological feathered serpent, worshipped as the creator god by the Aztecs and Mayas. The destruction of Tula by the Chichimecs in 1156 opened to way to invasion by the Aztecs.

AZTECS

The Aztec capital of Tenochtitlán, today's Mexico City, located on a lake island to the south of Teotihuacán, was founded only in 1370. No trace of the city remains, but some idea of it is provided by the description left by Hernán Cortés, who conquered it in 1521. Little remains of Aztec architecture, such as the temple of the god of war at Xampala, similar in type to the Toltec temples.

MAYAS

The Mayas were lords of a vast domain whose culture was intermingled with Toltec elements. The Maya civilization lasted more than three millennia, from about 2000 B.C.E. to 1697 C.E., when Martin de Ursua conquered Taysal, the last of the Maya cities. These cities were organized around pyramids that served as religious centers, with rooms for priests, plazas in which the people could assemble, and fields for playing pelota.

INCAS

The Inca Empire developed from about 1100 C.E., with the founding of the capital of Cuzco. It expanded rapidly in the fifteenth century, and collapsed in the face of civil war and Spanish invasion in the mid-sixteenth century. The most interesting Incan archaeological site is Machu Picchu in Peru, a splendid example of mountain architecture.

Andrea Palladio

Palladio was one of the great architects of the High Renaissance and, to the extent that stylistic definitions matter, of Mannerism as well. He drew inspiration from classical architecture through knowledge acquired in repeated excursions to Rome (1541, 1545, 1547, and 1549). Palladio recorded his observations in a treatise that would prove highly influential, *I Quattro Libri dell'Architettura* ("The Four Books of Architecture"), published in 1570. Along with designs for his own projects, the work included Palladio's detailed analyses,

with fine illustrations, of many Roman monuments. His study of Vitruvius, as well as such modern architects as Sebastiano Serlio, led him to rediscover proportional ratios based on fractions with musical values (p. 20). By no means does this suggest that Palladio slavishly imitated classical architecture. He reinvented (and herein lies the Mannerist component) the architectural language of antiquity in light of the luminous art of his native Veneto region, but so effectively as to go beyond the ancient style and create one of his own. This, indeed, is the sole explanation for the

phenomenon that became known as Palladianism. The movement is best understood as a function of the supreme skill of the architect himself, whose work came to seen in British, German, and American eyes as more truly classical than that of antiquity itself.

● LIFE

Of humble origins, Andrea di Pietro della Gondola was born in Padua in 1508 and apprenticed to a stonecutter at the age of only 13. In 1524, at age 16, he fled to Vicenza and enrolled in the city's "brotherhood of builders, stonecutters, and stonemasons." Sometime thereafter he was employed at a busy workshop, of which he seems to have become head at the age of about 30. But fate willed it that he would be summoned to work for Count Giangiorgio Trissino, the

Right and below:
Andrea Palladio,
View of the Basilica,
1549–1617.
Vicenza, Italy
The balustrade visually links the fullness of the building with the immense void of the sky. This solution, also employed by Michelangelo in the Palazzo dei Conservatori (pp. 296–297), is clearly of Mannerist inspiration.

Right:
Andrea Palladio,
Palazzo Chiericati,
1550–1557. Vicenza.
One of the few examples of an urban palazzo designed by

Palladio, it is also one of the rare cases of a design that went unchanged in the realization. The giant order is used here with striking effect.

most eminent intellectual in Vicenza. This was the turning point in his life. The count oversaw his cultural education, gave him the classical-sounding name of Palladio, and directed his studies in architecture and engineering with the intention of making him a kind of special assistant. Palladio's education was enriched by contacts with the Paduan circle of Alvise Cornaro, by the books of Serlio, and by repeated trips to Rome, the first of them accompanied by Count Trissino himself. In Rome, Palladio was attracted by modern architecture, too, as evidenced by his drawing of Bramante's Tempietto. He was, along with Michelangelo, the first to employ the giant order, which was to become so poplar in the Baroque Age. Interested in Latin literature as well, he published an edition of Caesar's *Commentaries*. Palladio died in Treviso at the age of 72.

● WORKS

His first important commission was the so-called Basilica of Vicenza: renovation of the exterior of the city's Palazzo della Ragione. As Alberti had done for the Tempio Malatestiano in Rimini, Palladio designed a facing like a jewelry box to preserve the original building. His preferred decorative scheme was Serliana which, repeated in close succession, created a solemn, cadenced rhythm. Palladio specialized in villas and palaces for the local nobility, and he also designed one of the most beautiful theaters of the Renaissance, the Olimpico of Vicenza (p. 58). In 1570 he was named chief architect of Venice, for which he designed his only two religious buildings, the Church of San Giorgio Maggiore and the Church of the Redentore, derived from the façade of the Pantheon in Rome.

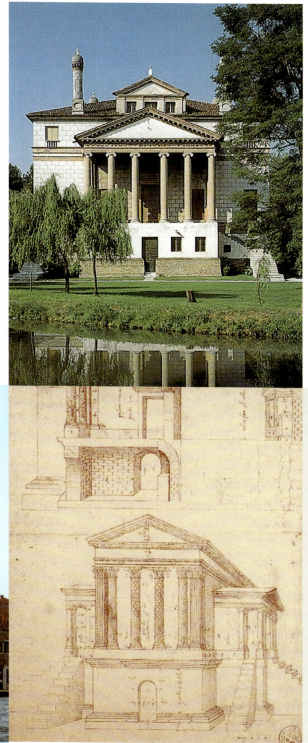

Above:
Andrea Palladio,
View of the Church of the Redentore,
1577–1592. Venice.

Right:
Andrea Palladio,
View of the right side of the Church of the Redentore,
1577–1592. Venice.

Above:
Façade of Villa Foscari with Ionic pronaos, 1588. Malcontenta di Mira, Venice.

Above:
Andrea Palladio,
Studies of the Temple of Clitumnus near Spoleto, c. 1560. Vicenza, Civic Museum.

Gianlorenzo Bernini

Below:
Giovanni Battista Falda,
*Church of Santa Bibiana
on the Esquiline Hill*
(1624–1626),
engraving from the
*Nuovo teatro delle
fabriche et edificii
in perspectiva di Roma
moderna*, Rome,
1665–1669.

Painter, sculptor, architect, and amateur playwright, Gianlorenzo Bernini epitomized the spirit of classicism, harmony, and balance that characterized the Baroque style. He might properly be called the "inventor" of Baroque, were the movement not so complex and derived from contributions in various fields of artistic endeavor. What is certain is that Bernini, who dominated sculpture and architecture with the same authority as Michelangelo (to whom he was sometimes compared), was the first to consider architecture in the universal sense, as encompassing the design and creation of every aspect of daily existence ("from the spoon to the city," as it was put some centuries later). Thus, the shop of Bernini the architect and artistic genius produced furniture, theatrical devices, stage settings for festivals, carriages, fountains, monumental sculpture, and whole cities. It was precisely this continuous transition from the small to the large, from the minor to the major, that favored the formulation of the Baroque style, in which a ciborium (Communion vessel) becomes a *baldacchino* (altar canopy) and a fountain resembles a centerpiece for the table.

● LIFE AND WORKS

A child of art, the eldest son of the Late Mannerist sculptor Pietro Bernini, Gianlorenzo was born in Naples on December 7, 1598. He trained under his father who, having gone to Rome to work on the Chapel of Paul V in Santa Maria Maggiore, managed through his contacts to have the young artist engaged in the shop of Cavalier d'Arpino and work on the Vatican Apartments, where he could study the masterpieces of Michelangelo and Raphael. His father's acquaintances included high-ranking prelates such as Scipione Borghese, who became Gianlorenzo's first patron, commissioning projects that were to leave an indelible mark in the history of art. Bernini's first independent projects succeeded his design for the great Baldacchino in St. Peter's, in many ways their predecessor. The first building constructed by Bernini was the Church of Santa Bibiana in Rome; his own work included the statue for the high altar, which was to serve as a model throughout the seventeenth century and into the eighteenth. Bernini's creative genius covered the full range of artistic endeavor, and a single project could bring to bear his skills as an architect, sculp-

*Above:
False bridge of the
Palazzo Barberini in
Rome (1625–1633).*

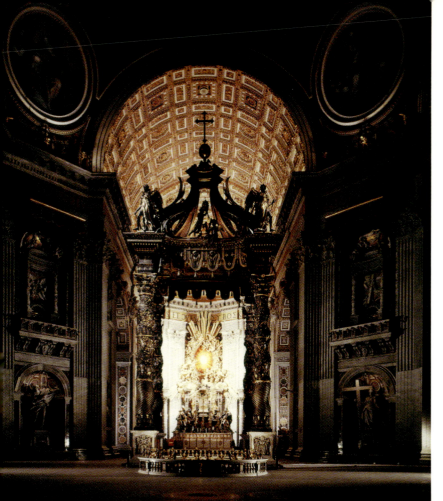

tor, and painter. In accordance with his own versatility, he developed the theory of the *bel composto*, in which all the arts are called upon in equal measure to contribute to the completion of a work. To fully grasp this concept, it is enough to observe the interior of St. Peter's and in particular the enormous transept, in which the architectural volumes, the pictorial polychrome marbles, the relief sculptures, and the statues come together as a magnificent whole.

Bernini loved artifice and surprise, treating the city like an immense stage set to be designed, as demonstrated by the Sant'Angelo Bridge. His most imposing achievements are the colonnade for St. Peter's Square (pp. 116, 299), for which he planned a third arm over the entrance, and his design for the Louvre, which was never built but which exerted a powerful influence on French architecture. Other noteworthy designs include the Palazzo Montecitorio and Sant'Andrea al Quirinale, both in Rome. Bernini died in 1680.

Gianlorenzo Bernini, *The Danube*, detail of the Fountain of the Four Rivers, c. 1650. Rome, Piazza Navona. To win the commission, Bernini created a silver centerpiece in the form of a fountain, which was donated to Donna Olimpia Maidalchini, the sister-in-law of Pope Innocent X.

Left:
View of a section of the Sant'Angelo Bridge looking toward Castel Sant'Angelo. Rome. The work carried out by Bernini and his assistants on this famous bridge consisted of adding two arcades and sculpting the statues of the ten angels as permanent structures to replace the previous temporary decoration.

Below:
Gianlorenzo Bernini, *Fireworks machine to celebrate the birth of the dauphin of France,* 1662, engraving by D. Barrière. Rome, Istituto Nazionale per la Grafica.

Above:
Gianlorenzo Bernini and others, *View looking toward the apse of the transept in St. Peter's (1634–1638) and the Baldacchino (1624–1633).* Rome, St. Peter's. Bernini drew inspiration from processional baldachins to create one of monumental size for St. Peter's.

Right:
Gianlorenzo Bernini, *Cornaro, or St. Teresa d'Avila, Chapel,* 1647–1651. Rome, Santa Maria della Vittoria.

Francesco Borromini

Borromini represents the other great spirit of Baroque style, and the one most frequently imitated. First a friend and collaborator and then a rival of Bernini, Borromini countered the solemnity of classicism with the daring genius and apparent caprice of an architecture, ever Baroque in tone, that seems at times to defy the very laws of nature. The surprising beauty of Borromini's creations sprang from his own imagination and experience, as demonstrated by the resemblance between the exterior of the dome over Sant'Ivo alla Sapienza and the continuous spiral of a seashell. He was fascinated by the unexpected but harmonious variations of which only nature is capable. Such an approach is typical, in fact, of the finest seventeenth-century tradition of the *Wunderkammer*, a kind of museum containing collections displaying the most unusual and bizarre aspects of the animal, vegetable, and mineral worlds. His sources of inspiration were not only naturalistic, however, deriving as well from a broad knowledge of the cultural and symbolic world, all of which combined to make him an inimitable figure in architectural history.

● LIFE AND WORKS

Like Bernini, Francesco Borromini, born at Bissone in Switzerland's Ticino Canton in 1599, was a child of art. His father, Giandomenico Castelli, was an engineer who specialized in hydraulics at the service of the Visconti family; his mother, Anastasia Garvo, came from a well-to-do family of building craftsmen. At the age of only nine, Francesco was sent to Milan as an apprentice. There, between 1613 and 1615, he attended the lessons of Muzio Oddi, a mathematician from Urbino who was to exert a strong influence on the young man. In 1621, his cousin Leone Garvo, who had been working on the construction site of St. Peter's, was injured, and Francesco was engaged to take his place. Two years later, he was chosen to replace Filippo Breccioli, the first assistant of chief architect Carlo Maderno. He thus found himself working beside the uncle who had involved him earlier in the Baldacchino and Palazzo Barberini (pp. 146–147).

Borromini's first entirely independent project was San Carlo alle Quattro Fontane in Rome, for which he designed the interior, cloister, and monastery for the Order of the Barefoot Trinitarians. He worked on this project

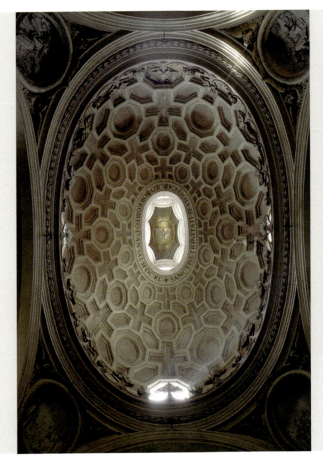

Francesco Borromini, *Interior of the dome of San Carlo alle Quattro Fontane*, 1634–1641. Rome.
The decorative motif of crosses and octagons is derived from the ornamentation of the Catacombs of Santa Costanza.

Francesco Borromini, *Nave of San Giovanni in Laterano*, 1646–1649. Rome. Borromini designed a masonry ceiling that was never built; the wooden one attributed to Daniele da Volterra has remained.

for four years, although he was commissioned at the same time to work on the Oratorio dei Filippini (p. 98). Borromini's methods were very different from those of Bernini, who defined the overall concept and directed the work. Borromini instead occupied himself with every detail. When Bernini was subjected to severe criticism after the bell tower of St. Peter's collapsed, Borromini was able to obtain papal commissions for San Giovanni in Laterano and Sant'Agnese. And when he was commissioned to work on the Collegio di Propaganda Fide, he took sadistic joy in demolishing everything that had been built by Bernini, who witnessed the destruction because he lived on the corner of the same street. As if guided by the hand of fate, the last work of Borromini was the façade of San Carlino, the church where he had worked more than 30 years earlier. When this project was over, Borromini fell into deep depression and, undone by the insolence of a servant, committed suicide in 1667.

Below:
Drawing of the façade of Sant'Agnese in Agone by Borromini (1653–1655) in Rome. This project was continued by Carlo Rainaldi because Borromini was expelled from the construction site due to disagreements with the client, Camillo Pamphili, who later fired Rainaldi as well. The work was finally completed by Bernini. This was a severe blow to the pride of Borromini, who fell into even deeper depression.

Left:
Francesco Borromini, *Spiral dome of Sant'Ivo alla Sapienza,* 1642–1660. Rome. The dome evokes the shape of the *Triton nodiferum* conch shell, known as the buccina, a symbol of mythological figures such as the Tritons.

Below:
Figure of Philosophy, from the *Iconologia* of Cesare Ripa (1618 edition). Wrote Ripa, "Its garments are of gossamer thread… on the border of these robes is a Greek Pi, and near the top is a T, and between one letter and the other are certain degrees which form a scale, proceeding from the lowest and inferior letter to the highest" (1603 edition). This image has been identified as the iconographic source for the roofing of Sant'Ivo, and in particular for the tiered steps below the lantern.

Above:
Francesco Borromini, *Sant'Ivo alla Sapienza,* 1642–1660. Rome. It was Bernini who obtained this commission for Borromini, hoping that he would fail in the attempt. Although the space available for the church was narrow and constricted by the presence of the courtyard built by Giacomo della Porta, the final result was a masterpiece.

The Royal Palace of Versailles

If there is one place in modern Europe where the opulence of power can be clearly seen, it is the Château de Versailles. Located about 12 miles southwest of Paris, the town of Versailles grew up around the royal residence in the second half of the seventeenth century. The first structure was erected at the order of Louis XIII (1601–1643), who, enchanted by the woodland setting, had a hunting lodge built on the site in 1624. Ten years later, the lodge was transformed into a château, which was to become the core of a magnificent new structure—and symbol of French royalty—completed before the end of the century.

● HISTORY OF VERSAILLES

The complex of Versailles centers around a human figure, that of Louis XIV (1638–1715), and around an idea, the architectural representation of absolute power and regality. Crowned king at the age of five, Louis XIV assumed direct sovereign power only after the death of Cardinal Mazzarin in 1661. His claim of absolute authority, and the spirit of Versailles, was captured in his famous remark, "*L'État c'est moi*" ("the State is myself"). Identifying completely with his royal status, he compared himself to the sun, around which the world revolved, and indeed came to be called the "Sun King." Louis XIV looked upon politics as the expression of his own personality and exercised his power directly, assisted by a secret state council and the ministers who made up his cabinet.

Right:
View of the Marble Courtyard, 1634. Versailles. Converted by Philibert Le Roi to its present state, this Late Mannerist building has a central body with a slightly projecting façade, distinguished by paired columns supporting a balcony onto which open three large windows.

Below:
Aerial view of the Royal Palace. Versailles, Yvelines, Ile-de-France.

Right:
Pierre Patel, *The Château of Versailles*, detail, c. 1668. Versailles, Versailles Museum. This bird's-eye view illustrates the appearances of the palace after the first stage of work carried out under Louis XIV to embellish and enlarge the original château of Louis XIII.

Above:
Louis Le Vau and Jules Hardouin-Mansart, *View of the western façade of the palace from the great ornamental pool*, 1679–1684. Versailles.

The government of Louis XIV inaugurated a policy of balancing the state budget and reorganizing the armed forces so paternalistic that historians still often refer to the 1600s as "the Sun King's century." Such supreme royal power demanded a scenario of supreme splendor, though its great expense contributed to worsening financial problems. Moreover, the château and park of Versailles were the ideal place in which to distract the court and keep it far from national affairs.

● THE ARCHITECTS

Two architects were responsible for the enlargement of Versailles: Louis Le Vau (1612–1670), who worked there from 1661 until his death, and Jules Hardouin-Mansart (1646–1708), who completed the work in 1690. Le Vau is recognized as the creator of the Louis XIV style. An extremely practical man, he directed the group of painters, interior decorators, sculptors, and gardeners who produced the royal palace par excellence, an embodiment of the concept of absolute power. Le Vau was responsible in particular for the façade overlooking the garden, designed with an uncommon sense of grandeur but later altered and enlarged by Mansart. The latter, the great-grandson of the eminent Parisian architect François Mansart (1598–1666), had trained at the school of Le Vau.

● THE SPLENDOR OF THE ROYAL PALACE

Versailles was created to astound. Visitors were awed first by the broad parade ground, surrounded by stables designed by Mansart. From there, two courtyards flanked by buildings for the sovereign and ministers (Royal Courtyard) lead to the original core of the palace, from the time of Louis XIII. At the back is the new façade, whose central element was designed by Le Vau, and the two long wings by Mansart, extending a total of 1,900 feet. The interiors are distinguished by opulent splendor, while the groomed gardens feature an enchanting succession of ponds, fountains, and groves.

Left:
Jules Hardouin-Mansart and Robert de Cotte, *Grand Trianon*, 1687. Versailles. The white-and-pink marble building is surrounded by gardens laid out by the famous André Le Nôtre (1613–1700). The peristyle with Ionic capitals, used by the king as a summer dining room, was designed by Robert de Cotte (1656–1735), the brother-in-law of Hardouin-Mansart, whose position as first royal architect he inherited.

Left:
Charles Le Brun, *Hall of Mirrors*, 1678–1684. Versailles. The masterpiece of the artist directly responsible for creating the Louis XIV style, this dazzling hall was 240 feet long and lit by seventeen windows, their light reflected by a mirror in front of each one.

Below:
Jules Hardouin-Mansart and Robert de Cotte, *Chapel of St. Louis*, 1698–1710. Versailles.

The Taj Mahal

A building may be constructed for many different reasons: for political or economic purposes, for defense or public entertainment, as a place to live, or as a place to pray. But it was none of these that led the Mogul Emperor Shah Jahan (r. 1628–1658) to build the Taj Mahal in Agra, India. The Taj Mahal was built for love. It is the tomb of Arjumand Banu Begum, the wife of Shah Jahan, known as *taj mahal* ("diadem of the palace"). The emperor was so deeply in love that he spent his days admiring his beautiful wife, enchanted by her grace and beauty.

After having been engaged for 14 years, they were married on April 12, 1612, when Shah Jahan, formerly Prince Khurram of the Mogul Dynasty, became emperor. Husband and wife were never apart, not even during the sovereign's difficult military campaigns, when she followed him with members of the court. After successfully bearing thirteen children, she died in the Deccan, far from the palace, while giving birth to a last child, who grew up to become the beautiful Gauharara Begum. Arjumand's death occurred on June 17, 1631, and was undoubtedly caused in part by the hardship endured in following her husband on his latest military campaign. Thus ended one of the most fabled love stories in history. Although Shah Jahan was obliged to marry twice again, he never recovered from his sorrow.

To pay homage to his wife and ensure that her memory would endure forever, Shah Jahan resolved to build a tomb of unparalleled magnificence, drawing inspiration from a vision Arjumand herself once had had. She had told him that she had dreamed of finding herself in a splendid palace made of white marble rich in inlaid stones and elaborate carving, surrounded by a flourishing garden with pools and fountains. Shah Jahan, in a last act of love, decided to bring her dream—now steeped in sorrow—to life.

● THE STRUCTURE

Made entirely of pure white Makrana marble, the Taj Mahal is most astonishing for its wealth of decoration, in which the typically Islamic use of Koranic inscriptions is combined with sinuous ornamentation of plant and floral inspiration, some inlaid in stylized forms and some carved in naturalistic bas-relief. Surrounded by a large ma-

Above:
Interior of the Taj Mahal with the tombs of the two sovereigns, 1632–1658. Agra, Uttar Pradesh, India.

Right:
The Taj Mahal seen from above, 1632–1654. Agra, Uttar Pradesh, India.

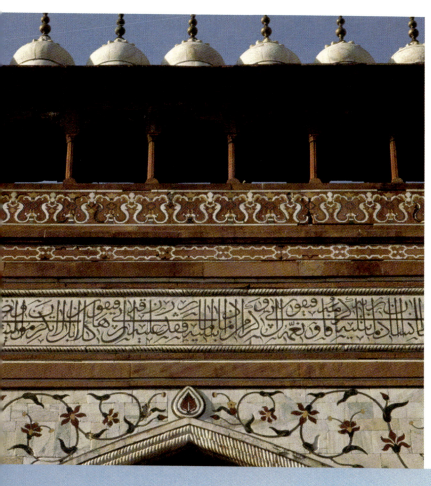

sonry enclosure (nearly 3,000 feet by 1,000 feet) that encompasses the gardens and a mosque, the Taj Mahal seems a glowing pearl (it is known as the "pearl of India") set in a verdant frame. The gardens, pools, and fountains that together animate the setting form a kind of avenue of approach to the mausoleum itself. Yet in spite of its splendor, the building is simple. It stands on a square platform some 23 feet high, visually framed by four minarets at the corners, each 135 feet tall. With a quadrangular plan and strongly beveled corners, the main structure is surmounted by an onion-shaped dome measuring 65 feet in diameter. In the interior of the main body, a lacy, perforated marble enclosure surrounds the tombs of the two sovereigns.

Shah Jahan had wanted to build an identical tomb for himself in black marble across from the Taj Mahal, but he died in 1658 without having had the chance to realize his plan.

Left
Detail of the façade of the Taj Mahal, 1632–1654. Agra, Uttar Pradesh, India. The decorative scheme is based on inscriptions from the Koran and inlaid floral motifs in polychrome marble and semiprecious stones.

Below:
The Taj Mahal seen from the gardens, 1632–1654. Agra, Uttar Pradesh, India.

Christopher Wren

The career of Christopher Wren is one of the most singular in the history of Western architecture. Turning from a brilliant career as a scientist (he was a professor of astronomy at Oxford), Wren became the most important British architect of the seventeenth century, and perhaps of any other time. He was one of the first, along with Inigo Jones (1573–1652), to bring the message of classicism to Great Britain. But while Jones interpreted classical style in the light of his knowledge of Palladio, Wren chose to emulate Bernini. Of his stay in Paris in 1665, he wrote, "Abbot Charles has revealed to me Bernini.... For Bernini's project for the Louvre I would have given my life." Wren was an ardent enthusiast of architecture, which he pursued with the training of an amateur but the talent of a genius.

● LIFE

The son of a Protestant pastor, Christopher was born at East Knoyle, Wiltshire, in 1632. After studying with some of the best minds of his century (the poet John Dryden and the philosopher John Locke were his classmates at the Westminster School), Wren took up a vigorous pursuit of the exact sciences, earning his bachelor's degree at the University of Oxford at the age of only 17. He was awarded a master's degree at 21 and became professor of astronomy at Freesham College in London at age 25. Not yet 30, he was appointed to the same position at Oxford. Recognized as one of Britain's leading experts in the field of geometry, he was a founding member of the Royal Society. Brilliant and well rounded, his career exemplified that of the true scientist.

His passion for architecture would lead him down other paths. Although designing buildings for Wren was almost an entertainment, his life's work and place in history were to be changed by one of the most tragic events in the history of England: the great fire of London in 1666. King Charles II, aware of Wren's passionate interest in architecture, requested his assistance. Wren submitted a plan for rebuilding the city, which the king approved. The amateur architect was commissioned to

Christopher Wren,
Interior of Saint Stephen's at Walbrook, 1672–1679. London.

build 52 churches, including the new Cathedral of Saint Paul's, the parish church of the British Commonwealth. It was to become Wren's masterpiece. He died in 1723 at the age of 91.

● WORKS

Wren's first project was the Sheldonian Theatre at Oxford, which was inspired by the Theater of Marcellus in Rome; his design demonstrated the interest of the budding architect in classicism and archaeology. Of the churches designed for the reconstruction of London and demolished in the centuries to come, many were of the central plan, reiterating a fixed scheme without great care taken in construction. Notable among those still standing is Saint Stephen's at Walbrook (1672–1679). Saint Stephen's is considered a masterpiece of harmony and equilibrium, with a dome reminiscent of the one on Saint Paul's. In the interior, 16 large Corinthian columns support projecting cornices in a central plan.

● THE CATHEDRAL OF LONDON

To replace the old Saint Paul's Cathedral, destroyed in the fire of 1666, Wren in 1673 presented a large wooden model already tending toward the Baroque. It was quite unlike the design proposed by Inigo Jones immediately after the fire, whose façade still showed the influence of the Quattrocento. In Wren's final design (the first not having been approved by the clergy, who judged it too bold for a cathedral), the general scheme of the building was transformed from a complex centralized plan to a basilican plan with the transept at the center, crowned by a dome. The dome itself remained essentially unchanged from the original plan. Modeled after the dome of St. Peter's, it is 366 feet high.

Johann Balthasar Neumann

Neumann was the leading exponent of Rococo architecture in Germany. He worked mainly in the Franconia region and was associated above all with the bishop's residence at Würzburg, for which he had the good fortune to find such exceptional collaborators as Giambattista Tiepolo and his sons.

Neumann was hailed by his contemporaries as "the architect of architects," his chief distinction being a masterful interpretation of the spirit of Rococo in mid-eighteenth century Germany.

● LIFE

The son of a humble cloth merchant, Johann Balthasar was born in 1687 at Egen, (today's Cheb, Czech Republic) in Bohemia. His career began in a cannon factory at Würzburg, the capital of the episcopal principality of Franconia, where he entered the artillery of the bishop-prince.

In 1717 and 1718, he traveled to various places to pursue his studies, including Paris and Milan. His talent soon came to the attention of Bishop-Prince Franz von Schönbrun, who first employed him as a military architect. By

1719, Neumann had been appointed director of construction at the court of Würzburg. Although he was to hold this position almost all his life, he did have the opportunity to display his talents beyond this small city in Lower Franconia. There, however, within the narrow confines of the urban environment, his talent could range over all fields of architecture, as he was called upon to plan streets and construct houses, including his own at 7 Kapuzinergasse. Neumann thus showed himself to be not only an architect for the wealthy residents of the town, but one able to deal with all aspects of the art of building in the early eighteenth century. He died in 1753.

● WORKS

Neumann's great initiative, to which he dedicated himself wholeheartedly and

on which his fame largely rests, is the residence of the bishop-prince. Germany, like the rest of Europe, was fascinated by the splendid mansions being built in France (such as the Louvre and Versailles) and the Italian architectural achievements of such masters as Bernini and Borromini.

The residential palace was considered such an important project that Neumann was first invited to Paris to consult with the Rococo masters Robert de Cotte and Germain Boffrand, after which he was assisted by the famous Johann Lukas von Hildebrandt and others, under the supervision of Johann Dientzenhofer. Still, the first design concept to gain approval was his own, albeit with such modifications as the elimination of a second monumental stairway (deemed too massive and clumsy).

In the final plan, the building was or-

ganized around a central core with four inner courtyards. The side that opened onto the courtyard was very different from the one overlooking the gardens, which, as at Versailles, became a sort of scenographic background.

The magnificence of the residence was not based entirely on its grandiose halls and structures, however, but also on the opulent beauty of its decoration. A splendid example is the Kaisersaal (imperial hall), in which Tiepolo's decoration harmonizes superbly with the architecture.

But Neumann did not produce civil works alone, including the royal mansions in Stuttgart and Karlsruhe, but also religious monuments, such as the Church of the Fourteen Saints (Vierzehnheiligen, 1743–1772) near Bamberg, where the influence of Borromini is immediately apparent.

Left:
Johann Balthasar
Neumann and others,
*Façade overlooking
the garden
in the Bishop-Prince's
Residence,*
1719–1744.
Würzburg, Lower
Franconia, Germany.

Above:
Johann Balthasar
Neumann and others,
with frescoes
by Giambattista Tiepolo,
*Kaisersaal in the
Bishop-Prince's
Residence,*
1719–1753.
Würzburg, Lower
Franconia, Germany.
The frescoes, painted
by Tiepolo between
1751 and 1753,
represent the epic story
of Frederick Barbarossa
and his wedding to
Beatrice of Burgundy.

Left: Johann Balthasar
Neumann and others,
*Façade overlooking the
courtyard of the Bishop-
Prince's Residence,*
1719–1744.
Würzburg, Lower
Franconia, Germany.

Above:
Johann Balthasar
Neumann and others,
with frescoes by
Giambattista Tiepolo,
*Great staircase
in the Bishop-Prince's
Residence,*

1719–1753.
Würzburg, Lower
Franconia, Germany.
The structure
of the monumental
staircase is supported
by a self-bearing
cross vault.

Thomas Jefferson, *Jefferson House at Monticello*, 1769–1775 and 1796–1809. Charlottesville, Virginia. Originally designed according to the model of Palladian villas with a central plan, the residence at Monticello was modified by Jefferson himself after his long stay in Paris as ambassador. Inspired by the new style of French architecture, the future U.S. president enlarged the plan, conferring on the building a more monumental aspect. He introduced many innovative features, such as folding beds and dumbwaiters.

Thomas Jefferson

On March 4, 1801, after delivering his solemn inaugural address to Congress, Thomas Jefferson, the third president of the United States of America, returned to his hotel for dinner. As he entered the dining hall, someone rose to give him the place of honor, but Jefferson went to sit in his usual place. At the time, the fledgling nation already numbered more than five million inhabitants and covered an area of nearly 400,000 square miles. It was, in fact, already a great sovereign state. As a political leader, Jefferson was reminiscent of the ancient Roman statesman Cincinnatus—unpretentious but strong. His ideal was Greek and Roman, or at least the idealized image of these two great civilizations as portrayed in history books.

Moreover, as a landowner from Virginia, Jefferson had strong ties to the land and viewed with strong disfavor the imminent arrival of forced industrialization or anything else deemed detrimental to human dignity (a principle compromised by his ownership of slaves). Jefferson's unswerving desire was to revive the democratic spirit of Periclean Greece and republican Rome, a desire that was reflected in American political terminology and institutions. The title of "president elect," in fact, was the exact equivalent of the Roman *consul designatus*, and the institution of the Senate was inspired directly by the classical model (though the House of Representatives reflected British tradition). Like that of Rome, in fact, the U.S. Senate was a council of elites, made up of educated landhold-

ers who were not popularly elected but designated by the various state legislatures. With these precedents, it would have been hard to conceive of any other architectural choice than the one that was adopted: Neoclassicism, as seen through the filter of Palladianism. Benjamin H. Latrobe (1764–1820), Jefferson's collaborator and the architect whom he appointed director of public monuments in Washington, was to write, "I am a fanatical Greek…. My canons of good taste are strictly oriented toward Greek architecture….The days of Greece can live again in the American forests." Behind these stylistic preferences lay well-defined political ideals.

● LIFE AND WORKS

The son of a wealthy landowner from Virginia who left him a vast estate, Thomas Jefferson was born in 1743 at Shadwell, in what is now Albermarle County. A man of great erudition, he was a jurist, economist, naturalist, and edu-

Below:
*Drawing of the Capitol
Building in Washington,
D.C., as designed
by Benjamin H. Latrobe,
before the fire of 1814.*

Right:
Aerial view of the
Capitol Building,
completed in 1865
by Thomas U. Walter.
Washington, D.C.

cator as well as a talented architect. His first programmatic work was his own residence, called Monticello, built on a picturesque hilltop site on the property inherited from his father. The plan was taken from a book by Robert Morris, *Select Architecture*, revised in light of the English edition of Palladio's *Quattro libri dell'architettura*, edited by Leoni (1721). It is not hard to identify Palladio's Rotonda as the model for Monticello. The building played the important role of importing to America a refined architectural style as a counterpart to the simplicity and spontaneity of colonial design. Jefferson's other achievements as an architect include the original buildings of the University of Virginia, of which he was the founder, and the state capitol building in Richmond. As George Washington's secretary of state, he established the guidelines for the urban plan of the District of Columbia and, as president, commissioned Latrobe to complete the new federal Capitol. Jefferson died on July 4, 1826.

Etienne-Louis Boullée and Claude-Nicolas Ledoux

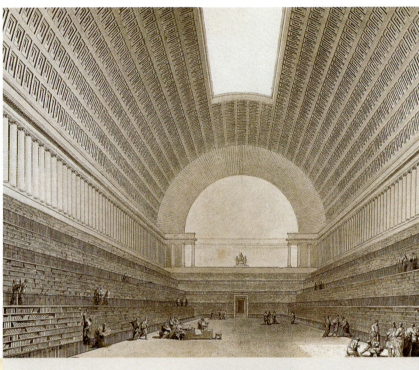

Another aspect of Neoclassical architecture that had never before emerged so clearly was its experimentation with forms that had no precedent in architectural tradition. In this sense, the Enlightenment philosophy underlying Neoclassicism marked a sharp break from the principles of previous artistic movements. In reaction to the excesses of Rococo, this new style was based on laws of nature and reason. In the theories formulated by the Germans Anton Raphael Mengs and Johann Joachim Winckelmann beginning in the second half of the eighteenth century, the ancient Greek ideal was adopted as the model of perfect beauty. Since rationality was deemed the only valid guide for approaching Beauty, there was no purpose

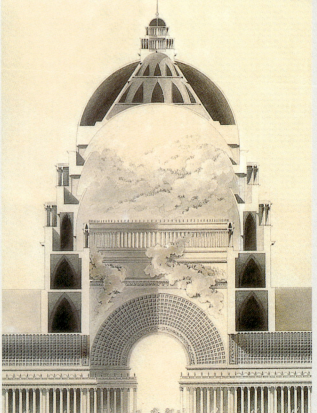

Above:
Etienne-Louis Boullée, *Design for a national library*, 1785, drawing from *Architecture: Essai sur l'Art.* Paris, National Library.

Left and below:
Etienne-Louis Boullée, *Design for a cenotaph for Newton*, 1784, drawing from *Architecture: Essai sur l'Art.* Paris, National Library.
The great central sphere would have been nearly 500 feet high.

Left:
Etienne-Louis Boullée, *Basilica,* c. 1786, drawing from *Architecture: Essai sur l'Art.* Paris, National Library.

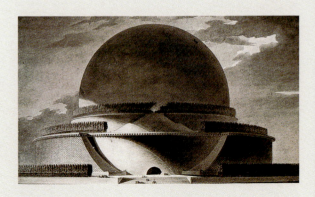

in being distracted by models that had developed outside the beneficent influence of the "goddess Reason." While on the one hand attention was thus focused on the function of an object or building (from which the form was to emerge), any models that might block the path of reason to the luminous realm of beauty were deemed useless. This was precisely the reverse of the political Neoclassicism that had been most extensively applied in the United States. The outstanding figures of this second aspect of Neoclassicism (in whose work all of its complexity is revealed) were the architects and architectural theorists Boullée and Ledoux, both of whom belonged to the circle of the *Encyclopédie* headed by Jean D'Alembert and Denis Diderot. Their reform was one of the primary components of the movement for cultural renewal, distinguished by a strong secularism, prior to the French Revolution.

● ETIENNE-LOUIS BOULLÉE

The rational approach that resulted in the adoption of simple geometric forms was accompanied in the works of Boullée by a love of the monumental and spectacular that, paradoxically, transformed the cold austerity of reason into a fantastic visionary dream. It was not by chance that Boullée, born in Paris in 1728, actually built very little (among his few surviving works is the Hôtel Alexandre in Paris, 1766–1768), preferring to illustrate his designs in the treatise *Architecture: Essai sur l'Art*, which remained unpublished until 1953. In this text, he theorized an architecture that would be rational, based on simple, universal figures alluding to the ideal, and therefore moral, representing the world of Enlightenment archetypes. In spite of his scarce production and the fact that his treatise went unpublished for centuries, Boullée exerted great

influence over his contemporaries, from his pupil Jean-Nicolas-Louis Durand to Benjamin Henry Latrobe (see preceding pages). He died in 1799.

● CLAUDE-NICOLAS LEDOUX

Born at Dormans-sur-Marne in 1736, Ledoux was educated in Paris but strongly influenced by the visionary world of Giovan Battista Piranesi. Although he built much more than Boullée, his finest works have been demolished. In 1773 he was named *achitecte du roi* ("architect of this king"), an appointment that stimulated his imagination still further, as demonstrated by his designs for the ideal city (1794–1804). Not unlike the "geometric" formulations conceived by Boullée, he theorized an architecture that would be highly expressive; his works were intended as *parlantes* ("speaking") structures whose form proclaimed their function.

Giacomo Quarenghi

Above:
Entrance to the State Bank in St. Petersburg (1783–1790) in an old photograph. The building, also called the "marble palace," now houses the Lenin Museum.

Right:
"Raphael's Loggias" in St. Petersburg (1783–1792), in a watercolor by Konstantin Ukhtomsky, 1860. In 1783, Quarenghi was commissioned to build a copy of the Vatican Loggias (p. 295) in a hall near the theater he had designed in St. Petersburg. The project had begun in 1780, when a group of artists headed by Christopher Unterberger was commissioned by Catherine II to faithfully copy the frescoes in the Vatican by Raphael and his school.

Above:
Watercolor of the Great Hall in the Winter Palace in St. Petersburg, early nineteenth century. This watercolor is a valuable record of the original appearance of the Great Hall (or Nicholas Hall), designed by Giacomo Quarenghi in 1780 and rebuilt by Vassili Stasov after the fire of 1837.

The historical context in which Giacomo Quarenghi worked was the Russia of Catherine II (1729–1796), the widow of Tsar Peter III, who had been assassinated in 1745. An unindustrialized nation still regarded as a great power by the other European nations, with an economy based on agricultural estates worked by the peasant class, Russia had been set on a path of modernization under the reformist policies of Peter I (the Great).

Catherine II, suspected of having plotted the assassination of her husband, continued to govern on the course laid out by her predecessor. A vital, exuberant, highly educated woman who was said to have had many lovers, Catherine surrounded herself with artists, writers, and Enlightenment intellectuals. Founded during her reign were the University of Moscow (1755) and the Academy of Fine Arts (1758), which took their place alongside the Academy of Science, established in 1725, as leading cultural institutions. Despite her intellectual and cultural activities, which began to yield fruit only in the following century, the Russia of Catherine the Great still looked to Europe as a model to be imitated. Eminent foreign artists and intellectuals were summoned to court and accorded the highest honors.

Among these was the Italian Neoclassical master Giacomo Quarenghi, who played a leading role in renovating old buildings and constructing new ones, conferring on St. Petersburg and Moscow a look more similar to that of the great European capitals such as Paris and Rome, if not even more grandiose.

● LIFE AND WORKS

Born in 1744 at Valle Imagna in Lombardy, not far from Bergamo, Quarenghi began his career as apprentice to a painter. At the age of only 19, he traveled to Rome and attended the school of Mengs and Pozzi, where he assimilated the theoretical premises of Neoclassicism. His interest soon turned to architecture, and he studied the classical monuments of Rome. He made trips to other cities, where he studied the works of Bramante, Antonio da Sangallo the Younger, and above all Palladio, who strongly influenced his style. But it was from Boullée and Ledoux that Quarenghi drew the concept of geometric simplicity. One of his first important commissions was the Church of Santa Scolastica at Subiaco, east of Rome. The fateful change in his life occurred when

Baron Grimm, a minister in the government of Catherine II, invited him to work in St. Petersburg. In 1779, Quarenghi became architect to the court, where he made a major contribution to the new urban aspect of the city. In one of his first projects, he renovated the style of the Winter Palace, which had been designed by the Italian architect Rastrelli (p. 151). In the same spirit, he built the Hermitage Theater, inspired by Palladio's Olympic Theater in Vicenza (p. 58). The State Bank, which he designed entirely himself, reflects the influence of Palladio, with decoration that is remarkably sober despite consisting of polychrome marble. With the same attention to proportion and harmony, Quarenghi designed the Academy of Science and several mansions. In Moscow he received major commissions, such as the Berborodko Palace. He died in St. Petersburg in 1817.

Above:
An old photograph of the riding stable of the cavalry regiment stationed in St. Petersburg.

Giuseppe Valadier

The most important Italian architect of the Neoclassical period, Valadier worked mainly in the Papal States and is credited with bringing Italian architectural style to the level of the great nations of the time. He went beyond the revival of sixteenth-century forms that had been strongly promoted by Pope Pius VI (r. 1775–1799), a style whose chief representative had been the architect Cosimo Morelli (1732–1812). Not by chance, all of Valadier's great achievements belonged to the new century. While in perfect harmony with the ruling class of the time, priests and the papal nobility, Valadier not only made Neoclassical principles acceptable (if still suspected of being based on Enlightenment concepts), but showed himself highly sensitive to the revival of the Roman classicism embraced by enthusiasts of the French Revolution. Valadier was clearly influenced by the architect and artist Carlo Marchionni (1702–1786), while attentive to the innovations of Quarenghi and the dictates of Francesco Milizia.

● LIFE AND WORKS

An archaeologist, architect, and urban planner, Giuseppe Valadier was born in

The Arch of Titus in Rome as it appears today, after the restoration by Giuseppe Valadier.

Below and at right: Giuseppe Valadier, Casina Valadier on the Pincio, 1810–1818. Rome.

View of Piazza del Popolo from the Pincio, in a nineteenth-century watercolor. Restored on the occasion of the Jubilee in 2000, the square has returned to its ancient splendor. Valadier began to plan its rearrangement in 1793. At first he considered a long line of buildings with a double order of columns, but the final project, approved in 1816, was that of the square as it appears today. The park on the Pincio, which he also designed, was laid out between 1810 and 1818. Valadier was always attentive to the use of gardens as an architectural resource.

Rome in 1762, the son of a sculptor, goldsmith, and smelter who worked in close contact with the Curia. Although little is known of his education, it is certain that he was a precocious boy. At the age of only 11, he executed and signed a relief on the Cybo Chapel in Rome's Piazza del Popolo, and two years later participated in a competition for restoring the Church of San Salvatore in Lauro, also in Rome. He then studied with Girolamo Toma, who taught him mathematics and descriptive geometry. In 1781, Valadier became a member of the staff of the Fabbrica di San Pietro, with the title of architect of the Holy Apostolic Palaces, then under the direction of Carlo Marchionni. A year after Marchionni's death, Valadier was appointed chamber architect and assistant for the Fabbrica di San Pietro. At this time he began to receive some important commissions. Pope Pius VI entrusted him with the restoration of the Duomo of Spoleto (from 1785) and the reconstruction of the Duomo of Urbino, severely damaged by earthquakes in 1781 and 1787.

Valadier's versatility and ingenuity also earned him commissions to attempt a reclamation of the Agro Pontino swampland and to conduct a survey of the damage caused by the earthquake in Romagna. One of his first major projects in Rome was the Church of San Pantaleo, renovated at the order of Duke Giovanni Torlonia, who asked Valadier to design the new façade. The Roman architect was soon engaged in problems of urban design as well, planning first the arrangement of Via Flaminia (1805) and then the pedestrian path through the Imperial Forums (1811). Fascinated by Roman antiquities, he restored the Ponte Milvio (1805) and the Arch of Titus (1811). In 1819 he designed the Teatro Valle, an elegant theater that still functions perfectly today. He also designed the Church of San Rocco, near the old port of Ripetta, whose façade (1833), with a single order of Corinthian pilasters, is inspired by the Palladian Church of San Giorgio Maggiore in Venice. On the urban scale, he definitively rearranged the square in front of the Church of San Giovanni in Laterano and the adjacent gardens. But the work on which his fame is principally based is the reorganization of the Piazza del Popolo, which was to complete the process of urban renewal already begun with the new arrangement of the Via Flaminia. The Piazza del Popolo was originally trapezoidal in shape, which Valadier at first considered retaining; but the presence of the Pincio Gardens next to it encouraged him to open out the space in the shape of an ellipse, thereby creating a more articulated and compelling space.

Below:
Giuseppe Valadier,
Façade of San Pantaleo,
1806. Rome.
The façade is divided into two registers by a stucco frieze executed by Pietro Aureli.
In the upper register, crowned by a dentiled tympanum, is a large window framed by a blind lunette. Below it is the portal, with a tympanum flanked by two Ionic columns. The façade is distinguished by smooth stonework (bossage).

John Nash

Claude Lorrain, *View of Delphi with a processional way*, 1650. Rome, Galleria Doria Pamphili.

The theme of the relationship between art and nature runs through much of the history of art and architecture, but there was a moment, in England during the eighteenth century, when it found explicit formal expression in the genre of the Picturesque. Developing in France as well, in the wake of Rococo, the Picturesque emphasized the creative vitality of nature and found beauty in its wild, irregular aspects. This gave rise to the aesthetic concept of an "educated" nature, cleansed of the harshness that exists in reality and thereby capable of appearing spontaneous without really being so. Not by coincidence, the finest expression of the Picturesque may be seen in the English garden architecture of the eighteenth and nineteenth centuries. Sources of inspiration were found in the works of such great seventeenth-century French painters as Nicolas Poussin and Claude Lorrain, who decisively contributed to the development of this new sensitivity to landscape. Many architects felt the fascination of this theme; outstanding among them were William Kent (1685–1748) and his friend and pupil Lancelot Brown (1716–1783), better known as Capability Brown. Kent and Brown may be considered the inventors of the English Landscape garden, with its copses of trees, gentle meadows, and small lakes (p. 39). John Nash was a product of the same cultural climate, but he cannot be considered a landscape architect alone, since his achievements in the field of urban planning are also outstanding.

● LIFE AND WORKS

The British architect and urban planner John Nash was born in 1752 in London, where he trained with Robert Taylor (1714–1788), a leading figure in the neo-Palladian current then sweeping Great Britain. Encouraged by his early successes, Nash opened his own studio before the age of 30. The decision was to prove disastrous, however, as bankruptcy soon threatened. Nash was forced to collaborate instead with the garden architect Humphrey Repton (1752–1818), with whom, in 1783, he established a successful partnership engaged in building cottages for the wealthy middle class and nobility. One of his most famous achievements is the Royal Pavilion at Brighton (p. 162), erected in 1818 in an almost visionary Mogul style mingled with aspects derived, especially in the interior, from an equally improbable Chinese manner. The success of projects such as this undoubtedly lay in a fast-growing interest in the exotic, attributed in turn to the new contacts, first

Right:
Aerial view of Warwick Castle and the garden designed by Capability Brown, 1750. Warwick, England.

The Chinese-style corridor in the Royal Pavilion at Brighton, designed by John Nash, in a contemporary watercolor.

commercial and then cultural, with the distant lands of the burgeoning British Empire. Colonial expansion also facilitated, although in ways that were not entirely orthodox, relations between different artistic worlds, which, when transplanted in the West, carried special appeal as curiosities. Nash's great opportunity came with the commission conferred on him by the prince of Wales, later to rule Britain as King George IV (1820–1830), to design Regent's Park in London and the surrounding residential area. In this project, the theme central to Nash's architectural enterprise—the picturesque—emerges once again. The park and gardens (inaugurated in 1838, three years after Nash's death) cover an area of more than 45 acres, bordered by elegant residential terraces (row houses; see illustration, p. 159). The plan provided for a processional route from the park to Buckingham Palace, along which were monumental plazas (including Piccadilly Circus and Trafalgar Square) and terraces in a pure Neoclassical style that changed the face of the British capital.

Left:
John Nash, *Trompe-l'oeil interior*, 1798. Grosvenor Priory, Southgate, London. For the breakfast room in the Neoclassical mansion at Grosvenor Priory, Nash created an illusionist setting that replicates the inside of a birdcage.

Above:
John Nash, *Nash Terraces*, 1825. Regent's Park, Langham Place, London. Nash used architectural style as a kind of garment, changed to suit a particular occasion.

Giuseppe Sacconi and the Vittoriano

It would be hard to find a monument that has been the object of harsher criticism than the so-called Vittoriano in Rome's Piazza Venezia—the Monument to Victor Emmanuel II, also known as the Altar of the Nation and the Tomb of the Unknown Soldier—designed by Giuseppe Sacconi. The criticism is summarized by the ruthless judgment of the journalist Giovanni Papini, who said it looked like a pompous public urinal. In a witty popular epithet, the structure is likened to a giant typewriter. Indeed, if one thinks of the crude mechanical typing devices produced at the turn of the century, the comparison is easy to understand. Yet it is precisely this kind of criticism that shows how rapidly tastes changed during the first decade of the twentieth century. The effect of the structure at its unveiling must have been like that of an archaeological discovery. At the time that it was begun, in 1885, Paris was ecstatic over the music emanating from the Opéra, finished in 1874. Thus, if not in the avant-garde, the Vittoriano was at least perfectly in keeping with the dominant stylistic trends of the period. By 1911, however, when the structure was finally inaugurated, the atmosphere had changed drastically. Italy was experiencing the shock of Futurism, Picasso had painted the *Demoiselles d'Avignon,* and the architecture now in vogue was that of Adolf Loos. In the light of all this, Papini's disrespectful opinion, published in 1913 in the magazine *Lacerba,* was understandable.

● GIUSEPPE SACCONI

Born in 1854 at Montalto delle Marche in east-central Italy, Giuseppe Sacconi won the design competition for the Monument to Vittorio Emanuele II, the project that launched his career as architect, at the age of only 30. He belonged to the generation of architects that had come to regard style as a kind of garment, to be changed with each passing season and for each new occasion. Accordingly, it was easy for Sacconi to move

Giuseppe Sacconi,
*View of the Monument
to Vittorio Emanuele II,*
1885–1911. Rome.

Giuseppe Sacconi,
*Monument to Vittorio
Emanuele II,*
1885–1911. Rome.
To make room for the
monument, the small

church of Santa Rita
by Carlo Fontana (1665)
and the viridarium
(garden) of the
Palazzo Barbo had
to be moved.

from the classical forms of the white Vittoriano to an imitation of the fifteenth-century Palazzo Barbo (p. 19) for the headquarters of the Assicurazioni Generali insurance company. The choice was in a way obligatory, as it created a symmetrical design on the opposite side of the square, which had been created as the site for the Monument to Vittorio Emanuele II by demolishing an entire block of houses from the past. In this sense, Sacconi may also be recognized as an urban planner, since he gave a new arrangement to the heart of the city by creating a new square and its scenic backdrop. His victory in the competition brought with it other major commissions, such as the tomb of Umberto I in the Pantheon, and his last project, the expiatory chapel in Monza. Dejected by the criticisms of the Vittoriano, however, he committed suicide in 1905, at age 51.

● THE MONUMENT TO VITTORIO EMANUELE II

To understand the atmosphere in which the Vittoriano was created, we may compare it with a famous early work by Gustav Klimt (right), celebrating the spirit of Rome. This seems to justify, in the Vittoriano, the choice of glaringly white Botticino marble, deemed the most appropriate material for recalling the splendor of Ancient Rome. Around the bronze statue of Vittorio Emanuele II on horseback, the grandiose structure rises before a colonnaded portico. At the ends are two bronze statuary groups, representing Thought and Action. Below them are two groups of Winged Victories. At the sides of the stairway are statues of the Adriatic and the Tyrrhenian Seas. The Tomb of the Unknown Soldier stands at the front of the monument.

Gustav Klimt,
*The theater of Taormina,
decoration on the ceiling
of the Burgtheater,*
1886–1888.
Vienna, Austria.
The white marble
building in the
background closely
resembles the stylistic
typology of the
Vittoriano. The
combination of marble
and bronze is also
in keeping with the taste
of the times.

Giuseppe Sacconi,
*Interior of the portico
on the Monument to
Vittorio Emanuele II,*
1885–1911. Rome.

Eugène-Emmanuel Viollet-le-Duc

Below:
Interior of Sainte-Chapelle, restored in 1840. Paris.

Below:
Façade of the Church of the Madeleine, restored in 1840. Vézelay, Burgundy, France.

Above:
View of the citadel, restored starting in 1849. Carcassonne, Languedoc, France. The citadel of Carcassonne is the most significant example of military architecture from the French Middle Ages.

Right:
Eugène-Emmanuel Viollet-le-Duc, *Drawing of the restored façade of the Narbonese Gate in Carcassonne*, after 1849.

The revival of the Gothic style during the nineteenth century is in large part attributable to the architectural projects and writings of Viollet-le-Duc. His studies explored various forms and expressions of Gothic style: from clothing, jewelry, and utensils to interior design and architecture. Moreover, there was new interest in the Middle Ages among groups of contemporary painters, such as the Nazarenes and Pre-Raphaelites, further demonstrating that the Gothic Revival was taking hold in a broad cross-section of nineteenth-century culture. The cultural activities of Viollet-le-Duc covered three separate fields: art history, the restoration of medieval monuments, and architecture itself. His importance, however, is fully apparent only in considering the effects of his work and teachings on succeeding generations. His principles of Gothic architecture exerted a clear influence on those who apparently had nothing in common with his aesthetics, ranging from Victor Horta (1861–1947) and Antoni Gaudí (1852–1926) to Frank Lloyd Wright (1869–1959) and Le Corbusier (1887–1965), all of whom were, in one way or another, indebted to Viollet-le-Duc.

● LIFE AND WORKS

The scion of a wealthy family and son of a high government official, Eugène-Emmanuel Viollet-le-Duc was born in Paris on January 21, 1814. A grandson of the then famous art historian and painter Etienne Jean Delécluze (1782–1863), he was surrounded in his family by the cultural atmosphere of a progressive, highly cultivated France. After a period of apprenticeship to the architects Jean-Jacques Huvé (1783–1852) and Achille Leclère (1785–1853), he began to travel extensively in France and Italy to complete his professional training. His talent for drawing won him recognition at the Salon of 1834, but his fierce aversion to the classical instruction at the École des Beaux-Arts prevented him, from the time of his student years, from embarking on an academic career. Instead he attended the École des Dessins, cultivating his interest in medieval architecture and archaeology, in keeping with the dictates of nineteenth-century romanticism. The decisive turn in his life and career occurred when Prosper Mérimée (1803–1870), at the time inspector of historical monuments, commissioned him to restore, at the age of

Left:
Eugène-Emmanuel
Viollet-le-Duc,
Gargoyles
at the top of the
western tower
of the Cathedral

of Notre-Dame,
c. 1844–1864. Paris.
These downspouts
(gargoyles) were
designed in Gothic
Revival style
by Viollet-le-Duc

as part of the sweeping
restoration of the
Parisian cathedral.

Below: *View of Notre-
Dame*, restored
in 1844. Paris.

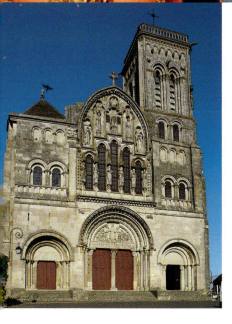

only 26, one of the greatest medieval churches surviving from the twelfth century: Sainte-Madeleine at Vézelay. This was followed by commissions for such important monuments as the Sainte-Chapelle in Paris, which he also began to restore in 1840, in collaboration with Jean Baptiste Lassus (1807–1857). Viollet-le-Duc soon became France's most renowned expert in medieval culture, and in 1844 he was commissioned to restore the country's most famous cathedral, Notre-Dame of Paris (1163–1320), the recent setting for Victor Hugo's great historical romance, *The Hunchback of Notre Dame* (1833). But the most demanding restoration proj-ect undertaken by the French architect was that of the walled citadel of Carcassonne in southern France, beginning in 1849, the same year in which he also restored the Cathedral of Amiens. Viollet-le-Duc attempted to record his vast architectural knowledge in voluminous reference works, long regarded as the finest studies of medieval art (in particular, *Dictionnaire raisonné de l'architecture française*, 1854–1868). At the time, however, his aesthetic convictions met with hostility in classicist circles, and he was forced to resign his chair in art history at the École des Beaux-Arts in 1864. He died at Lausanne, Switzerland, in 1879.

Below:
Charles Barry
and Augustus Welby
Northmore Pugin,
Houses of Parliament,
1839–1888. London.

The Houses of Parliament

In the mid-nineteenth century, the rejection of classicism in favor of such other styles as Gothic Revival, which was fast emerging, was not a painless option. This was demonstrated, for example, in the career of Viollet-le-Duc, who was forced by the classicists at the École des Beaux-Arts in Paris to resign his chair in the art history department. The reason for the hostility had to do with the fact, at least in the minds of opponents, that unconditional acceptance of the Neo-Gothic would irrevocably cancel the centuries-old, universally shared conviction that the style derived from

Greco-Roman culture was the only one appropriate to represent Western civilization. Moreover, acceptance of the classical style constituted a reference to the Latin roots of Europe, which had produced the only Mediterranean-wide empire, that of Ancient Rome, followed by the Holy Roman Empire in its various manifestations (French, German, Hapsburg, Napoleonic, etc.). Acceptance of the Gothic style thus meant embracing what could be called, albeit improperly, "local independent styles," representing specific national vocabularies and situations. And here it would seem

only natural to choose this style for the British Houses of Parliament in London. In this case, the Gothic Revival style had important political significance, emphasizing the country's pride in its own roots (at least its Norman ones). Not by coincidence, the building stands on the site of the ancient royal palace, founded in the eleventh century and designated by King Edward VI in 1547 as the seat of parliament. Destroyed by fire in 1834, the great complex was rebuilt from 1839 to 1888 in highly ornate vertical Gothic style.

● THE ARCHITECTS

The work was carried out through the collaboration of two British architects. Charles Barry (1795–1860) won the design competition held in 1834–1835, immediately after the fire. Ground was

Below: Augustus Welby Northmore Pugin, *Interior of the House of Commons*, rebuilt after World War II. Houses of Parliament, London.

Right: Augustus Welby Northmore Pugin, *Staircase in the House of Lords*, c. 1847. Houses of Parliament, London.

Right: Augustus Welby Northmore Pugin, *Royal Gallery in the House of Lords*, c. 1847. Houses of Parliament, London.

Below: Augustus Welby Northmore Pugin, *Interior of the House of Lords*, c. 1847. Houses of Parliament, London.

broken in 1839, and the building was inaugurated in 1852, although work on it continued until 1888. The plan and general layout were the work of Barry, who had employed different styles in previous projects (such as the Royal Institution of Fine Arts of Manchester, classically Greek). The ornamentation and decoration were then designed by Augustus Welby Northmore Pugin (1812–1852) in minute detail. Pugin was also responsible for the arrangement of the interior, the furniture, and all other internal objects, down to the inkwells. The son of the equally famous Augustus Charles Pugin, he also designed a number of churches in his own right, including the cathedrals of Nottingham (1842–1844) and St. George in London (1840–1848) and wrote highly influential treatises on Gothic Revival, which he considered the "style par excellence."

● THE STRUCTURE

Covering an area of over 350,000 square feet, the building contains the House of Commons (rebuilt in 1941 after having been damaged by bombs during World War II), the House of Lords, and Westminster Hall, which housed the courts of law from the thirteenth to the nineteenth century. Roughly rectangular, it has a straight façade overlooking the Thames and a more irregular one on the side that faces Westminster Abbey. Famous for its most striking feature, the 316-foot-tall Clock Tower, which contains Big Ben (named after Sir Benjamin Hall, who installed the clockworks and carillon), the building has a purposefully austere look. In the southwest corner stands the 336-foot Victoria Tower, the tallest in the world upon its completion in 1860, two years after the Clock Tower.

Gustave Eiffel

Above:
Photograph of the Galerie des Machines at the Universal Exposition, Paris 1889. The building, designed for the 1889 Expo by the architect Charles-Louis-Ferdinand Dutert (1845–1906) with the collaboration of the engineers Contamin, Pierron, and Charton,

was a daringly bold structure of metal and glass measuring 1,380 feet long, 375 feet wide, and 160 feet high. Mobile bridges were purposely installed to allow the public to observe the machines on display.

Below:
Aerial view of the Universal Exposition in a contemporary illustration.
Thanks to the Eiffel Tower and the Galerie des Machines, the success of metal architecture was definitively established at the Universal Exposition of 1889.

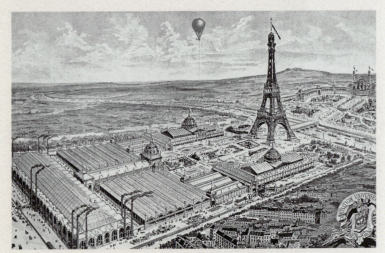

Originally intended for use only during the Universal Exposition of 1889, the great wrought-iron tower designed by Gustave Eiffel still dominates the skyline of Paris as a tourist landmark and enduring symbol of a naive faith in progress and modernity. It is the only work, out of the many he built, for which "Monsieur Eiffel" remains famous.

● THE UNIVERSAL EXPOSITIONS

Beginning with the first held in London in 1851, international expositions occupied a prominent place in European public life in the late nineteenth century. Those held in the following century were less frequent and carried less of the aura of their predecessors. The primary objective of the "Expos" was to herald the wonders of new technologies and display their capabilities to the general public. For this purpose, large exhibition pavilions were constructed, only to be demolished soon after the close of the fair. The expositions also had a significant effect on the development of technologies for speeding up the construction process, a necessary requisite for the erection of imposing but temporary buildings in a short time. This was precisely the challenge faced by the engineer Eiffel: to construct within a relatively brief period of time a metal tower no less than 300 meters (984 feet) high.

● THE EIFFEL TOWER

The idea was conceived five years before the Paris Expo; it was in 1884 that Gustave Eiffel assigned the project to two engineers employed by his firm, Émile Nougier and Maurice Koechlin. The realization of iron-frame bridges had

Eiffel Tower, 1884–1889. Paris. The famous tower is built on three levels resting on enormous supporting pylons.

Right:
The Eiffel Tower during construction in a photograph from around 1885.
In the background is the Rotonda designed by the architect Jean-Camille Formigé (1845–1926) during the same period.

spurred engineers to develop techniques for solving the problem of constructing metal pylons. In other words, the future tower originated as an experiment to test the flexibility and strength of the material required to raise a giant pylon. Many problems had to be addressed, not least of them that of wind stress. It was the solution to this technical problem, rather than aesthetic considerations, that finally determined the form of the Eiffel Tower; although, according to its inventor, its curves, determined on the basis of precise calculations, would emanate "a great impression of strength and beauty." The technical decision was critical, reflecting a revolution in building methodology that soon passed from engineers to architects. Indeed the revolutionary aspect of the Eiffel Tower lay in this area as much as any, although at the time it was apparent to no one. Outcries against its aesthetic quality were heard from Émile Zola and Guy de Maupassant, among others, and many engineers predicted the collapse of the tower; local property owners sued the Eiffel company because they found it difficult to rent out buildings in the area. Construction began in January 1887 and was completed, to the amazement of all, on April 15, 1889.

● LIFE AND WORKS

Alexandre-Gustave Eiffel was born in Dijon, France, in 1832. He earned a degree in chemistry at age 18, but opted instead for a career in construction engineering, specializing in new materials and technologies. He earned a reputation as a builder of bridges and viaducts, and in 1867 he established his own firm, the Maison Eiffel. Notable accomplishments included the Maria Pia Bridge over the Douro River in Oporto, Portugal, and a viaduct over the Truyère River in Garabit, France. Eiffel was not satisfied with carrying out his commissions through traditional techniques, but made each of them an occasion for applying original technical solutions aimed at improving the structural integrity, as well as the aesthetic appeal, of his projects.

Right:
Gustave Eiffel,
*Garabit Viaduct
over the Truyère*,
1880–1884. Cantal,
Auvergne, France.
For the viaduct, Eiffel
designed an arched
bridge 525 feet long
with metal trusses,
which provide maximum
strength and flexibility
with minimal wind
resistance.

Charles Rennie Mackintosh

Right: Charles Rennie Mackintosh, *White bedroom in the Hill House*, 1902–1906. Helensburgh, Glasgow, Scotland. Mackintosh was assisted in the design of interior fabrics and the stucco facings on the walls of the bedrooms and living rooms by his wife, Margaret MacDonald.

Charles Rennie Mackintosh, *Hill House*, 1902–1906. Helensburgh, Glasgow, Scotland. The house stands on a hilltop overlooking the estuary of the Clyde River, 14 miles from Glasgow. At the request of the owner, Walter Blackie, Mackintosh also designed the surrounding garden.

In the late nineteenth and early twentieth centuries, the hotly debated issue in cultural circles was the interrelationship among industry, craftsmanship, and art. The development of industrial capabilities by which objects could be mass-produced at a relatively low cost was seen by some as depriving the objects themselves of their inherent dignity and as threatening the quality of life and the human spirit everywhere. Such was the conviction of William Morris, who, beginning in 1861 with his own furnishing and decoration company, attempted to raise the level of artistic craftsmanship while still serving the demands of industrial production. His efforts gave rise to the so-called Arts and Crafts Movement, whose echo was to resound throughout Europe. Particularly sensitive to these issues was the Belgian designer and architect Henry Van

de Velde, who promoted the concept of *Gesamtkunstwerk* ("total work of art"), which would unite all forms of expression—architectural, pictorial, and sculptural. The career of the Scottish architect and designer Charles Rennie Mackintosh unfolded against the backdrop of these trends. In late nineteenth-century Great Britain, the Viennese experience of Art Nouveau was viewed with some diffidence, as it was still deemed overly concerned with aesthetics. This point of view anticipated positions that later would be expressed by Van de Velde himself, who, in a text dating from 1924, called for "a rationalizing aesthetics" in which beauty and form would be "immunized against the recurrent infections of that harmful parasite, fantasy." In this sense, Mackintosh represents the British response to the aesthetics of Art Nouveau: the Modern Style (p. 165).

● LIFE AND WORKS

Born in Glasgow in 1868, Mackintosh studied architecture at the School of Art in his native city. From 1884 to 1889, he attended night school while working by day in the studio of the architect John Hutchinson. It was during these student years that he established lasting friendships with Henry MacNeir and the sisters Frances and Margaret MacDonald, who were to become the wives of the two architects. The four friends also had professional interests in common; as artists and painters they formed a group known as "The Four," collaborating on a number of successful design projects. At age 22, Charles won a grant that allowed him to travel through Europe and hone his professional skills. Upon returning to Great Britain, he was employed by the architectural firm of Honeyman & Kep-

Right:
Reconstruction of the dining room designed by Charles Rennie Mackintosh for his own house at 78 Southpark Avenue, in the suburbs of Glasgow.

Below:
Charles Rennie Mackintosh, *Façade of the Glasgow School of Art*, 1897–1909. Glasgow, Scotland. The building of the Glasgow School, finished in 1899, was enlarged in the years 1907–1909.

pie, becoming a partner in 1894. Two years later, The Four were invited to participate in the Arts and Crafts exhibition in London, where their work attracted considerable attention. In 1897, Mackintosh won the competition for the new Glasgow School of Art, designed according to precise rationalist principles that anticipated, albeit in a different style, the ideal of the Bauhaus. His design for the new building of the Glasgow School of Art (1897–1909) combined Scottish baronial, geometric, and Art Nouveau motifs. Mackintosh's furniture designs at the Viennese Secession exhibition in 1900 and the Universal Exposition of Turin in 1901 expanded his reputation and attracted new commissions. Notable among these was the Hill House in Glasgow, acclaimed for its harmonious blend of architectural design and furnishings. Mackintosh died in London in 1928.

Antoni Gaudí

While stylistic definitions help classify and catalogue the artistic currents of a particular period, thereby investing them with historical significance, it is also true that some artists and architects defy categorization under any heading. Such is the case with Antoni Gaudí, whose work is truly unique in the history of architecture. Although the designs of this Catalonian architect are often considered within the sphere of Art Nouveau, his stylistic solutions also anticipated certain aspects of Expressionism—as evident in a comparison of windows on the Batlló House in Barcelona with one of Mendelsohn's sketches for the Einstein Tower (p. 173). Aside from the obvious differences, there is a clear similarity in the use of an aggressive, incisive line, which only the spirited imagination of Gaudí manages

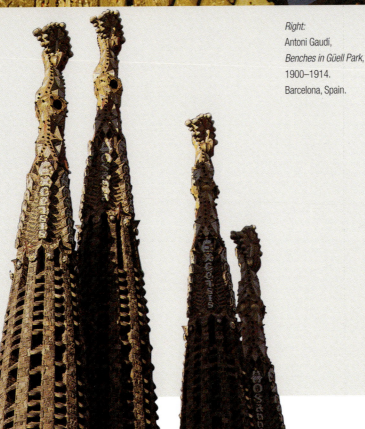

Above and at right:
Antoni Gaudí, *Detail of the spires on the Sagrada Familia,* 1883–1926. Barcelona, Spain.
In this reinterpretation of the Gothic spire, the architect's familiarity with the work of Borromini is clearly evident.

Right:
Antoni Gaudí, *Benches in Güell Park,* 1900–1914. Barcelona, Spain.

to render gentle and light-hearted. Moreover, the Spanish architect's world of form shows an obvious debt to Viollet-le-Duc, whose books helped mold his artistic taste. This is well demonstrated by the work widely regarded as his masterpiece, the Church of the Sagrada Familia in Barcelona, on which he labored assiduously for the last decades of his life. The original plan (set by his predecessor) was Gothic Revival, re-envisioned in an exuberant fantasy that did not hesitate to twist and distort architectural elements as if they were made of soft colored sand. Indeed, the general impression conveyed by the cathedral is that of a sand castle built by children on the beach. Nevertheless, the engineering approach employed by Gaudí was highly refined, achieving effects apparently free from the laws governing static behavior. One of his boldest solutions was

the use of tilted columns capable of absorbing thrust and weight simultaneously, thereby making rampant arches unnecessary. Another characteristic feature of Gaudí's work is its manifestly pictorial quality, which emerges in the soft, enveloping rendering of volumes and the use of simple but brilliantly colored materials capable of transfiguring surfaces already vibrant in their own right. In these aspects, Gaudí was also influenced by the principles of John Ruskin and the Arts and Crafts Movement.

● LIFE AND WORKS

Antoni Gaudí y Cornet was born at Reus, Catalonia, in 1852. He came from a family of craftsmen (his father was a coppersmith from whom he acquired his exceptional manual dexterity) and studied architecture at the Barcelona Acad-

emy. The formation of his complex personal aesthetic was influenced by a variety of factors, including the courses he took in philosophy and romantic aesthetics and his study of the writings of Viollet-le-Duc. One of Gaudí's first clients was Count Güell, a wealthy and highly cultivated Barcelona industrialist for whom he designed the Güell Residence (1885–1889) and Güell Park (1900–1914), the latter entirely tiled in ceramics. Gaudí's prodigious imagination enabled him to satisfy the most traditional commissions without betraying his aesthetic principles, finding inimitable solutions in virtually every instance. A case in point is the Milà House, which revolutionized the aesthetics of the conventional apartment building. He was commissioned in 1882 to complete the Sagrada Familia, which remained only one-quarter finished at the time of his death in 1926.

Antonio Sant'Elia

None of the projects conceived, planned, and designed by the Italian Futurist architect Antonio Sant'Elia was ever built, except for the modest Villa Elisi at San Maurizio near Como, still in the wake of the Secession movement. This was not due to neglect on the part of clients nor to any lack of recognition for his creative talents, but only to a lack of time: Sant'Elia died in World War I at the age of only 28. Although his career was brief and his designs captured only in pencil, paint, and sheets of paper, his ideas left a profound mark on the architectural aesthetics of the new century. Sant'Elia was an early adherent of the Futurist movement, after an early foray into the Liberty style, the Italian version of Art Nouveau, during his years of training. He was, in fact, the author of the "Manifesto of Futurist Architecture" (1914), quoted below in the amended version by Filippo Tommaso Marinetti. Sant'Elia gets to the heart of the matter in the very first sentence, specifically in response to the Liberty experience: "The problem of modern architecture is not a question of linear rearrangement. It is not a question of finding new contours, new framing for doors and windows, of replacing columns, pillars and corbels with caryatids, with blue-bottle flies, with frogs [an obvious reference to Liberty ornamentation]; it is not a question of leaving bare brick on a façade or plastering it over or facing it with stone; it is not a question, in short, of determining formal differences between the new building and the old one, but of creating *ex novo* a new house, constructing it by skillfully applying every resource of science and technology… determining new forms, new lines, a new *raison d'être* only in the unique conditions of modern life."

In other words, the "new house," designated as the image par excellence of the new architecture, should be the "daughter" of this new age, reflecting an inner transformation and not content with *seeming* modern because the windows are oval rather than rectangular in shape. Because the new age cannot be compared with any in the past, architecture must not draw inspiration from tradition or precedent, but must be guided only by science and technology. Sant'Elia continues: "This architecture cannot be naturally subject to any law of historical continuity. It must be as new as our state of mind and the circumstances of our historical moment." Sant'Elia saw an unbridgeable gap between the con-

Above:
Antonio Sant'Elia,
Electric power station,
1914.

Left:
Antonio Sant'Elia,
Eastern end of the Villa Elisi, 1911. San Maurizio, Como, Italy.

tinuity of the previous centuries (which, on the whole, may be regarded as "variations on the theme" of style) and the historical moment of his own time, in which "the perfection of mechanical means, the rational and scientific use of material" were inaugurating a new era in the art of building. He was perhaps the first to interpret the historical moment with such lucid clarity, anticipating the positions later taken by Le Corbusier and Gropius, even if his drawings offered no complete solutions. Despite their sense of the monumental, they continued to reflect the atmosphere pervading in the first decade of the twentieth century after the Viennese Secession.

● LIFE

Antonio Sant'Elia was born in 1888 at Como in northern Italy, where he pursued technical studies. At the age of only 17, he began work as master builder for the city of Milan while attending classes at the Brera Academy. He received his degree in architecture from the University of Bologna and then opened a studio in Milan. He built the Villa Elisi at San Maurizio in 1911, joined the Futurist movement in 1912, and began his visionary project of the *Città Nuova* ("New City") the following year. A volunteer in the Italian army, he died in battle at Monfalcone in October 1916.

Above:
Antonio Sant'Elia,
Electric power station,
1914.

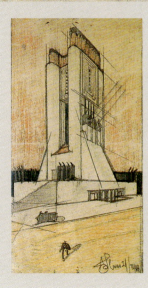

Left:
Antonio Sant'Elia,
*Study for the new
Milan station,* 1914.
Como, Musei Civici.

Antonio Sant'Elia,
Lighthouse Tower,
1914. Como,
Musei Civici.

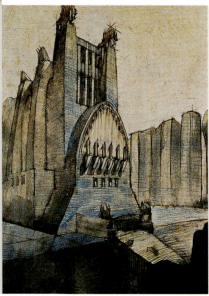

Antonio Sant'Elia,
Monumental building,
1915. Como,
Musei Civici.

Louis Henry Sullivan

The famous dictum "form follows function" summarizes the thought of this modern American architect and characterizes his influence in the renewal of architectural style that took place from the end of the nineteenth century through the first three decades of the twentieth. Sullivan's vision was, however, much more complex than this simple statement might suggest. In an article published near the end of his career, he explained that "Architecture is not a simple art to be practiced more or less successfully: it is a social manifestation. If we want to know why certain things are as they are in our architecture, we must look to our people…. Accordingly, under this light, a critical study of architecture becomes, in reality, a study of the social conditions that produce it." Thus, to amplify the architect's oft-quoted phrase, function is nothing less than a social necessity, and form should follow transformations in the fabric of society, attempting to satisfy its needs. To do so, says Sullivan, architects should invent appropriate forms. He does not claim that society is changed through architecture, but he does believe that the discipline can help society solve its problems. Hence he states, "It is not my purpose to discuss social conditions; I accept them as a fact, and say immediately that the tall building for offices should be taken into consideration and confronted from the start as a problem to be solved; a vital problem, which calls for a vital solution." Thus he commits himself to searching for solutions suitable to a specific purpose. Moreover, as he says in an article published in *Lippincott's Magazine* in 1896, "I am convinced that, by the laws of nature, any problem, in its deepest essence, contains and suggests its own solution." Here again, Sullivan organizes his thinking around the key concept cited above.

In the same long article, Sullivan gives a simple, direct prescription for the design of skyscrapers. In short, the building should include five general levels: a basement containing the heating system and other utility services; a ground floor with banks and shops; a first floor, reachable by stairs, with large meeting rooms and reception halls; above them, an indeterminate number of floors for offices ("one row above another, each office identical to all the others"), which he likened to a honeycomb; and at the top an attic, where "the circulatory system concludes and completes its imposing ascending and descending cycle."

Exemplary in this regard is the Guaranty Building in Buffalo, inaugurated in 1895, a year before the publication of this article.

Below:
Louis H. Sullivan, *Guaranty Building,* 1895. Buffalo, New York.

● LIFE AND WORKS

The "father of the skyscraper" was born in Boston in 1856 and studied briefly at the Massachusetts Institute of Technology before working at architectural offices in Boston and Chicago in 1873. He completed his training at the École des Beaux-Arts in Paris (1874–1876) and in 1879 joined the Chicago firm of Dankmar Adler (1844–1900), the city's leading structural engineer. Their 15-year partnership produced such innovative structures as the Auditorium Building and Stock Exchange Building in Chicago, and Wainwright Building in St. Louis. Sullivan thus emerged as a leading figure the Chicago School of architects, known for steel-skeleton commercial high-rises. But the Chicago World's Fair of 1893 marked the rise of academic classicism, after which Sullivan's success began to decline and his partnership with Adler was dissolved. Later works include the Schlesinger & Mayer (now Carson, Pirie, Scott & Co.) department store in Chicago. He died in 1924 at age 78.

Below:
Louis H. Sullivan, *Façade of the Farmers & Merchants Union Bank*, 1919. Columbus, Wisconsin. Note the elaborate decoration on the entrance, a reference to both Gothic Revival and the Viennese Secession.

Left:
Louis H. Sullivan and Dankmar Adler, *Auditorium Building*, 1887. Chicago. The building, designed to hold up to 4,000 persons, shows the influence of Henry Hobson Richardson, of whom Sullivan was a great admirer. The latter once said that he had decided to become an architect after seeing the Marshall Department Store in Chicago, built by Richardson between 1885 and 1887.

Above:
Schlesinger & Mayer Department Store (1899–1904) in Chicago, in a photograph from the 1920s.

Below:
Louis H. Sullivan, *Schlesinger & Mayer Department Store (now Carson, Pirie, Scott & Co.)*, detail of the entrance portal, 1899–1904. Chicago.

Frank Lloyd Wright

At left and below:
Frank Lloyd Wright, *View of the Winslow House*, 1910. River Forest, Illinois. The design is clearly inspired by traditional Japanese culture.

Above:
Frank Lloyd Wright, *The Willits House*, 1902. Highland Park, Illinois. Wright preferred houses, like this one designed for Ward Willits, organized around the intersection of perpendicular axes.

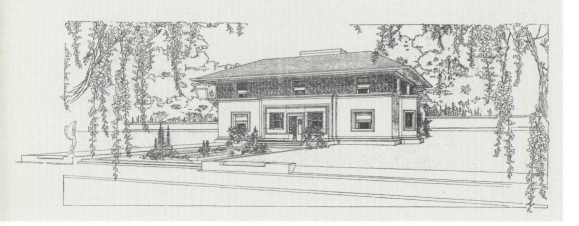

The legacy of Louis Henry Sullivan did not consist only in the realization of buildings that established a new direction (vertical) in building design and construction. The measure of his influence must also take into account the fact that Frank Lloyd Wright, the greatest figure in twentieth-century American architecture, worked for no less than six years in Sullivan's studio and frequently acknowledged his importance, referring to him as "beloved master." Wright developed and extended the concepts of the Adler & Sullivan Studio, influencing at least three generations of architects, not American alone, and constructing more than 300 buildings.

● ORGANIC ARCHITECTURE

The main difference between pupil and master was that Sullivan had European training and felt obligated to defend his own ideas against conventional thinking. Wright, by contrast, took it for granted that conventional architecture had to be revitalized and did not preoccupy himself with defense or diatribe. The driving force behind his renewal was the lifestyle of America society, based on individual initiative. As Wright explained, "Organic architecture more or less means organic society. An architecture inspired by this ideal cannot acknowledge the laws imposed by aestheticism or mere taste, just as an organic society should reject any external impositions on life that contrast with nature and with the character of the man who has found his work and the place where he can be happy and useful in a form of existence suited to him." In short, a society that governs itself according to its own needs creates a new architecture to meet social demands. This was not

Below:
Frank Lloyd Wright, *View of Taliesin West*, 1938–1959. Maricopa Mesa, Paradise Valley, Scottsdale, Arizona.

Erected at Maricopa Mesa in the desert north of Phoenix, the Taliesin West complex includes several buildings designed by Wright, among them his home and teaching center. Wright had bought this vast expanse of land in the foothills of the McDowell Mountains as a place to build his winter residence.

Above:
Frank Lloyd Wright, *Staircase leading to covered walkway of the Hollyhock House*, 1920. Barnsdall Park, Hollywood, Los Angeles, California.
The decorations in this California home are inspired by Native American culture.

Below:
Frank Lloyd Wright, *Fallingwater*, 1936. Bear Run, Pennsylvania. The famous house designed by Wright for Edgar J. Kaufmann, known as Fallingwater, dates from a stage in his career when he made ample use of reinforced concrete.

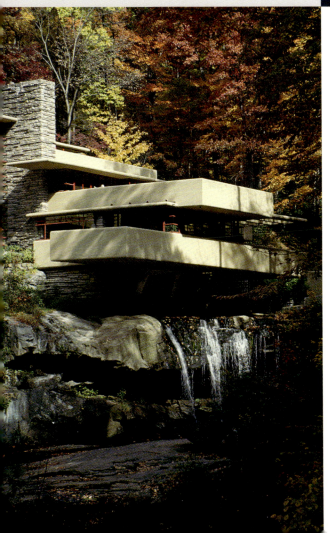

a society of pioneers, strictly speaking, but a society animated by the American pioneer spirit, unbound by the ideological concepts that held sway in Europe. Accordingly, the residential structure preferred by Wright was the single-family house of American and British tradition, but re-elaborating the construction ingenuity of the pioneers to reflect the modern American experience: wide roofs extending over porches, horizontal spaces, and an unbroken relationship between the exterior environment and interior space. The concept culminated in his celebrated Fallingwater (Kaufman House, 1936) near Bear Run, Pennsylvania. It is impossible to understand Wright's work, however, without taking into account the influences of Japanese culture (p.168), the effects of which can be seen in his private home designs up to 1925, and Native American culture. Thus were born the "prairie houses" he designed for wealthy industrialists and professionals, including the famous Robie House (1908–1909) in south Chicago.

● LIFE AND WORKS

Born at Richland Center, Wisconsin, in 1869, Frank Lloyd Wright studied at the Faculty of Engineering of Wisconsin University. At the age of 18, he entered the studio of architect James Lyman Silsbee in Chicago and then that of Sullivan. After traveling in Europe for two years, he settled in 1911 at Spring Green, Wisconsin, where he designed his own home, called Taliesin. Rebuilt several times (as Taliesin II and Taliesin III), it was a crucially important example of architectural experimentation. From 1916 to 1922 he lived in Japan, and from 1931 to 1935 he was engaged in the field of urban planning with the Broadacre City project, an ideal city merging technology and nature in the middle of a prairie. In 1938 he built Taliesin West, a synthesis of all his thoughts on organic architecture. Between 1943 and 1958, he created another of his landmark works, the Guggenheim Museum in New York City (p. 63). Wright died in 1959 at the age of 90.

The Katsura Imperial Villa

Dripstone and fireplace in the antechamber of the Music Pavilion, 1662. Katsura Imperial Villa, Kyoto, Honshu, Japan.

Above:
Room of three mats in the Music Pavilion, 1662. Katsura Imperial Villa, Kyoto, Honshu, Japan. The interiors of the Katsura Imperial Villa show the pronounced tendency toward linearity, lightness, and simplicity that strongly appealed to Wright.

Below:
Piet Mondrian, *Composition with Red, Yellow and Blue,* 1921. The Hague, Gemeentemuseum.

The Japanese imperial residence of Katsura, located near Kyoto, dates from the early Edo period (seventeenth century). It is included in this section of the book in consideration of the fact that it was through Frank Lloyd Wright, Le Corbusier, and some of their contemporaries that the architecture of the Western world was able to assimilate Japanese tradition. Not that Japonism (the taste for things Japanese) was born at this time; one need only recall James McNeill Whistler's famous painting the *Peacock Room* (1876–1877) to recognize that this civilization had been the object of fascination in the West for many years. But it was only starting with Wright that Western architects found themselves not only attracted by Japanese architecture, but actually designing in the same spirit, recognizing in it the confirmation of some of their own intuitions (p. 168). Telling in this regard is a passage from Wright's autobiography, published in 1932, in which the American architect ends by observing that the process of formal simplification toward which he had been tending for years was already clearly present in Japanese prints and architecture: "I later realized that Japanese art and architecture have a truly organic nature… it was a more autonomous product… thus it approached the modern age much more closely than did the art of any European civilization, either present-day or ancient." A few years later, the German architect Bruno Taut (p. 173), who lived and worked in Japan from 1933 to 1936, was to find in the imperial residence at Katsura—which he defined as "an eternal entity"—a model that could be applied to enrich and improve the quality of twentieth-century Western architecture. Furthermore, the linear interiors of the residence closely resemble the simple structural geometry of Mondrian's paintings, although there is no direct relationship between them.

● THE EDO PERIOD

The name comes from the city of Edo (modern Tokyo), which became the seat of government in 1615, under the rule of Shogun Tokugawa Ieyasu, who had established himself as the absolute lord of Japan after destroying the army of his rival, Toyotomi Hydeioshi (died in 1598), and capturing the castle of Osaka. The 264-year Edo (or Tokugawa) Period, distinguished by isolation from the outside world and rejection of foreign influence, especially European, lasted until 1867. During this period, the Japanese nation broadly accepted the ideas of Confucianism, and the feudal structure grew stronger. Economic policy was equally strict, authorizing the recon-

View from the east of the three main buildings. Katsura Imperial Villa, Kyoto, Honshu, Japan.

struction of temples only when destroyed by fire. Japan's isolation was abruptly ended by the cannonades of American battleships (p. 168) in the second half of the nineteenth century.

● THE VILLA OF KATSURA

The Katsura residence belonged to a collateral line of the imperial family, that of the Hachijo, founded in 1590 by the Shogun Toyotomi Hydeioshi, who put it under the leadership of his protégé, Prince Kosamaru, later called Toshihito. The Hachijo imperial villa (see also p. 39), designed by the tea-ceremony master and architect Kobori Enshu (1579–1647), is set in a large garden of the *tsukiyama* ("artificial hill") type, characterized by a vast expanse of land, man-made mounds, and a lake. The serene succession of landscapes is arranged to create the impression of randomness and harmony. The scenery motifs are se-

lected with the greatest care, however, and each theme is isolated as if the garden were a picture gallery of diverse landscapes. Such a design is called "composite," inspired by narrative scroll paintings (*emakimono*) in which the scenes unfold one after another like separate paintings. The villa consists of three main structures: the *Ko-shoin* (old main building), *Chu-shoin* (intermediate building), and *Shin-goten* (new palace). The first two were built for Prince Toshi-hito (1579–1629) and the last for his son, Prince Toshitada (1619–1662). The Music Pavilion dates from 1662. The result is a mingling of different styles: the *shoin*, typical since the Middle Ages of temples and the solid, imposing residences of the Samurai; and "Japanese free style" (later known as *sukiya*). As observed by the famous contemporary architect, Arata Isozaki, Katsura has been fundamental to the development of Japanese modern architecture.

Gate of the garden adjacent to the main entrance of the Ko-shoin, early seventeenth century. Katsura Imperial Villa, Kyoto, Honshu, Japan.

Marcello Piacentini

An exploration of the role played by Marcello Piacentini and his work introduces the complex issue of Italian architecture before and after the rise to power of the Fascist regime (1922–1943). The architect's long career and the superior quality of his work make him well-suited to illustrate the course of an artistic period that is often dismissed as marginal but that in fact intersected with major trends across Europe.

● LIFE AND WORKS

A child of the profession, Marcello Piacentini was born in Rome in 1881. After attending the Institute of Fine Arts in Rome, he trained in the studio of his father Pio Piacentini, a successful architect. In keeping with the fashion of the day, Marcello's work tended toward an eclectic classicism. His achievements were mainly in the field of temporary architectural structures, designs presented at the Brussels Exposition of 1910 and the San Francisco Exposition of 1915. His Corso Cinema in Rome, however, dating from a few years later (1915–1917), aroused heated debate for its modernism. Piacentini differed from his colleagues in other European countries in that he considered the Modernist style to be only one possible solution, and not one imbued with moral or existential imperatives (a view reflected in Hotel Ambasciatori, still suspended between eclecticism and modernist linearity). This helps explain, on the one hand, his untroubled acceptance of Fascist rule and, on the other hand, his equally effortless compromise between Rationalist premises and those deriving from the propaganda of the regime. This led Piacentini to open conflict with the movement of young Rationalist architects known as the MIAR (p. 186). Although he clearly understood the need for a modern, functionalist architecture, he believed that it had to be attentive to tradition and versatile enough to adapt to different contexts—in other words, not radical. This, in addition to his impressive body of work, explains why he was chosen as a project director and special consultant by a number of Italian municipalities. The first was Turin, where he was responsible for the stylistic rearrangement of the Via Roma Nuova between 1934 and 1938.

Piacentini may be called the *arbiter elegantiarum* ("arbiter of taste") of Italian

Left:
Marcello Piacentini,
*Dome on the Church
of Cristo Re*,
1933–1934. Rome.

Above:
Marcello Piacentini,
*The Rectorate
in University City*,
1936. Rome.

architecture during the 20 years of Fascist domination, during which he attempted to create a national image in keeping with the ideals of the regime—a country that was at once Roman, modern, and highly efficient. Some of his finest work may be seen at University City in Rome, where he assumed the role of project director and designed both the Rectorate and the Chapel of Divine Wisdom. He acted in the same capacity at the site of E42, an exposition intended to celebrate the triumph of Fascism but annulled by war and later transformed into the Roman suburb of EUR. There he designed the Palace of Italian Civilization, in which the purity of the lines and volumes serves as a bulwark against rhetoric and complacency. Piacentini faced his harshest criticism after the fall of the Fascist government for his design of Via della Conciliazione, a grandiose approach to St. Peter's Square, intended to fulfill the old dream of Pope Alexander VII. Piacentini died in 1960.

Above:
Marcello Piacentini
and Attilio Spaccarelli,
Via della Conciliazione,
1934–1950. Rome.

Right:
Marcello Piacentini,
*Chapel of Divine
Wisdom in University
City,* 1948–1950.
Rome.

Below:
Marcello Piacentini,
Hall of Justice,
1933–1934. Milan.

Le Corbusier

Defining Le Corbusier is an all but impossible task. In seeking comparisons, one may think of Picasso: just as the painter dictated trends in contemporary art, so the architect, with a steady hand, laid down the lines for the development of contemporary architecture. At the same time, however, it might be noted that the pictorial style of Le Corbusier more closely resembles that of Fernand Léger, with whom he established both a friendly and collaborative relationship. In any case, Le Corbusier may be regarded as the most important architect of the twentieth century on the strength of his imagination, creativity, range of enedavors, and influence on subsequent generations. He was an artist in the broadest sense of the term—an architect, painter, sculptor, furniture designer, urban planner, and architectural theorist—which he understood as a social mission and means of renewing the human spirit. Passages from his "Charter of Athens," a kind of manifesto and handbook for the design of the new city, serve to clarify his positions not only with regard to urban planning. In this text, compiled in 1933 for the fourth congress of the CIAM and published anonymously in 1942, he observes: "Most cities today appear as the image of disorder. These cities do not correspond in any way to their objectives, which should be to satisfy the fundamental biological and psychological needs of their inhabitants…. The violence of private interest causes a catastrophic disruption of the balance between the pressure of economic forces on the one hand and the weakness of administrative control and the impotence of social solidarity on the other…. The size of anything within the urban grid can only be regularized on the human scale." A leading figure in Rationalist architecture (p. 180), Le Corbusier was convinced that logic and reason are the best antidote to unhappiness and disorder. Hence he revived the Renaissance concept of the "golden section," applying it not only to architecture but also to the human figure, according to the principle of the "modulor" (see pp. 8–9). For the same reason, he made every effort to build rational structures in which everything is planned in relation to human experience.

In the end, however, this coolly logical approach proved unsatisfactory even to him, and, rediscovering the emotional potential of exposed reinforced concrete, he inaugurated a new style, Brutalism (p. 183). This crack in the monolithic faith in Functionalism and Rationalism was the first step in a process that would lead to the overall revision of architecture in the twentieth century and to the revival of other styles.

Left:
Le Corbusier, *Detail of the exterior of Villa Savoye*, 1928–1930. Poissy, France.

Above:
Le Corbusier, *Plan Voisin*, 1925. Paris, Le Corbusier Foundation.

● LIFE AND WORKS

Charles-Edouard Jeanneret, known as Le Corbusier, was born in 1887 at La Chaux-de-Fonds, Switzerland, where he attended the School of Applied Arts from 1900 to 1905. Between the ages of 19 and 33, he traveled through Europe and the Middle East to sketch and take notes on architecture. He worked in the studios of Joseph Hoffmann in Vienna (1907), Auguste Perret (1908) in Paris, and Peter Behrens (1911) in Berlin. His first design (never built) was for the so-called Dom-Ino houses (1914–1915), simple, prefabricated, two-story structures. In 1917 he moved to Paris, where he dedicated himself to painting. In 1922 he opened an architecture and design studio with his cousin, Pierre Jeanneret. In 1925 he presented his "Plan Voisin" for the rearrangement of Paris, one of several influential works in the field of urban planning. In 1948 he published *Le Modulor*, a manual of proportions. A leading figure in both the Modern Movement (p. 178) and the International Style (p. 182), Le Corbusier died in 1965.

Above:
Le Corbusier, *Houses of Parliament*, 1956–1965. Chandigarh, India.

Below:
Le Corbusier, Charlotte Pierrand, and Pierre Jeanneret, *Chaise longue*, 1928. This chaise longue was produced by the Cassina furniture company beginning in 1965.

Right:
Le Corbusier, *Convent of Sainte Marie de la Tourette*, 1957–1960. Eveux, Rhône-Alpes, France.

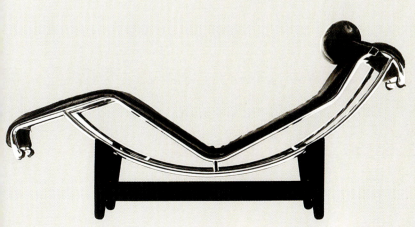

Walter Gropius

The career of Walter Gropius is divided into two distinct periods, separated by World War II. The Gropius of the first period was German and was the more revolutionary and creative architect, influenced by Peter Behrens. In the second phase, he was an American who was both an architect and businessman. The early Gropius was one of the leading proponents of Rationalism; the second Gropius continued to pursue, albeit sometimes wearily, the rationalist formulas of the International Style (pp. 182 and following).

● LIFE AND WORKS

A son and grandson of architects, Walter Gropius was born in Berlin in 1883. He studied architecture first in Munich (1903–1904) and then in Berlin (1905–1907). After traveling through Spain, he worked for the next three years in the studio of Peter Behrens. Under Behrens's guidance, he received training not only in specific technical aspects, but also in experiencing first-hand the contemporary German reality, based on the relationship between creativity and the new industry. It was at this time of rapid in-

Above:
Walter Gropius and Adolf Meyer, *Indoor stairway in the Fagus Works*, 1911–1914. Alfeld-an-der-Leine, Lower Saxony, Germany.

Below:
Walter Gropius and Adolf Meyer, *Fagus Works*, 1911–1914. Alfeld-an-der-Leine, Lower Saxony, Germany.

dustrialization that a group of architects, including Behrens, welcomed the heritage of William Morris's Arts and Crafts Movement and founded an association called the *Deutscher Werkbund* (German Work Association), whose stated purpose was "to select the best from art, industry, craftsmanship and the forces of manual labor." The lack of a recent architectural tradition in Germany comparable to those in England and France meant that the new concepts could be implemented more rapidly here than elsewhere. In 1910, Gropius opened an independent studio and worked in collaboration with Adolf Meyer, who compensated for his lack of drawing skills until 1925. The *Deutscher Werkbund* (with which Gropius was affiliated from 1907 to 1914) had no prejudices with regard to mass-production and was to become the foundation of the Bauhaus

experience (pp. 31 and 179). During this time, the Fagus Works were completed (see also p. 64), establishing Gropius's reputation. Amid the era's enthusiasm for technological progress, the aim of his design was to enable humans and machines to work in perfect symbiosis. It was chiefly the realization of interiors, however, that earned Gropius teaching offers from a number of universities. After World War I, he accepted the directorship of two schools in Weimar that were united under the name of Staatliches Bauhaus in 1919. In 1925, after breaking with Meyer, Gropius designed the building for the new school in Dessau (p. 178). This was one of the most creative periods of Gropius's career, including designs that ranged from the utopian Totaltheater (1926, p. 59) to innovative apartment buildings, from the urban renovation of Dessau (p. 179) to

the realization of such unique building types as that city's employment bureau. With the ascendancy of the Nazi Party in 1933, Gropius was scorned as a "Bolshevik of architecture," increasingly ostracized and finally forced to emigrate to Great Britain, where he was offered the chance to found a British Bauhaus. The more concrete opportunity, however, was a 1934 commission to design a residential complex at Windsor. It was in London also that Gropius published his celebrated book, *The New Architecture and the Bauhaus* (1935). In 1937, having accepted a chair at Harvard University, he moved to the United States. In 1945 he joined with a number of younger architects in forming The Architects Collaborative (TAC), a studio in which he designed such monumental projects as the Pan Am Building in Manhattan (p. 185). Gropius died in 1969.

Above:
Walter Gropius,
The director's house viewed from the southeast, 1926.
Dessau, Germany.
Gropius's design for the Bauhaus in Dessau

included several faculty residences in the woods near the school. Among these were two houses for the professors and a one-family house for the director, who was Gropius himself.

Right:
Walter Gropius and Adolf Meyer, *Sommerfeld House*, 1920–1921. Berlin. This building, the first great project realized by the Bauhaus, is considered the finest architectural example of a "unitary work of art."

Above:
Walter Gropius,
Auditorium of the Bauhaus furnished with seats designed by Marcel Breuer, 1925–1926.
Dessau, Germany.

Ludwig Mies van der Rohe

Reconstruction of the German Pavilion at the International Exposition of Barcelona of 1929, designed by Mies van der Rohe and Lilly Reich. The pavilion, which had been destroyed, was rebuilt in 1986.

Considered one of the principal founders, along with Frank Lloyd Wright and Le Corbusier, of twentieth-century architecture, Mies van der Rohe had a long and brilliant career marked by achievements of the highest order, without compromising his Rationalist principles or aesthetic standards.

● LIFE AND WORKS

Ludwig Mies was born in Aachen, Germany, in 1886. (Van der Rohe was his mother's family name, which he added to his own in 1922). His manual dexterity and attention to detail came from his father's teachings and practice in designing stucco ornamentation, a craft for which his native city was known. He never took a degree in architecture but,

after moving to Berlin at the age of around 20, worked as an apprentice in various architectural firms, one of them specializing in wood constructions. Having joined the studio of Peter Behrens in 1908, he worked with the likes of Walter Gropius and Le Corbusier. He opened his own studio in 1912 and, over the next ten years, formulated the ideas that were later to prove revolutionary. His skyscraper designs presented for the first time the possibility of utilizing exterior walls made of glass to achieve effects of luminosity and transparency (pp. 99, 184–185). In 1922, along with Gropius and others, Mies van der Rohe became a member of the Novembergruppe, an Expressionist movement (named for the month of the Weimar Revolution in 1918) that defined itself as "an association of radical artists—radicals in rejecting the traditional forms of expression—radicals in employing new means of expression."

These principles perfectly suited the German architect, who sought to apply them in his 1923 design for an office building: a simple box made of reinforced concrete and glass, providing an unimpeded view of the landscape. A more traditional application of these principles was evident in the Wolf House in Guben (now destroyed), while a more innovative approach was taken in the Berlin monument to Karl Liebknecht and Rosa Luxemburg (also destroyed). In another important experience of this period, Mies van der Rohe directed the construction of the Weissenhof residential center in Stuttgart, in whose realization many architects, among them Le Corbusier, participated. His highest achievement during these years was the German pavilion for the Internation-

al Exposition of Barcelona of 1929. At the request of Gropius, who had left the Bauhaus, Mies van der Rohe served as the third director of the school from 1930 to 1932, when pressure from the Nazi regime forced him to shut it down. In 1938, he left Germany for the United States, where he served as director of the School of Architecture at the Armour Institute of Technology in Chicago, later known as the Illinois Institute of Technology (ITT). For this institution he designed the Crown Hall, bringing to full maturity his experiments in continuity between exterior and interior. Mies van der Rohe focused on horizontal organisms such as the Neue Nationalgalerie in Berlin and vertical buildings such as skyscrapers. In the first case, he strove to ensure that space, like fluid, traverses the body of the structure; and in the second, that the volume of the skyscraper is a shining, reflecting prism.

Above:
Ludwig Mies van der Rohe, *Neue Nationalgalerie,* 1962–1968. Berlin.

Below:
Ludwig Mies van der Rohe, *Crown Hall at the Illinois Institute of Technology,* 1950–1956. Chicago.

Alvar Aalto

Above:
Alvar Aalto and Elissa Mäkiniemi, *Library of the municipal center, project begun in 1951.* Seinäjoki, Finland.

Right:
Alvar and Aino Aalto, *Armchair made of curved birch wood,* 1935.

A European version of the organic architecture of Louis Henry Sullivan and Frank Lloyd Wright developed independently and incorporated features entirely its own. Among the leading exponents of this style was the Finnish architect Alvar Aalto, along with such others as Hugo Häring, Hans Scharoun, and Louis I. Kahn. The core concept of this movement is that things develop according to their own form, so preconstructed geometric "cages" should never be applied to buildings. The corollary of this theorem is that, wherever possible, synthetic materials should be avoided in favor of natural ones, such as wood, of which Aalto makes extensive use. A classic example is the auditorium of the public library in Viipuri, Finland, widely believed to have been destroyed in World War II but in fact abandoned for a decade and recently restored. The shape of the ceiling was specially designed by Aalto to optimize the acoustics in the auditorium. The ceiling thus appears as a molded cast of emitted sounds, developed on the basis of the "organic" diffusion of sound waves rather than a predetermined geometric form.

● LIFE AND WORKS

The son of a woodskeeper, Hugo Alvar Henrik Aalto was born in Kuortane, Finland, in 1898. His first architectural undertaking, while still a student at the Helsinki Polytechnic Institute, was the construction of a house for his parents at Alajärvi. Having graduated in 1921, he worked for two years in the Projects Department of the Göteborg Exposition. In 1924 he married and took the classic tour to Italy; both of these events eventually had a major influence on his pro-

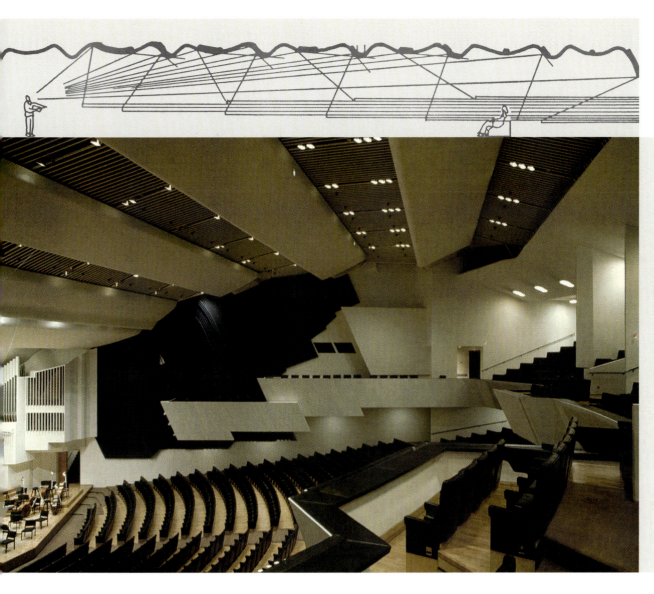

Above:
Alvar Aalto, *Diagram of sound distribution in the conference hall of the municipal library of Viipuri, Finland (1927–1935).*
The ceiling, with the aesthetic quality of abstraction, was designed on the basis of refined logarithms and their geometric application to hall acoustics.

Alvar Aalto, *Interior of the Finlandia Concert Hall*, 1971. Helsinki, Finland.

fessional life. With his wife, Aino Marsio, in fact, he maintained a highly productive working relationship that attached her name to all projects until 1949, the year of her death. The architect's trip to Italy provided the inspiration for his first major work, the Workers' Club in Jyväskylä (1924–1925), a tribute to Florence. The project that made Aalto famous, however, was the Sanatorium in Paimio (p. 61), which spreads across a wide stretch of green landscape, perfectly adapted to the terrain. The design of the building takes into account the path of the sun during the course of the day, allowing patients to benefit from the greatest possible light and heat (precious in a country like Finland). Aalto did not limit himself to the "container," but de-signed all aspects of the building, ex-ternal and internal. To realize his de-signs for furniture made of plywood and curved wood, he even set up a work-shop, which was later transformed in-to a company, called Artek, directed by Aino until 1942. Such intense efforts won the architect his first international recognition in 1937, when the New York Museum of Modern Art organized an ex-hibition of his work. His relationship with America continued in various stages; in 1939 he returned to the United States to set up the Finnish Pavilion at the New York World's Fair, a structure highly praised by Wright. ("Aalto is a genius," he declared). In the years immediately after World War II and the Russian-Finnish War of 1944, the architect was engaged in major urban planning projects, such as that of Rovaniemi in Lapland. He remarried in 1952, and his second wife, Elissa Mäkiniemi, also an architect, began to collaborate with him. With her he designed, among oth-er things, a municipal center in the city of Seinäjoki, grouping together the town hall, an Episcopal church and parish house, a library, and a commu-nity theater. Also fundamentally im-portant was his urban and architectural renovation of Helsinki, beginning in 1960. Aalto worked in many other lo-cations as well: in the Far East, Ger-many, Denmark (the Ålborg Art Muse-um), and Italy (the Cultural Center in Siena and a parish house at Riola di Ver-gato near Bologna). He died in 1976.

Brasília

Above:
*View of Brasília with its
residential islands.*

Below:
*Lucio Costa, Pilot
plan for the Brasília
project,* 1954.

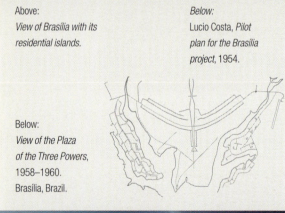

Below:
*View of the Plaza
of the Three Powers,
1958–1960.
Brasília, Brazil.*

The need to create a national architectural style, thereby promoting a common civic identity, was one of the many challenges faced by countries established through the process of decolonization, among which was Brazil. The foundation of a city such as Brasília thus represented a unique opportunity to put into practice, on a broad scale, theoretical premises that would align the architecture of Brazil with the European Rational style and with the concepts of Le Corbusier in particular. The great French modernist, in fact, had been engaged by the Brazilian architect and urban planner Lúcio Costa to consult on designs for the new city. The dual goal was achieved, and international critics have recognized in the development of Brazil's modern architecture an autonomous voice in the worldwide panorama. The other great opportunity was the possibility of studying, as in a laboratory, the formation of an urban organism. Research conducted in 1936 by the Viennese mathematician and architect Christopher Alexander demonstrated that the mental process of designing an "artificial" city can be likened, in the final analysis, to the diagram of a tree. The historical or "natural" city, by contrast, developed according to a more complex model that experts today can reproduce only with sophisticated computer aids.

● HISTORY OF A CITY

The creation of Brasília should be viewed within the context of Brazil's favorable economic circumstances from the late 1950s to the mid-1960s. The new federal capital, built at the initiative of the Ministry of Education and Public Health and of President Juscelino Kubitschek de Oliveira, is located in a federal district along the banks of an artificial lake on the plateau of Goiás state, about 600 miles from Rio de Janeiro. Inaugurated on April 21, 1960, Brasília (see also, p. 17)

Right:
Oscar Niemeyer, *Detail of the city's cathedral*, 1958–1960. Brasília.

Below:
Oscar Niemeyer, *Government buildings*, 1958–1960. Brasília.

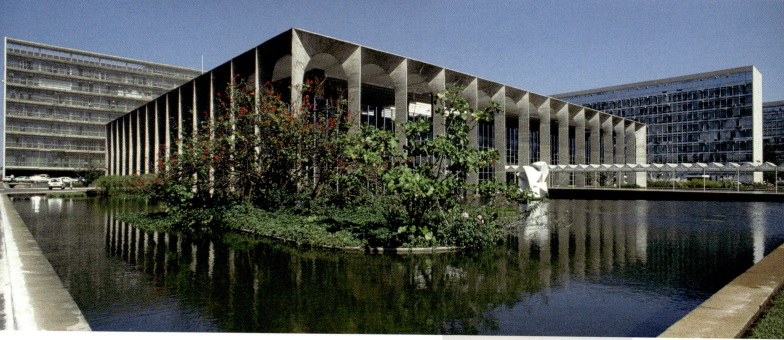

was designed for a population of seven to eight million inhabitants. The basic layout resembles a jet airplane, with residential and commercial areas occupying the wings and government buildings centralized in the fuselage. The main thoroughfare, about six miles long, separates the sections containing residential "superblocks," each with its own school, church, and market, all within a radius of a few hundred yards. Bridges and underpasses take the place of road crossings. Settled areas follow the course of a curved roadway about seven miles long. The solution reflects in part the studies of Le Corbusier, who in 1929 was involved in planning initiatives for several South American cities.

● THE ARCHITECTS

In 1956, when he won the competition to build the city of Brasília, Lucio Costa (1902–1998) was already a world-renowned architect. Among other things,

he had built—with the collaboration of his celebrated countryman, Oscar Niemeyer (1907–1998) and the consultation of Le Corbusier—the seat of the Ministry of Public Education and Health, now known as the Palace of Culture, in Rio de Janeiro. The airplane shape conferred on Brasília was intended as a metaphor of progress and modernity, perhaps also expressing the hope that Brazil would "take off" toward democracy after the overthrow of its dictatorship in 1954. Not by chance, the main inspirers of this great urban initiative were the architects of the "Charter of Athens" (p. 348). The monumental buildings in the heart of the city were designed by Niemeyer. Noteworthy among the new structures is the Plaza of the Three Powers, the seat of the three branches of government (executive, legislative, and judicial). The square is marked by the vertical thrust of a double skyscraper containing administration offices and the horizontal volume of the Houses of Congress.

Lucio Costa and Oscar Niemeyer, *Ministry of Public Education and Health, now the Palace of Culture*, 1936–1943. Rio de Janeiro, Brazil.

The Sydney Opera House

View of Sydney Harbor and the Sydney Harbor Bridge from the Opera House, 1957–1973. Port Jackson, Sydney, Australia.

The Opera House in Sydney, Australia, designed by the Danish architect Jørn Utzon in the late 1950s and completed in 1973, was regarded for years as the avant-garde architectural design par excellence. With its striking visual impact, it was the building most frequently cited as pointing to the future of architecture. Its impact was enhanced by a sort of "Eiffel Tower effect," in that it became an icon universally associated with the Australian continent. Accordingly, Utzon's masterpiece is rightfully included in the "family album" of architectural landmarks of the second half of the twentieth century.

● THE ARCHITECT

Jørn Oberg Utzon was born in Copenhagen in 1918 and trained at the Royal Academy of Art in the Danish capital, where he studied with Kay Fisker (1893–1965). Between 1940 and 1945, Utzon lived in Stockholm, where he was influenced by the designs of Gunnar Asplund (1885–1940), typified by large glass panels supported by a slender steel skeleton. Upon returning to his native land, Utzon worked intensively for a year and in 1946 moved to Helsinki, where he joined the studio of Alvar Aalto. Three years later he traveled to the United States, where he met Frank Lloyd Wright. From there we went on to Central America, visiting remains of the Maya civilization, from which he derived the concept of buildings that comprised only two elements: a platform base and roofing. In 1950, the 32-year-old Utzon opened his own studio in Copenhagen. His first important project was his own house in Hellebaek (north of Copenhagen), inspired by the organic architecture of Wright. The year that definitively changed his life was 1957, when he won the competition for the Sydney Opera House. To supervise the work more closely, he moved to Australia in 1962 and remained there until 1966. Among his other works are the residential complex of Kingo in Helsingør and one in Fredensborg (Denmark), where the arrangement of houses faithfully follows the contours of the land. In 1964 he won the competition for the Zurich Theater and worked on this project until 1970, though the building was never constructed. Between 1972 and 1987, Utzon designed the Parliament House of Kuwait City, considered the finest work of his later period. Here, drawing inspiration from desert bedouins, he seemed to illustrate a statement by Asplund: "It is more important to follow the style of the place

Jørn Utzon and Peter Rice, *Detail of the roofing on the Opera House*, 1957–1973. Port Jackson, Sydney, Australia.

Above and right:
Jørn Utzon and Peter Rice, *Opera House*, 1957–1973. Port Jackson, Sydney, Australia.

Aerial view of Port Jackson and the Opera House. Port Jackson, Sydney, Australia.

than the style of the time." Among his more recent achievements is a house he designed for himself in 1995, located in the mountains of Majorca.

● THE BUILDING

The Opera House has three distinct but harmonious parts: the base, four auditoriums, and multiple roofs. This last element created problems, until Utzon realized that each roof had to form a separate segment of the same ideal sphere, with a diameter of 245 feet. The exorbitant costs forced him to leave the project to others. The building's signature roofs, resembling billowing sails, are flexible structures of pre-stressed reinforced concrete faced with Swedish white Högans tiles, with concrete panels anchored to the roofing shells (installed by the engineer Peter Rice).

Kenzo Tange

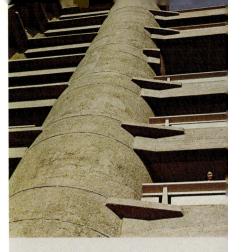

By the mid-twentieth century, the Rationalist style had been exported throughout the world and had emerged as a sort of universal idiom, interpreted in various ways in different cultures. The Japanese architect and urban planner Kenzo Tange, one of the outstanding exponents of the International Style, played a critically important role in two respects: on the one hand, he helped to disseminate in his own country the new concept of architecture elaborated by the West, and on the other hand enriched that concept with his own exquisitely Japanese sensibility.

● LIFE AND WORKS

Kenzo Tange was born in Imabari, southern Japan, in 1913. After studying at the University of Tokyo from 1935 to 1938, he completed his training in the studio of Kunio Maekawa (1905–1986), who had collaborated with Le Corbusier in Paris. In 1946, a year after taking a specialized degree at the University of Tokyo, Tange was granted a professorship,

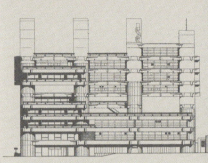

Right:
Kenzo Tange and collaborators, *Olympic gymnasiums in the Sports Palace*, 1961–1964. Tokyo, Japan. The contour of the distinctive roofing recalls that of a pagoda.

Above:
Kenzo Tange, *Press and Broadcasting Center*, detail of a tower and design diagram, 1961–1966. Yamanashi, Kofu, Japan. This multipurpose center was designed so that it could be expanded virtually to the infinite, according to the principles of architectural metabolism. The facilities are contained in 16 towers that could, in theory, be multiplied.

Left:
Kenzo Tange, *Model for the Tokyo urban planning project (1960).* The critical need behind the project was to alleviate traffic jams in the center of Tokyo. Tange, believing that automobile traffic should be facilitated, conceived a "civic axis," or a system of streets connecting self-sustaining districts designated as residential, administrative, or commercial—individual cells in the organism of the city.

Right:
Kenzo Tange, *View from above the Olympics complex*, 1961–1964. Tokyo, Japan.

which he kept until 1974. He opened his own studio in 1946, which was to operate under a succession of names (since 1985, Kenzo Tange Associates). In 1949 he received his first important commission, for the Hiroshima Peace Center, in which he paid homage to the city devastated by an atomic-bomb explosion only four years earlier. His debut on the national scene aroused heated controversy in Japanese cultural circles, however, with the main target of criticism being the Tokyo Town Hall. The building itself is suspended on classical *pilotis* (pillars) in the manner of Le Corbusier, but Tange took care to create spatial continuity between the paved square in front of the building and the area around it, with the refinements of a traditional Japanese garden. Yet it was not until he won a prestigious international award, the Grand Prix

d'Architecture et d'Artbroad, in 1959, that Tange was finally accepted in his homeland without critical reproach. After this he designed a number of important projects, ranging from the Yamanashi Press and Broadcasting Center (1960–1966) in Kofu to St. Mary's Cathedral (1963) in Tokyo, for which he used a type of roofing employed in his dual gymnasium complex for the 1964 Tokyo Olympics. That facility, designed to hold 15,000 spectators, is distinguished by an elegant curvilinear roof made of chain cables, which, in their variety of articulations, form the decorative motif of the entire complex. In the 1960s, Tange's interests turned to the field of urban planning, in which his work effectively melded the two ancient "souls" of Japan: those of the Yayoi and Jomon Cultures, which have permeated artistic tradition from the first

century C.E. to the present. His experiments in structure, meanwhile, looked toward the concepts and theories of architectural metabolism (p. 183), focusing on the realization of a "protean" structure that could in theory, based on a principle similar to that of animal metabolism, be extended infinitely. His 1960 plan for reorganizing the Tokyo metropolis called for the development of a series of megastructures along a main thoroughfare that would be suspended over the bay; commercial, administrative, and residential "islands" would be organically connected by a network of secondary streets. Active throughout the world since the 1970s, Tange soon developed a more international style, as reflected in the New Tokyo City Hall Complex and the towers of the Fiera District Center in Bologna.

Below:
Kenzo Tange,
*Administration Center
(New Tokyo City Hall),*
1986–1995. Shinjuku,
Tokyo, Japan.

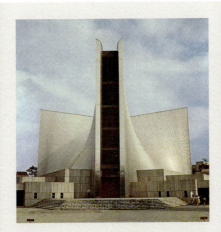

Above:
Kenzo Tange,
*St. Mary's
Cathedral,* 1963.
Tokyo, Japan.
The paraboloid roof

expresses a symbolic
upward thrust imbued
with mystical meaning.
The plan of the building,
designed to hold 1,500,
is cruciform.

Arata Isozaki

The greatness of a master can be measured by the achievements of his pupils as well as by his own work. The impact of Kenzo Tange on Japanese architecture has been immense, bringing to it a sudden and sweeping new way of thinking about the art of building. Through him and thanks to him, the Land of the Rising Sun has added a prominent new voice, at times provocative but always elegant in the extreme, to the artistic panorama of the twentieth century. From his teachings, in the academic as well as the practical arena, a true school of architecture has been born, some of whose members have attained international standing. Among these is Arata Isozaki.

● LIFE AND WORKS

Arata Isozaki was born in Oita, Japan, in 1931. At the University of Tokyo, he studied under Kenzo Tange, entering his studio upon graduating and remaining there until 1963.

The stylistic evolution of Isozaki—who is still active at the international level—has gone through several stages, beginning with his rejection of Metabolism, a current to which he had adhered in the 1960s. As long as he remained in Tange's studio,

Isozaki was chiefly committed to large-scale projects such as the new urban plan for Tokyo, for which his creative contributions consisted of advice and implementation. Years later, Tange involved his former pupil in such projects as the reconstruction plan for the city of Skopje in Macedonia (1965–1966) and the Festival Plaza at the International Exposition of Osaka (1970), projects in which the Metabolism component is clearly evident.

Beginning in the 1970s, however, Isozaki has taken a stylistic direction tending toward simple geometric forms, albeit with a tendency toward fragmentation and combinations that make use of sophisticated new technologies. A good example may be seen in the Kitakyushu Central Library (Fukoka prefecture), whose entrance, composed of cubes and triangles, opens onto an immense reading tunnel that snakes over the terrain like a gi-

Arata Isozaki, *Okanoyama Graphic Art Museum*, 1982–1984. Nishiwaki, Hyogo, Japan.

Above:
Arata Isozaki, *Model for the new exit at the Uffizi,* 1996.

Below:
Arata Isozaki, *Town Hall,* 1975–1978. Kamioka, Japan.

ant worm. Since the late 1970s, Isozaki has tended toward a style close to historicism, a movement still in its early stages at the time. His declaration of purpose can be gleaned from the famous "Strada Novissima" exhibit at the Venice Biennale of 1980, in which, along with such other leading architects such as Hans Hollein (p. 191), he presented fragments of his thinking.

During this period, which continued well beyond the 1980s, albeit with modulations, the Japanese architect enthusiastically embraced influences from the past (Giulio Romano, Étienne Louis Boullée, Claude Nicolas Ledoux, Karl Friedrich Schinkel, and others) as raw material for his own imagination. One example is the Sant Jordi Sports Palace in Barcelona (p. 57), evocative of Palladio's basilica in Vicenza but reinterpreted through the use of advanced technology. The Country Club of Fujimi as well, with a rounded arch

resting on an architrave, could be a free interpretation of a Palladian villa, while his design for a new exit at the Uffizi in Florence alludes to the medieval Loggia dei Lanzi in Piazza della Signoria. In recent years, Isozaki has also followed the model of hetoropia (p. 197), emphasizing the contrast between a building and its environment.

He explains it this way: "A town hall may look like a spaceship docked in a quiet city, another construction may resemble a whale beached at the base of a castle...." The remark seems well suited to his Center of Japanese Art and Technology (1990–1994) in Cracow, Poland, standing on the slope of a hill dominated by a castle. Other later works include the Museum of Contemporary Art in Los Angeles (opened 1986), the Tokyo University of Art and Design (1990), and new galleries for the Guggenheim Museum (1992) in New York.

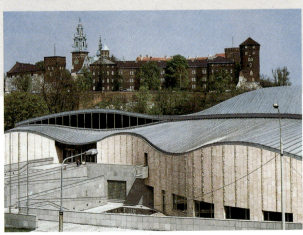

Left:
Arata Isozaki, *Center of Japanese Art and Technology,* 1990–1994. Cracow, Poland.

Above:
Arata Isozaki, *Cultural center and conference hall,* 1999. Shizuoka, Japan.

The Louvre
and Ieoh Ming Pei

The work that cemented the reputation of I.M. Pei, the only Chinese-born architect of note on the current world scene, is the glass pyramid he designed in 1983 for the entrance to the Louvre Museum in Paris. With the building's Renaissance façade as a backdrop, the pyramid was intended not only to rejuvenate the image of the great French art museum but also to adapt the structure to contemporary needs: specifically, to properly welcome a growing number of visitors and to modify, without transforming, the architectural balance of a building that is itself a work of art. Pei's project was therefore carried out in two stages. The first consisted of arranging the main entrance, created in a vast area under Napoleon's Courtyard. Visitors would now be routed along three underground arms to the wings of the historic building. The new structure, in keeping with modern museum standards, provides services of every kind: information desks, a coatroom, several ticket offices, cafés and a cafeteria, a large library, and an auditorium. In short, the pyramid on the ground level, assisted in its function as a skylight by two smaller ones, is only the tip of the technological and architectural iceberg conceived by Pei for the Louvre. The first phase, completed in 1987, was followed by the one concluded in 1993, in which the Richelieu Wing, until then occupied by the Ministry of Finance, was converted into an exhibition area. Promoted by then President François Mitterrand, the overall initiative transformed the Louvre into one of the world's most modern museums.

● LIFE AND WORKS

Ieoh Ming Pei was born in Canton, China, in 1917, and emigrated to the Unit-

Below: Pei Cobb Freed & Partners, *View of the Puget Courtyard in the Richelieu Wing of the Louvre,* 1987–1993. Paris.

Top:
Ieoh Ming Pei & Partners, *Entrance pyramid of the Louvre,* 1983–1987. Paris.

Above:
Ieoh Ming Pei & Partners, *Access stairs to the Louvre underground,* 1983–1987. Paris.

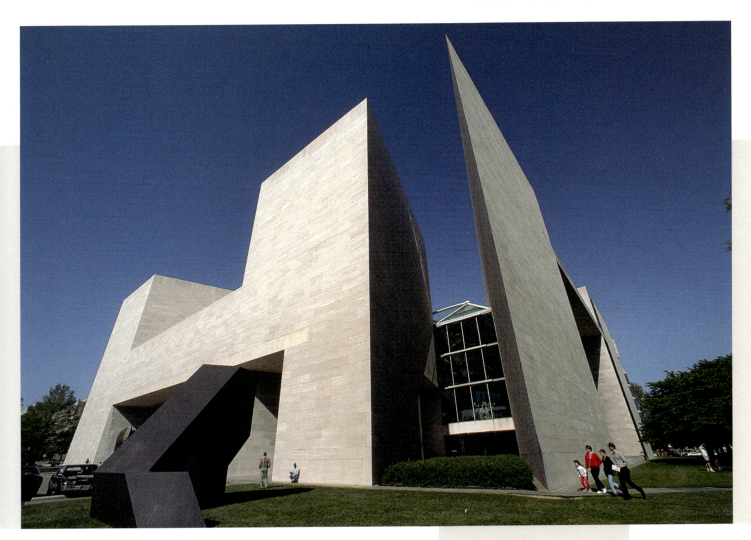

ed States at the age of 17. He studied at Massachusetts Institute of Technology and then with Walter Gropius at Harvard University. In partnership with the New York real estate developer William Zeckendorf, he earned his first major commissions in the period 1948–1955. At the age of 38 he established his own firm in New York City, which remains one of the most prominent in the United States today. A number of private and public commissions were forthcoming, including the East Wing of the National Gallery of Art (1978) in Washington, D.C. As if extolling Rationalist concepts, the clean, solid forms of the structure create a sense of the monumental evocative of the classical and the elemental. The wide range of projects handled by Ieoh Ming Pei & Partners (renamed Pei Cobb Freed & Partners in 1989) has nevertheless al-lowed the firm to develop specific stylistic aims, attentive to the latest innovations, all with the primary purpose of optimizing the functionality of the designs regardless of individual aesthetic choices. Paradoxically, the work of Pei at the end of the twentieth century and beginning of the twenty-first has revived concepts that were typical of the nineteenth. But the studio has also produced designs tending toward the Postmodern (such as the Holocaust Museum in Washington) and of a decidedly high-tech inspiration. An example of the latter is the skyscraper erected as headquarters of the Bank of China in Hong Kong, which has rapidly become a symbol of both the city itself and the advent of capitalism in the People's Republic. Modern luxury hotels in Beijing and elsewhere in China further attest to that transformation.

Above:
Ieoh Ming Pei, *East Wing of the National Gallery*, 1968–1978. Washington, D.C.

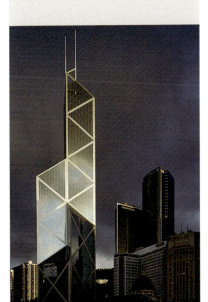

Left:
Ieoh Ming Pei & Partners, *The Bank of China tower*, 1982–1990. Hong Kong, China.

Robert Venturi

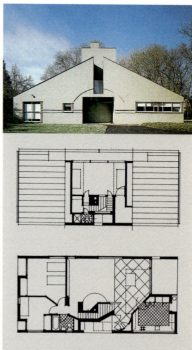

Right:
Robert Venturi
(with Arthur Jones),
House for Vanna Venturi,
1959–1964. Chestnut
Hill, Pennsylvania.
For his mother's house,
Venturi drew inspiration
from traditional
American home
designs. In the plan
shown here, the
fireplace acts
as the "fulcrum"
of the entire residence;
from it departs
the staircase leading
to the upper floor.

During the 1960s, the contribution of Robert Venturi to the debate on architecture and its new stylistic trends was, at first, little more than theoretical. Indeed his publications and critical assessments were much more important than his architectural achievements, although his designs were consistent with the concepts expressed in his books. In his essay on contemporary trends, "Complexity and Contradiction in American Architecture" (1966), he offered a controversial interpretation of the interwoven but not entirely coherent stylistic currents in Western architecture and proposed a revival of the so-called "vernacular" architecture. In Venturi's opinion, vernacular design could claim an impor-

tant place in the American heritage and had been unjustly sacrificed on the altar of architectural Rationalism. International recognition was accorded to Venturi in 1972 when, along with Steven Izenour and Denise Scott Brown, he published *Learning from Las Vegas*, in which he focused on the "lesser" architecture made up of advertising, lights, neon signs, and false façades, and promoted it as a paradigm in opposition to the stilted seriousness of the International Style. Suddenly, a form of architecture previously regarded as trash became a source of *learning*, an architectural culture full of life and irony. In expressing this concept, Venturi's books made an essential contribution to the formulation of the Postmodern movement (pp. 189–191), demolishing the reverential aura that had surrounded the International Style. With the "Strada novissima" exhibit presented, with others, at the Venice Biennale of 1980, Venturi became one of the high priests of Postmodernism.

Right:
Robert Venturi,
John Rauch,
and Denise Scott
Brown, *Brant House,*
1970–1973.
Greenwich, Connecticut.
This luxurious home
was inspired by the
work of Adolf Loos.

Above:
Venturi, Scott Brown
and Associates,
*Emergency Service
RCID for Disney World,*
1993. Orlando, Florida.
Here Venturi makes use
of what he had learned
from Las Vegas.
The building is tiled
with ceramic panels
in bright, gaudy colors
that camouflage
a utilitarian facility—
a fire department
headquarters.

● LIFE AND WORKS

Born in Philadelphia, Pennsylvania, in 1925 to a family of Italian origin, Robert Venturi studied at Princeton University. After receiving his degree in architecture, he worked, starting in 1958, with such celebrated professional firms as those of Louis I. Kahn and Eero Saarinen. At the same time, until 1977, he also taught at the University of Pennsylvania in Philadelphia. In 1964 he formed a partnership with John Rauch and three years later with Denise Scott Brown, who then became his wife. (Since 1989 their studio has been known as Venturi, Scott Brown and Associates). During the same period in which he was launching his invectives against the International Style, Venturi put his convictions into practice in the house he built for his mother, Vanna Venturi, in Chestnut Hill, Pennsylvania. Here the architect exploited the traditional repertoire of the typical American one-family house, giving it a new interpretation with an unusual sense of space. The

Above and right:
Venturi, Scott Brown
and Associates,
*Sainsbury Wing
of the National Gallery*,
1991. London.

ironic aspect of his style clearly emerged in his later projects, such as the Franklin House in Philadelphia, where a slender metal contour evokes the volumes of the house owned by Benjamin Franklin on the same site. Decidedly oriented toward the Postmodern, instead, is his design for the Sainsbury Wing extension of the National Gallery in Trafalgar Square, London, in which a visual tie to with the original building is provided by the adoption of the Corinthian order for columns and pilasters, which gradually become fewer as the new construction takes shape. By contrast, the RCID fire-department building for Disney World has an ironic, cartoonist look.

Frank Owen Gehry

With Frank Gehry, we reach the generation of architects who rely on the computer not only to execute drawings, outlines, and other design documents, but also to bring the design process from the realm of intuition and ideas into the concrete world of feasibility and realization. As Gehry has declared, not without irony, "My sketches are gestures: How could I ever build them? I have been able to do so thanks to the computer; otherwise I wouldn't even have tried." His comment reflects how greatly the architectural profession has changed since three-dimensional digital models have made it possible to visualize a building even before it has been constructed. Yet imagination and inventiveness remain the greatest attributes of Gehry, who, since the late 1980s, has conceived of buildings as sculptures or quasi-organic assemblies of volumes rather than as mere containers. The Guggenheim Bilbao Museum in Spain (1991–1997), for which he is rightly celebrated, is the expanded, protean elaboration of a concept he had formulated in 1987 (when electronics did not yet offer the astonishing possibilities of today) with the realization of the Vitra Design Museum at Weil am Rhein, Germany.

In the Bilbao museum, Gehry's obective was to create a building with a spectacular visual impact, and the result was like a work of art carved in a gleaming film of titanium. Future and past mingle in references to Cubism and Futurism, or perhaps a fanciful *Nautilus* from the imagination of Jules Verne. A spaceship or protean life form, the Bilbao museum covers more than 250,000 square feet with nonchalant disregard for the laws of statics, narcissistically admiring its own image in an artificial lake on the

Below:
Frank O. Gehry, *Sketch for the Guggenheim Museum in Bilbao,* 1991–1997.

Above and right:
Frank O. Gehry, *Guggenheim Museum,* detail of the roof and view of the exterior, 1991–1997. Bilbao, Spain.

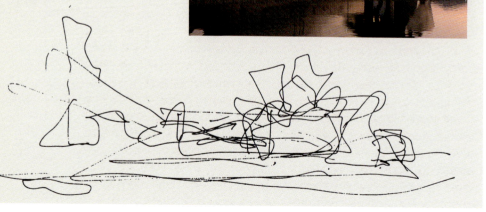

Left:
Frank O. Gehry,
*Detail of the exterior
structure of the Vitra
Design Museum,*
1987–1989. Weil
am Rhein, Germany.

Below and left:
Frank O. Gehry,
Venice Beach House,
1987. Venice, California.

Below:
Frank O. Gehry,
Chiat-Day-Mojo Offices,
1985–1991.
Venice, California.

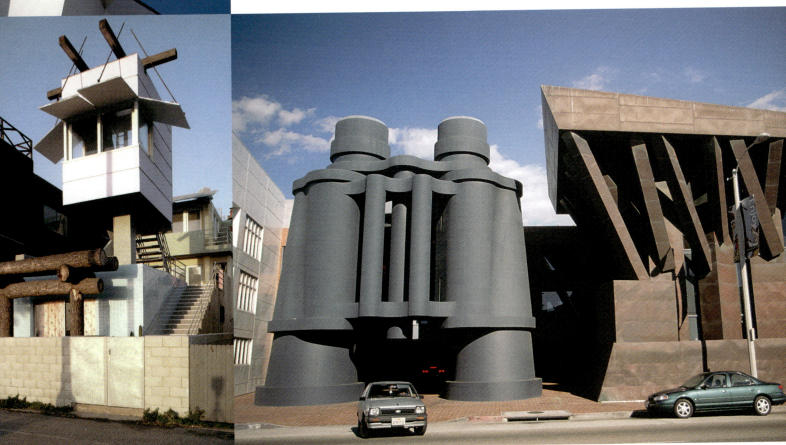

banks of the Nervión River. The museum is also a masterpiece from the point of view of structural engineering, exploiting every potential of galvanized steel in order to limit the cost, and maximize the impact, of the structure. The surface of the roof is covered in titanium scales with a thickness, or rather a thinness, of one-hundredth of an inch.

● LIFE AND WORKS

Frank Owen Gehry was born in Toronto in 1929 and studied in the United States at the University of Southern California at Los Angeles and Harvard University. Beginning in 1953 he worked at various professional studios, finally opening his own in 1962. The ear-

ly stage of his career was not marked by any major commissions, as he was engaged mainly in designing stores and one-family houses, but his tendency toward architectural deconstruction emerged emphatically. This path was to culminate in the reinvention of his own house, a conventional Dutch Colonial in Santa Monica, California, which he transformed into an internationally acclaimed expression of Deconstructivist principles (p. 193). Yet it is impossible to classify Gehry in this or any other stylistic category. In works such as the Chiat-Day-Mojo offices (1985–1991) in Venice, California, based on a sketch by the sculptor Claes Oldenburg, Gehry fully embraced the language of Pop Art while confer-

ring on it a monumental dimension. The pair of binoculars conceived by Oldenburg becomes a portico that enlarges, but in no way conceals, an everyday object. Deconstructivism makes a return in the Nationale-Nederlanden Building in Prague (1992–1996), whose two towers, one leaning against the other in apparent partial collapse, is a comment on the vernacular of modern urban life. More recent commissions include the new Guggenheim Museum in New York City, a design in which the rigid form of skyscrapers is fragmented and re-elaborated in a curvilinear body evoking the motion of water and the energy of the city, and the Walt Disney Concert Hall in Los Angeles, opened in 2003.

Renzo Piano

Above and below:
Renzo Piano and Peter Rice, *Tjibaou Cultural Center*, 1991–1998. Nouméa, New Caledonia.

Above:
Piano & Rogers, *Georges Pompidou Center*, 1971–1977. Paris. Underlying Piano's formal choices are an allusion to the visionary drawings of Sant'Elia (p. 338) and the "early-futurist" style developed by Archigram, a group of London architects and designers (1960).

Below:
Renzo Piano and Peter Rice, *The Menil Collection building*, 1981–1986. Houston, Texas.

The steel-and-concrete roof is designed to optimize natural light falling on the works of art.

In the collective memory, the figure of Renzo Piano is still closely associated with the work that brought him to the forefront of the international architectural scene: the Georges Pompidou Center (1972–1978) in Paris. The reason for such lasting identification may have to do with the fact that the Beaubourg, as it is familiarly known, was the first building to overturn common assumptions about the visible boundaries of construction. Until then, even the most innovative designs had taken care, if not to conceal, at least not to display the structural "secrets" of the building. In other words, ventilation ducts, air-conditioning systems, elevators, stairways, and the like were carefully walled off and concealed, leaving the visual field open to the clarity of volumes and interplay of aesthetic elements. In this sense, the Beaubourg, however engaging or even agreeable, was like a punch in the stomach. Looking at it was like observing an organism in perpetual X-ray. Nothing if not revolutionary, the building inaugurated the current in modern architecture that goes by the name of High Tech (p. 194) and makes use of the most advanced technologies. The Beaubourg was not, however, a gratuitous exhibition of eccentricity or an indulgent exercise in bravura, but was designed to meet demands for functional flexibility. It was, in a word, an enormous container, appropriately called a "cultural machine," with no less than 80,000 square feet entirely free of structural encumbrances.

Left and above:
Renzo Piano and others, *Reconstruction of Potsdamer Platz,* 1992–2000. Berlin. Promoted by the Daimler-Benz Company after the fall of the Berlin Wall, the reconstruction plan has upgraded the area, devastated during World War II and then gutted during the erection of the Wall. The initiative, based on a master plan by the Renzo Piano Building Workshop, involves such other notable architects as Isozaki, Rogers, Kollhoff, and Moneo. The plan included 19 buildings, to be used as offices, apartments, and an IMAX movie theater.

All such elements had been moved to the perimeter of the building (200 x 560 feet), while the steel-and-cast-iron skeleton spanned an interior space of no less than 160 feet. The Pompidou Center is thus fully entitled to be called "multipurpose." From a purely aesthetic viewpoint, it represented a major turning point on the issue of a building's relationship with its setting, inaugurating a trend that was to develop into Heterotopia (p. 197).

● LIFE AND WORKS

Born in Genoa in 1937, Renzo Piano studied at the University of Florence and the Milan Polytechnic Institute, earning a degree in architecture in 1964.

Immediately involved in international projects, he worked at the studio of Louis I. Kahn in Philadelphia (p. 187) and then in London. In 1971, in collaboration with Richard Rogers (p. 194), he designed the Pompidou Center. In 1977 he began to work with Peter Rice, the engineer who had helped solve the structural problems of the Sydney Opera House, with whom he was to collaborate until 1993. In 1981 he founded the Renzo Piano Building Workshop, with offices in Paris and Genoa, carrying out projects throughout the world. Piano's artistic vision has found expression in various fields, such as urban planning and theater, and his versatility in architecture itself is evidenced by such works as the Menil Collection building in Hous-

ton, which in some sense can be considered "anti-Beaubourg." Its halls lit by natural sunlight, the building is far removed from technological exaggeration. Piano has also frequently employed high-tech forms of expression, as in the Nouméa Cultural Center in New Caledonia, in which the use of a traditional material like wood is used to produce a surprisingly new form. With the same creative freedom, the architect has designed the Museum of Science and Technology in Amsterdam, which looks like an immense ship about to set sail for the unknown, in perfect harmony with its seaport environment. Along with other architects, Piano collaborated in the rebuilding of the Potsdamer Platz, where the Berlin Wall once stood.

Santiago Calatrava

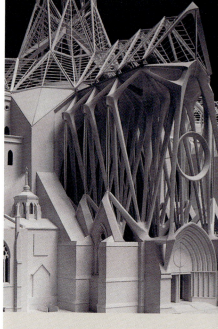

Above:
Santiago Calatrava,
*Model of the south
transept for the church
of St. John the Divine in
New York* (1991).

The debate between architects and engineers since the middle of the nineteenth century as to whether construction employing new technologies called for a director who was more an architect or an engineer, has found, at least in part, an answer in the work of Santiago Calatrava, who is both. On the basis of his training, the Spanish architect falls within that creative current whose starting point was the work of Gustave Eiffel (p. 332) and which, during the twentieth century, could boast outstanding achievements by the Spanish architects Eduardo Torroja y Miret (1899–1961) and Felix Candela (1910–1997), the Italians Pier Luigi Nervi (p. 186) and Riccardo Morandi (1902–1989), the Englishman Ove Arup (1895–1988), and the German Frei Otto (b. 1925). Calatrava's orientation is, obviously, that of high tech, but with a personal interpretation that focuses attention on organic forms of striking and disturbing effect. In an innovative creative process, he originates his designs in sculpture, watercolor, and drawings without particular regard to structural realization. Yet, gifted with prodigious technical skill, he never betrays the original plan, a case in point being the Montjuic Telecommunications Tower (1991) in Barcelona, which soars upward like an arrow aimed at the sky; the form was based on a Calatrava sketch of a kneeling figure making an offering. His chief interest, in fact, is the dynamism inherent in certain forms, as exemplified by the

Santiago Calatrava, *Rhône Alpes Satôlas TGV Station*, 1989–1994. Lyon (Rhône, France). The construction is highly evocative in appearance, suggesting a hybrid between a train and an airplane, a sort of modern technological animal that evokes an intense dynamism.

Above:
Santiago Calatrava,
*Watercolor designs
for the Rhône Alpes
Satôlas TGV station in
Lyon,* c. 1989.

Alameda Subway Station Bridge in Valencia, bent like a bow drawn taut.

● LIFE AND WORKS

A leading figure in the fields of contemporary architecture and engineering, Santiago Calatrava was born in Benimamet, not far from Valencia, Spain, in 1951. From 1968 to 1969, he studied at the Valencia School of Art and until 1973 at the Escuela Técnica Superior de Arquitectura. After moving to Zurich in 1975, he graduated from the Polytechnic Institute there in 1981, presenting a doctoral thesis on the behavior of flexible structures, trusses in particular. With his sound technical background, Calatrava began to conceive works in which the determining element consists of the structure itself, not a simple element supporting a roof but a form dynamically projected into space, "from inside to outside," as he has repeatedly affirmed. An example of great visual impact, ever evocative of speed, is the high-speed train (TGV) terminal of the Lyon-Satôlas station, which links the city to its airport. His interest in forms projected into space is not, however, a sterile exercise born of a craze for modernity, but rather a reflection of the heart of Calatrava's endeavor: to explore the relationship between structure and form. "Mine is… a research in the direction of what I am sometimes presumptuous enough to call sculpture," he has said. This may also explain why he participated in the competition held in 1991 for the rebuilding of the Cathedral of St. John the Divine in New York, one of the city's great landmarks. The design presented by Calatrava called for the addition of a transept revisited in Gothic style; a biosphere suspended 165 feet above the crossing of the transept and the central nave; and a hanging garden on the roof, a clear allusion to biblical paradise. While most famous for his bridge designs, Calatrava in January 2004 unveiled a typically soaring plan for the new World Trade Center transportation hub in New York City.

Above:
Santiago Calatrava,
Alamillo Bridge, 1992.
Seville, Spain.

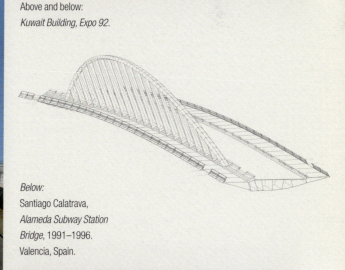

Above and below:
Kuwait Building, Expo 92.

Below:
Santiago Calatrava,
*Alameda Subway Station
Bridge*, 1991–1996.
Valencia, Spain.

Index of names

The numbers in italics refer to illustrations and captions, those in boldface to pages in this volume.

Credits

Archivio Giunti (in alphabetical order): 230b, 275a (Atlantide/Stefano Amantini); 14-15b, 19al, 133 (Atlantide/Massimo Borchi); Giuliano Cappelli, Florence: 201cr; Claudio Carretta, Pontedera: 28b; Dario Coletti, Rome: 82cr, 229b; Patrizio del Duca, Florence: 81br; Giuseppe De Simone, Florence: 103bl; Antonio di Francesco, Genoa: 125br; Jona Falco, Milan: 48a; Stefano Giraldi, Florence: 35bl, 101bl, 161al, 165ar, 279ar, 279bl, 287a, 287br; Nicola Grifoni, Florence: 16b, 17b, 19br, 28-29, 33, 34bl, 34r, 44, 50, 54al, 60b, 63bl, 66al, 69a, 72-73, 73al, 76-77, 79, 80ar, 80bl, 80-81, 81ac, 86bl, 88ar, 89bl, 89br, 90b, 91ar, 92-93, 94, 94-95, 98bl, 100 bl, 103a, 106-107, 112a, 114br, 116, 124r, 135b, 139bl, 140al, 143c, 143br, 144al, 144ar, 145ar, 146r, 214bc, 214br, 215al, 216ar, 216-217, 217ar, 217bl, 217br, 220, 220-221, 222-223a, 222-223b, 224al, 224-225, 225a, 225cl, 225cr, 227b, 228cr, 228b, 229cl, 233br, 234al, 234-235, 235r, 236cl, 238a, 259ar, 290; Aldo Ippoliti, Rome (Concessione S.M.A. no. 945 of 18/11/1993): 43c; Nicolò Orsi Battaglini, Florence: 62ac; Marco Rabatti-Serge Domingie, Florence: 62l, 142, 278a, 286-287, 296; Humberto Nicoletti Serra, Rome: 99bl, 118l, 146, 147a, 147cl, 230a, 232r, 305br, 322ar, 326-327, 326-327; Gustavo Tomsich: 305ar.

Atlantide, Florence (in progressive order): 40-41 (Massimo Borchi); 41a (Stefano Amantini); 55br, 69b (Massimo Borchi); 160br (Guido Cozzi); 163a (Stefano Amantini); 186ar (Concessione S.M.A. n. 01-295 del 21/06/1995); 294bl (Guido Cozzi).

Contrasto, Milan: 98a, 215br, 262cr, 302-303, 307bc, 315bl (Erich Lessing); 317c (Gamma), 329cr (Erich Lessing), 330 (Gamma), 352a, 352b (Erich Lessing); 356a, 356bl, 357a (Gamma); 358-359 (Massimo Mastrorillo); 359a (Wes Thompson); 359c (Massimo Mastrorillo); 359bl (Alexis Duclos); 364bl (Craig/ Rea); 368b (Massimo Mastrorillo); 370al (Gamma); 371a, 371c (Gianni Berengo Gardin).

Corbis/Contrasto, Milan: 14c (Karen Huntt Mason); 16-17 (James Davis); 26-27 (Yann Arthus-Bertrand); 27 (Roger de la Harpe/Gallo Images); 32al (Earl & Nazima Kowall); 34al (Archivio Iconografico, S.A.); 35r (Paul Almasy); 36b (Ric Ergenbright); 37a (Ruggero Vanni); 43br (Adam Woolfitt); 48bl (GE Kidder Smith); 49a (Chris Lisle); 51c (Paul A. Souders); 52r (John Slater); 55a (John Dakers); 56 (Macduff Everton); 58-59 (Angelo Hornak); 60-61 (Christine Osborne); 61ar (Eric Dluhosch, Owen Franken); 66ar (© Bettmann/Corbis); 67br (Chris Bland); 68-69 (Joseph Sohms/Visions of America); 71a (Oriol Alamany); 71br (Philip Gendreau); 73br (Dave G. Houser); 74al (Sandro Vannini); 78r (Adam Woolfitt); 83l (Werner Forman); 96ar (Ruggero Vanni); 97b (© Bettmann/Corbis); 100br (Gillian Darley); 101a (Adam Woolfitt); 104 (Archivio Iconografico, S.A.); 104-105 (Adam Woolfitt); 107b (Harald A. Jahn; Viennaslide); 110b (© Bettmann/ Corbis); 111 (Gianni Dagli Orti); 112-113 (Roger Wood); 113 (Kevin Fleming); 117 (Paul Almasy); 119br (Diego Lezama Orezzoli); 121al (Sandro Vannini); 124l (Mimmo Jodice); 125bl (Vittoriano Rastelli); 129b (Paolo Ragazzini); 130-131 (Robert Holmes); 134-135 (Kevin R. Morris); 136-137 (Pierre Colombel); 137a (John T. Young); 141 (Mimmo Jodice); 146l (Araldo de Luca); 148-149 (Yann Arthus-Bertrand); 149ac (Philippa Lewis); 149br (Macduff Everton); 152a (© Historical Picture Archive/Corbis); 152br (Lindsay Hebberd); 153a (Sheldan Collins); 153b (Stephanie Colasanti); 154al (Paul Almasy); 154b (Charles Lenars); 154-155 (Kevin Schafer); 155c (Gian Berto Vanni); 157a (Robert Holmes); 157b (Joseph Sohm); 158bl (Cuchi White); 159a (Robert Holmes); 161br (Dallas and John Heaton); 163cl (Marc Garanger); 163cr (© Corbis); 164b (Andrea Jemolo); 165al (José F. Poblete); 166 (Paul Seheult); 167b (Sakamoto Photo Research Laboratory); 168-169 (Michael S. Yamashita); 170cl, 170br (Andrea Jemolo); 171b (Archivio Iconografico, S.A.); 178 (Ruggero Vanni); 181r (© Bettmann/Corbis); 182 (Archivio Iconografico, S.A.); 183c (Gillian Darley); 184b (© Lake County Museum); 188cl (Layne Kennedy); 188cr (Angelo Hornak); 189al (Raymond Gehman); 190c (Werner H. Müller); 193ar (Richard Schulman); 194r (Macduff Everton); 195a (Yann Arthus-Bertrand); 195c (Pawel Libera); 196ar (Grant Smith); 196bl (Craig Lovell); 197bl (G.E. Kidder Smith); 201b (Michael S. Yamashita), 202a (Michael Nicholson), 202-203 (Gian Berto Vanni); 203 (Michael S. Yamashita); 204 (Yann Arthus-Bertrand); 206-207 (Paul Almasy); 207b (Diego Lezama Orezzoli); 208al (Dean Conger); 209a (Nik Wheeler); 209b (David Forman/Eye Ubiquitous); 210l, 210r, 211c (Roger Wood); 211a (Paul Almasy); 211b (Nik Wheeler); 212-213 (Charles & Josette Lenars); 213bl (Chris Lisle); 213br (Roger Wood); 218 (© Bettmann/Corbis); 218-219 (Michael Maslan Historic Photographs); 221c (Roger Wood); 222b (Wolfgang Kaehler); 223br (James Davis); 226c (Chris Lisle); 227cl (Richard T. Nowitz); 227cr (Ruggero Vanni); 231c (Jonathan Blair); 233bl (Richard T. Nowitz); 234bl (Roger Wood); 236cr (Chris Ellier); 237c (David Lees); 238b (Paul H. Kuiper); 239a (Adam Woolfitt); 239b (Andrea Jemolo); 240l (Vanni Archive); 241l (Ruggero Vanni); 242 (Aaron Horowitz); 243l (Sandro Vannini); 243r (David Lees); 244l (Carmen Redondo); 244r (Lucidio Studio Inc.); 245cl (Pierre Colombel); 245cr (Archivio Iconografico, S.A.), 245b (Dave G. Houser); 247r (Adam Woolfitt); 248 (Roger Wood); 249cr (Carmen Redondo); 250 (Richard T. Nowitz); 251a (Luca I.Tettoni); 251b (Christophe Loviny); 252b (Charles & Josette Lenars); 252a (Jack Fields); 253c (Lindsay Hebberd); 253b (Earl & Nazima Kowall); 255 (Ruggero Vanni); 256a (Paul Almasy); 256c (Gian Berto Vanni); 257a (Patrick Ward); 257c, 259cl (Angelo Hornak); 258b (Vanni Archive); 260a (Franz-Marc Frei); 260b (Gail Mooney); 262cl (Carmen Redondo); 262b (Bob Krist); 263cl (Vanni Archive); 263cr (Mimmo Jodice); 264b (Michael Busselle); 265b (Andrea Jemolo); 266, 267ar (Archivio Iconografico, S.A.); 266-267,267br (Adam Woolfitt); 268cr (Ruggero Vanni); 268b (Paul Almasy); 270c (Richard List); 272a (Dennis Marsico); 273b (Ruggero Vanni); 274cr (Sandro Vannini); 274b (Dennis Marsico); 275c (Bob Krist); 275b (Chris Bland/Eye Ubiquitous); 276cl (Martin Jones); 276cr (Archivio Iconografico, S.A.); 277a (Carmen Redondo); 277cl, 277b, 280-281, 281cr (Wolfgang Kaehler); 282ar (Paul Almasy); 283al, 283b (Adam Woolfitt); 284a (© Alfred Ko); 285br (Pierre Colombel); 288, 288-289 (Macduff Everton); 296-297 (Araldo de Luca); 298-299 (John Heseltine); 299ar (Araldo de Luca), 300cl (Francesco